ON CASE GRAMMAR

CROOM HELM LINGUISTICS SERIES

edited by Roger Lass

DEFINITENESS AND INDEFINITENESS

John Hawkins

COREPRESENTATION OF GRAMMATICAL STRUCTURE

Michael B. Kac

ON CASE GRAMMAR

PROLEGOMENA TO A THEORY OF
GRAMMATICAL RELATIONS

JOHN M. ANDERSON

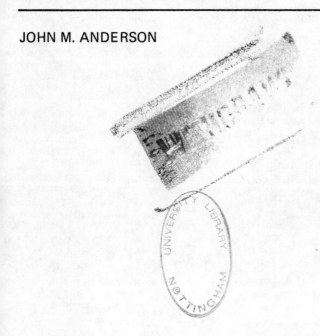

CROOM HELM   LONDON

HUMANITIES PRESS

© 1977 John M. Anderson
Croom Helm Ltd, 2-10 St John's Road, London SW11

British Library Cataloguing in Publication Data

Anderson, John M
  On case grammar.
  1. Case grammar
  I. Title
  415   P163

  ISBN 0-85664-449-8

First published in the USA 1977 by
Humanities Press, Atlantic Highlands, N.J.

ISBN 0-391-00758-0

Reprinted 1982

Printed and bound in Great Britain by
Biddles Ltd, Guildford, Surrey

CONTENTS

to
Nicola
Samantha
Miranda

PREFACE

The chapters which follow had their ultimate origin in research contributing to the first part of a longer work, still uncompleted, on quantification in a case grammar. As such they were to be devoted to a description and justification of the particular grammatical framework invoked in the subsequent discussion of quantifiers. However, it seemed to me that the phenomena dealt with were of sufficient intrinsic interest and the conclusions offered sufficiently provocative to warrant a more extended presentation in their own right. Such is the present volume. It represents an attempt to arrive at a preliminary definition of the role of case and grammatical relations in the grammar.

An earlier version of parts of ch.1 appears as Anderson, 1975*c*, and an intermediate version of §§1.8-.9 as Anderson, 1975*d*. Some idea of the direction the discussion might take following on from the present work can hopefully be gained from the preliminary versions in Anderson, 1974*b*, 1973*d*, 1974*a* (in that order).

I am grateful to Maurício Brito de Carvalho, Paul van Buren, Ramu Reddy and Dave Roberts for their many insightful comments on the manuscript which forms the basis for this version. To the last in particular the reader should be grateful for a number of important improvements in content and presentation. Parts of the material have been presented before audiences at Aarhus, Copenhagen, Edinburgh, Lancaster and Odense. These more formal occasions and numerous informal ones have made significant contributions to the present work. Among my many interlocutors I would like to thank especially Paul van Buren, John Dienhart, Hans Hartvigsson, Leif Kvistgaard Jakobsen, John Lyons, Jim Miller, Sheena Macrae and Dave Roberts. Thanks too to Roger Lass, who is responsible for the removal of many imperfections, and to Colin Ewen, who suffered some proof-reading. My wife would like to express her gratitude to me for having finished this before it drove her quite crazy. So too Anne MacDonald, who womanfully transformed into typescript the ancient Venutian calligraphy of the original manuscript.

My absolutions on them all of course.

J.M.A.

Edinburgh
December, 1975

1 GRAMMARS OF CASE

1.1 A Traditional Notion of Case

The grammatical terminology of most languages which incorporate the European tradition in such matters displays a systematic ambiguity in the use of the term 'case'. Usually, it is employed to refer both to a certain inflexional category (and the forms that manifest it) and to the set of semantic distinctions carried by the forms of that category. We can differentiate these as case-forms and case-relations or case-functions respectively. Thus in *Lutetiam veni,* it might be said that the noun is in the ACCUSATIVE form and that in this instance it indicates, or functions as, the 'goal'. Much controversy has depended simply on the confusion of these two senses. Certainly, such an ambiguous usage has the disadvantage that case-functions clearly can be expressed in other ways, notably by prepositions or postpositions, by word order or in the morphology of the verb rather than the noun. In what follows I shall use the term CASE-FORM (henceforth CF) more inclusively, to cover any form that serves to express a CASE-RELATION (henceforth CR), where the latter are interpreted as labels for the semantic role that a particular NP fulfils in the predication.

Most traditional accounts posit a complex mapping between the set of CRs and the set of CFs (either in the narrow sense or interpreted, as I propose, more widely). For instance, the same accusative form of Latin we noted above as a marker of the goal relation can also express the (DIRECT) OBJECT, as in *puellam amo.* And the goal can alternatively be associated with a form which includes a preposition: *ad urbem veni.* There have been rather few attempts to arrive at more NATURAL accounts, that is, descriptions of the CR/CF relationship which involve less of a discrepancy. Notable, however, have been various LOCALIST proposals, the character of which we shall return to below.

All such accounts encountered considerable difficulties in attempting to provide a unitary, or even unified function for such CFs as (particularly) the accusative and NOMINATIVE. Even if the goal/object distinction is disregarded, it is apparent that it is difficult to attribute to the objective accusative itself a constant semantic value, as reflected in a set like that in (1):

(1)   a. The policeman struck the student

     b. Marilyn gave John the whisky
     c. My uncle built a chalet
     d. John killed Bill
     e. Columbus discovered America
     f. The procession crossed the square
     g. Fred left home

Compare the even greater diversity of the SUBJECTIVE nominatives in (2):

(2)   a. The student was struck by the policeman
      b. The student tickled the policeman
      c. Nobody knew the truth
      d. That trunk contained eight books
      e. My dentist suffered terribly
      f. John received the whisky from Marilyn
      g. The truth was known to nobody

In each instance, the set of NPs partake of a range of semantic roles, some of them traditionally distinguished as subtypes of subject or object, such as 'object of result', 'indirect object', etc. But what (if anything) these different types of subject or object have in common semantically has remained uncertain.

    Thus, to be more particular, grammars written within the classical tradition almost invariably have extensive sections which under one guise or another document at some length the often multifarious 'uses of the cases'. So in Gildersleeve & Lodge (1895), for instance, out of fewer than 200 pages devoted to the 'simple sentence expanded', the description of the cases in their role of 'qualification of the prediction' is accorded almost 100. And Woodcock's (1959) more recent though still traditionalist treatment devotes five of its total of twenty-five chapters to 'the functions' of the cases. For the individual cases Gildersleeve and Lodge are typical in providing a detailed and intricate classification of 'uses'. The accusative, for example, may mark either an inner or outer object (or both in the same clause); and the former divides into the object of result, the cognate accusative and the accusative of extent, the latter may be partitive or not; and so on.

    Often, however, such classifications appear to impute to the cases (case forms) distinctions which are signalled elsewhere. For example, it could be argued that rather than an object of result in Latin, we have 'creative' verbs (like English *make*) whose objects (or rather their denotata) come into existence as a result of the action denoted by the verb. Is it then necessary to recognise a distinct relation/use/function? Many, perhaps all, of the object 'uses' are reducible in this way. A more interesting hypothesis would involve (as we have observed) minimising such recourse to syncretism. And it is some such natural view which has led to attempts to discover where possible a Grundbedeutung (or at least a single source, be it semantic or syntactic) for linguistic elements, including the case forms (cf. e.g. Jakobson, 1936). For the Latin cases this is illustrated already by the work of Key (1958) and Laurie (1859). The latter in particular pursues essentially a localist strategy such as we shall investigate in ch.2. Typically, however, the form that marks the subject in a language appears to be non-reducible. Apart from correlating with subject-hood such a form simultaneously neutralises uses distinguished in other (non-subject) constructions (as in (2)). Nevertheless, it would seem obvious that the least we can expect of any grammatical theory as far as cases are concerned is that it should provide a principled articulation of the relationship between case relation and case form, distinguishing neutralisation and syncretism from the natural. But this is lacking throughout much of the history of studies of case. The two characteristic polarisations are aptly summarised by Haudry (1968, 141):

> Le problème central de l'étude des cas est dans la difficulté qu'on éprouve à les décrire en termes de 'signes', c'est-à-dire à poser en face de chaque signifiant (la désinence), un signifié correspondant. La grammaire historique oscille entre deux attitudes: admettre une polysémie du cas, en la justifiant par un syncrétisme, ou tenter de réunir sous un concept les emplois les plus divers.

It is, however, not my intention here to discuss such traditional preoccupations at any length. Rather, I take as familiar such a context for the following investigations, which are concerned in the main with a consideration of specific proposals made within current frames of reference.[1] My concern is simply to sketch in something of this immediate background as a preliminary to an examination of relevant aspects of contemporary linguistic theory. In particular, we shall be concerned with some developments in what has come to be called 'case grammar'; and I shall attempt to maintain the adequacy of a variant of this especially in the face of objections that have been raised to particular aspects. In such a discussion, nevertheless, the traditional theme that we have broached in the present section, viz. the articulation of the relationship between CFs and CRs, will underly much of the debate.

1.2 Case relations and the Aspects theory

1.2.1. It might have been anticipated that the development of generative
grammar, and in particular the elaboration of the distinction between
deep and surface structure, would lead, if not to more natural accounts,
at least to an articulation of how the neutralisation of roles typical of
subjects and objects might arise. But this was not the case. In the
framework established in the early 1960s and culminating in the
position formulated in Chomsky (1965) (henceforth 'the *Aspects*
theory'), the ambivalences associated with surface subjects and
objects were carried over into their deep equivalents. Transformations
like the passive simply redistribute the NPs in a sentence without
increasing or decreasing their ambivalence with respect to CRs. And this
is not surprising. The passive, for instance, was conceived of as having
purely syntactic motivation. What remains mysterious, however, is
exactly what this motivation might be.

The arguments invoked by Chomsky (1957, §§5.4, 7.5) involve the
avoidance of a duplication of selectional restrictions (in 'corresponding'
actives and passives) and the difficulties in specifying restrictions on
the distribution of the passive marker *be . . . -en,* together with the
problem created for an analysis whereby passives are not derived from
the structure more immediately underlying actives but rather vice versa
by there being 'no structural way to differentiate properly between
[The wine was drunk by the guests] and *[John was drunk by midnight]*
if both are taken as kernel sentences' (1957, 80). I cannot see that this
last assertion can be accorded any force in the absence of any supporting
arguments for an analysis which fails to make such a differentiation.
Why should we accept that there is 'no structural way to differentiate
properly' between such sentences? Moreover, even if it is just, it and
the other arguments carry weight only within a grammar one of whose
goals is the establishment of a set of 'kernel sentences', which are
chosen 'in such a way that the terminal strings underlying the kernel
are easily derived by means of a [phrase structure] description, while
all other sentences can be derived from these terminal strings by simply
statable transformations' (Chomsky, 1957, 48). And they are decisive
only against the alternatives envisaged by Chomsky, viz. an analysis
whereby 'the passive of "John loves Mary" would be "John is loved by
Mary" ' (1957, 78) and one in which actives are derived transformationally from passives.

But other possibilities can be and have been envisaged. The original
considerations adduced by Chomsky do not enable us to select the
simplex-sentence transformational accounts of the derivation of passives

over a lexicalist formulation (Freidin, 1972*a*, 1975; Starosta, 1973) or a complex source in which the 'active' predication is embedded as a complement to the verb *be* (Hasegawa, 1968; R. Lakoff, 1968) or one in which neither the active nor passive variant is structurally closer to their source (Fillmore, 1968*a*). In *Aspects*, Chomsky (1965, 103-6) provides no new argument, but simply the suggestion, based on the observation that some transitive verbs which fail to undergo passivisation also 'do not take Manner Adverbials freely', that 'the Manner Adverbial should have as one of its realisations a "dummy element" signifying that the passive transformation must obligatorily apply'.[2] It therefore is unwarranted to cite a putative rule like passive as one of 'the traditional battery of transformations' (Jackendoff, 1971, 284) against which proposed transformations are to be evaluated. It is not sufficient to assert 'differences in the kinds of arguments given as motivation' (*ibid.*); this must be shown to be the case. We shall find, on the other hand, as our discussion develops, particularly in ch.2, that a functional view of transformations (as investigated by e.g. Langacker, 1974) will provide us with a means of articulating the CR/CF relation.

1.2.2. We return below to some more recent attempts to provide arguments for the deep structure of the *Aspects* theory (§§1.8-.10) and for the passive transformation (there and in §3.3). Let us rather at this point give our attention to the *Aspects* characterisation of underlying (deep) CRs, or 'grammatical functions'. This is of some interest in that although the introduction of such notions as 'deep subject' represents an innovation over most traditional positions (as I shall argue below), their presence does not provide any explanation for the discrepancy traditionally observed between CRs and CFs. The motivation for such an innovation therefore requires careful scrutiny, particularly since it seems to represent a retreat from naturalness in comparison with the traditional view which invoked only semantically relevant CRs and the CFs motivated on simple distributional (and ultimately perceptual) grounds (cf. Postal, 1974, preface). In this section we are concerned with the original arguments offered by Chomsky (1965, ch.2).

At the beginning of ch.2 Chomsky presents three sets of information which, he claims (without exemplification) 'traditional' grammar might provide concerning a sentence like:

(3)   Sincerity may frighten the boy

viz. a categorisation or constituent analysis, a description of functions,

and a subcategorisation or componential analysis of the formatives. The
following three subsections in that chapter are devoted to showing how
a generative grammar can and should express each of these sets of
information. Such a presentation is however somewhat misleading,
particularly with respect to the functional information which is our
present concern. For the functional descriptions provided by 'traditional'
grammars concern what would for Chomsky be 'surface structure' (or
perhaps 'shallow structure') and thus the subject of (4):

(4)   The boy may be frightened by sincerity

would be the NP *the boy*. Whereas Chomsky's own proposals (as
expanded in §2.2 of ch.2) are addressed primarily to the definition of
deep structure functions. Thus whether or not the functional
information concerning (3) ascribed to 'traditional' grammars is
'substantially correct' (as affirmed by Chomsky), it is quite irrelevant to
decisions concerning the character of 'deep functions'; in particular, there
is no (empirical?) support for such notions as 'deep subject' of the kind
that Chomsky appears to be appealing to deriving from 'traditional'
grammars. And unfortunately, no further 'evidence' for Chomsky's
conception of 'deep subject' etc. (i.e. for the constitution of the set of
'underlying functions') is offered — except in so far as his own proposals
concerning selectional restrictions presuppose such.

Similarly the 'evidence' which Chomsky advances (in ch.2, § 2.2)
against a categorial interpretation of 'deep' functions in general also
simply does not bear on the point at issue. Chomsky (1965, 68) states
that 'functional' notions like 'Subject', 'Predicate' are to be sharply
distinguished from categorial notions such as 'Noun phrase', 'Verb', a
distinction that is not to be obscured by the occasional use of the same
term for notions of both kinds. To include nodes bearing functional
labels 'is mistaken in two ways', according to Chomsky. The first way
lies in failing to distinguish formally between categorial and functional
notions. However, since Chomsky provides no generally applicable
criteria whereby this distinction is to be drawn but merely provides
a formal means of presenting some 'functional information' in a way that
distinguishes it from 'categorial information', on the assumption that it
is desirable to draw the distinction in the manner he himself proposes,
this 'failure' does not in itself count as evidence against the presence of
such nodes. The argument is circular: it is a mistake to collapse
'functional' and 'categorial' elements because it is a mistake not to
distinguish between such elements.

Chomsky's second objection looks at first to have more force. He observes that representations like (5):

(5)

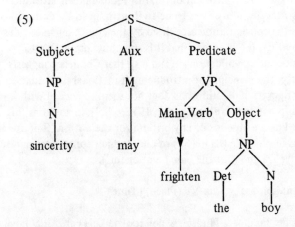

'and the grammar on which it is based are redundant, since the notions Subject, Predicate, Main-Verb and Object, being relational, are already represented in the Phrase-marker (6)

(6)

and no new rewriting rules are required to introduce them. It is necessary only to make explicit the relational character of these notions by defining 'Subject-of' for English, as the relation holding between the NP of a setence of the form NP Aux VP and the whole sentence, 'Object-of' as the relation between the NP of a VP of the form V NP and the whole VP, etc. (1965, 69).'

But this too involves rather a strange argument, which again depends upon the assertion of the relational/categorial distinction. It is not at all clear, for instance, why information that is 'redundant' if introduced by the phrase structure rules ceases to be so if introduced by definitions associated with the configurations specified by the (function-free) rules of the base. However, let us accept that it is somehow preferable to introduce 'functional' specifications in the way that Chomsky suggests.

Unfortunately, the principle of introducing 'functional' information in terms of configurational definitions does not seem to accord with Chomsky's own practice (cf. here Freidin, 1972*b*, 8-9), in so far as this can be evaluated in the absence of any criteria for the notion 'functional'. Consider, for example, rule (ii) in (57) of ch.2 (which constitutes part of 'An illustrative fragment of the base component'):

(7)   Predicate-phrase → Aux VP (Place) (Time)

(Let us leave aside 'Predicate-Phrase', which looks like a categorial label derived from the function of the category: the distinction 'is not to be obscured by the occasional use of the same term for notions of both kinds' (Chomsky, 1965, 68).) Presumably 'Place' and 'Time' are to be expanded as prepositional phrases (PPs), though this is not illustrated by the fragment. In this case, as far as I can tell, the most plausible interpretation of 'Place' and 'Time' is as functional labels: they indicate the function of these PPs in the predicate phrase. They are not, however, redundant. Since PPs of both types are immediately dominated (in the absence of the 'Place' and 'Time' labels) by the same category, a configurational definition is excluded. Not even the invoking of relative sequence (provided this can be motivated) will suffice, in that either kind of PP may be absent. (For further discussion, see e.g. Meisel, 1973; Starosta, 1974.)

Thus it appears that only some 'functions' are to be excluded from the categorial rules. Of course perhaps it is possible to exclude 'Place' and 'Time' and the like from deep structure configurations and introduce the functional information by an interpretative rule which takes into account the character of the lexical items in the appropriate PPs (though problems are presented by examples like *He turned off the road just after Carlisle*). And the diverse functions associated with subjects and objects (recall (1) and (2)) can be provided for in like manner (cf. Chomsky, 1972*a*). But in neither case do these need to apply to 'deep' configurations rather than 'shallow' (cf. Freidin, 1972*a*, 1975). Under the latter and (in the absence of strong counter-evidence) preferable proposal, the interpretative rules will merely replicate a case grammar account (see below) of the course of the neutralisation associated with (surface) subjects and objects. There remains of course the issue of the character of the 'rules' that relate role-or-case-structures to surface structures, which is a quite distinct question.

Moreover, more crucially, no motivations are indeed offered either for the presence of the configurationally defined functions in the grammar or for the presence in deep structure (as opposed to some derived level) of configurations of the character proposed as bases for the definitions. Motivations for subject-object deep structures have since been offered, as noted above, and we shall consider one such attempt below; but the discussion in *Aspects* is quite a prioristic in this regard. Further, it is far from clear what is intended to be the status of the relation 'deep subject', for instance, in the grammar (cf. Matthews, 1967: 133-5). It does not appear to contribute to the semantic interpretation (Lakoff and Ross, 1967): it is not a semantic element. Nor is it necessary as a basis for the rules of semantic interpretation, which can refer to the same configurations in terms of which 'deep subject' etc. were defined. Katz (1972, 109) shows that Chomsky's proposal to distinguish 'the true grammatical relations . . . from the pseudo-relations . . . by the fact that in the former case there are selectional restrictions governing the paired categories whereas in the latter there are none' is untenable, and goes on (1972, 111) to offer the following criterion:

an ordered *n*-tuple of grammatical functions is a grammatical relation just in case it is required in the semantic component as part of the statement of a specific type of combination that readings can undergo in the process of forming semantically interpreted underlying phrase markers from lexically interpreted underlying phrase markers.

But the relations so defined remain unnecessary to a semantic component to which underlying phrase markers are available. It is still unclear why it is necessary to make a distinction between 'true' and 'pseudo-relations': what motivations are there for such a distinction independent of Katz's criterion? And the need for the 'true' / 'pseudo' distinction appears moreover to be simply an artefact of the unsubstantiated deep structures upon which the relations are defined.

Chomsky in addition appears to accord these relations no role in the formulation of transformational rules, which again refer to

categories. Though recently Postal (1974), for instance, has claimed
such a role for 'grammatical relations', it remains to be seen whether
such formulations are preferable or indeed alternative to accounts
incorporating CRs: see § 1.9 and ch.3, where it is argued that syntactic
generalisations refer to CRs and derived subjects etc. In this respect,
'deep subject' contrasts both with CRs, which have a clear role in
underlying representations as labels for argument types, and with a
neutralised function like '(surface) subject', which is associated in
certain languages with the provision of an unmarked position for topics.
Given this, it is not surprising that there developed in the immediately
succeeding period proposals in which underlying predicate-noun
functions were given a unitary, categorial interpretation, and whereby
the configurations associated with 'deep subjects' and 'objects' were
absent from deep structure; such that 'subject' and 'object' are not in
fact CRs in the sense proposed in § 1.1. Grammars incorporating such
proposals have come to be labelled 'case grammars'.

1.2.3. We now must turn to these, and some further apparent
motivations for rejecting 'deep subject' etc. But firstly there is one final
objection of Chomsky's which we must give some consideration to,
since if it were wellfounded the development of 'case grammars' would
have been inconceivable. For Chomsky claims (1965, 70) that there are
sentences with respect to which 'functional categories' are not merely
redundant but which are such that 'the impossibility of a categorial
interpretation of functional notions becomes at once apparent'.
   The following are allegedly crucial instances:

(8)   a. John was persuaded by Bill to leave
       b. John was persuaded by Bill to be examined
       c. What disturbed John was being regarded as incompetent

Chomsky observes: 'In [(8.a)] *John* is simultaneously Object-of
persuade (to leave) and Subject-of *leave;* in [(8.b)] *John* is simultaneously
Object-of *persuade (to be examined)* and Object-of *examine;* in [(8.c)]
John is simultaneously Object-of *disturb,* Object-of *regard (as
incompetent),* and Subject-of the predication *as incompetent.'* Without
further argument, he advanced his conclusion concerning 'the impossibility
of a categorial interpretation of functional notions'. Now, this may be
(or have been) 'at once apparent' to Chomsky, but I quite fail to see in
what way these examples bear upon the point at issue at all. Again the
argument is couched in terms of unmotivated 'Subject of' and 'Object of'

deep structures; let us, however, even concede the appropriateness of
such an analysis. What (8) do appear to show is that a single NP in
surface structure 'corresponds to' (in a sense we can make precise) three
deep structure functions. But since each of these functions will be
associated with a different instance of the NP realised in (8) as *John* in
deep structure, no problem of principle arises in providing either a
categorial or an interpretative characterisation (redundant or not) of the
deep structure functions involved. These examples do not even show
that a categorial status for surface functions is necessarily excluded; and
they certainly do not support the conclusion asserted by Chomsky as far
as deep functions are concerned.

1.3 Fillmorean Case Grammar

1.3.1. Within the *Aspects* framework subject and object are associated
with both deep structure and derived, especially surface representations.
And the range of roles characteristic of surface subjects and objects (cf.
again (1) and (2)) also pertains to their deep equivalents. Indeed, the
number of widely accepted transformational rules, apart from 'raisings'
(and cf. Chomsky (1973) on even these), which result in a change of
functional status for a particular NP — say, from Object to Subject — are
very few: the existence of even the passive is in some doubt (cf. again
Freidin, 1972*a, b;* 1975). It is not at all clear in fact that there are any
motivations for distinguishing deep from surface Subjects and Objects.
This is now accentuated by any admission that 'thematic relations' (see
below) are interpretable at surface structure (Jackendoff, 1975). There
have thus been developed grammars wherein the Subjects and Objects in
(1) and (2) are surface Subjects and Objects only, and each of them is
associated with a distinct underlying function, role or CR. Configurations
of the subject/object type are removed from deep structure representations;
the Place/Time situation, in which the functional information is
necessarily given categorial status, is generalised throughout the base.
Subject and Object are 'neutralised', derived functions: such NPs may
correlate with any one of the set of underlying functions or CRs.

   A well-known proposal of this kind is associated with the name of
Charles Fillmore, who in a series of papers[3] has elaborated a grammatical
framework that he dubbed 'Case Grammar'. Instead of underlying
representations like that in (6), Fillmore (1968*a*) proposed such as are
indicated in (9):

(9)

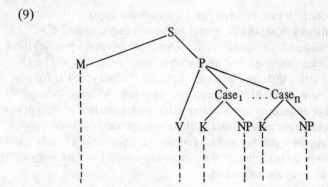

wherein each underlying function is assigned a case node, i.e. a categorial representation, and these in turn are expanded as K(asus) + NP, K dominating the case marker, typically in English a preposition. The cases constitute a finite universal set. M is the Modality node which 'will include such modalities on the sentence-as-a-whole as negation, tense, mood, and aspect'. The P(roposition) involves 'a tenseless set of relationships involving verbs and nouns'. It consists of a predicate (V) together with one or more case phrases. Fillmore (1968a, 24-5) proposes that at least the following distinct functions can be motivated (and more are added in the course of the discussion), and he provides for each a notional characterisation:

(10)   *Agentive* (A), the case of the typically animate perceived
       instigator of the action identified by the verb.
       Instrumental (I), the case of the inanimate force or object
       causally involved in the action or state identified by the verb.
       Dative (D), the case of the animate being affected by the state
       or action identified by the verb.
       Factitive (F), the case of the object or being resulting from
       the action or state identified by the verb, or understood as a
       part of the meaning of the verb.
       Locative (L), the case which identifies the location or spatial
       orientation of the state or action identified by the verb.
       Objective (O), the semantically most neutral case, the case of
       anything representable by a noun whose role in the action or

state identified by the verb is identified by the semantic
interpretation of the verb itself; conceivably the concept should
be limited to things which are affected by the action or state
identified by the verb.

A subject is normally created (in languages in which 'subject' is motivated)
by, in English etc., moving one of the case phrases to the left of the
modality constituent under the immediate domination of S, and
removing the K subconfiguration. Similarly, objectivisation juxtaposes
V and some case phrase whose K is then removed. In both instances the
case node is pruned, resulting in configurations analogous to (6), which
now can only represent a derived structure. Let us illustrate these
processes, and the hierarchisation of the cases with respect to subjectivisation, with a set of examples discussed by Fillmore, namely those
involving the verb *open*.

Consider the sentences in (11):

(11) a. The door opened
      b. John opened the door
      c. The wind opened the door
      d. John opened the door with a chisel

In (11.d) the predicate is associated with three cases:

(12)

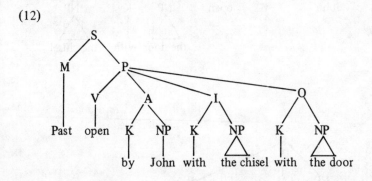

(We consider the choice of prepositions below.) Subjectivisation (of A)
and objectivisation (of O) result in the series of representations in (13):

(13) a.

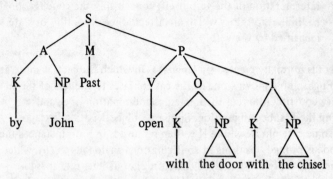

b.

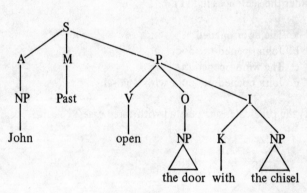

c.

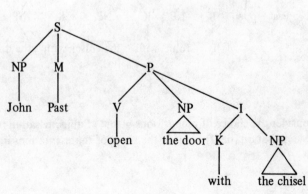

In (11.b-c) one of the cases is lacking, and in (11.a) two. Thus the lexical entry for *open* will contain the information that it is a verb that 'takes' obligatorily an objective case, and optionally an agentive and instrumental, which Fillmore expresses as in (14):

(14)   +   [————O (I) (A)]

i.e. *open* is insertable in a deep structure which contains an O and optionally A and I. (11) also reveal a HIERARCHY FOR SUBJECT SELECTION that seems to be rather general, such that an A if present is preferred (as in (11.b) and (11.d)); otherwise an I is preferred to an O (as in (11.c)). Fillmore proposes that the various features of passive sentences (in particular the presence of *be* and the form of the main verb) are there to indicate that the hierarchy has been overruled, that a 'marked' subject selection has been made, as in *The door was opened by John,* in which O rather than A is subject. Observe that this account of passives is quite compatible with the arguments of Chomsky's noted in § 1.2. There are however problems associated with such a treatment of subjects and objects and of the passive, and we shall take up some of the criticisms it has aroused below. The effect is to remove the passive as such as a transformation, since all sentences involve the same process of subject-formation illustrated in (12) and (13). It is in terms of such a process that the range of roles associated with the subjects in (2) (and not merely the alternation between (2.a) and (2.b)) is allowed for. Thus the subject in (2.b) is an A, in (2.c) a D, in (2.d) an L, etc.

1.3.2. It seems to me however that much of the interest that has been aroused by such case grammar analyses derives from the illumination it has been claimed they shed upon the classification of lexical information and of lexical items.[4] Thus *open*, for example, can be provided with a single lexical entry, given in particular the facultative case notation: compare the difficulties in a subject-object grammar, wherein the selectional restrictions on the subject of the intransitive verb *open* match those on the object of the transitive.

As will be apparent from what I say below, it is not at all clear to me (and cf. Fillmore, 1972, §§ 10-15) that in this instance such an analysis is preferable to one involving in the case of the transitive the embedding of the intransitive structure in a predication containing an 'abstract' verb of causing (despite such problems as have been raised by Fodor (1970) and Gregory Lee (1971); see too the discussion involving Kac, McCawley and Shibatani in Kimball, 1972; also Seuren, 1973*a*;

McCawley, 1973*a*, 67-8). It is not even certain that the two analyses are mutually exclusive (cf. e.g. Anderson, 1971*b*, ch.11). Each such choice of analysis (involving cases *v.* abstract predicates) is obviously to a large extent an independent empirical issue. Notice in the present instance however that even the analysis involving a complex derivation must incorporate the property that the conditions governing insertion of *open* etc. involve one constant element and some optional. How this is expressed depends on the place of lexical insertion. If however it occurs after predicate raising (or whatever collapses the component predications) then a case notation enables us to mark the constant in both the transitive and intransitive instances as O, whatever its superficial function (object or subject). That is, the possibility of a complex source for transitive sentences containing *open* does not necessarily in itself render the case nodes redundant; they may have a role in the expression of a lexical generalisation. It seems to me, on the other hand, that Katz's (1972, 357-60) attempt within a 'non-abstract' subject-object grammar to capture such a generalisation by means of a complex and ad hoc notation whose role is to undo the inappropriate information provided by subject-object 'deep structures' is far from persuasive. A distinct but similarly unconvincing expedient is adopted by e.g. Chvany (1974), who suggests that intransitive sentences including such predicates derive from underlying structures with 'empty subjects'. We return below to the semantic and syntactic roles of CRs and further reasons for preferring case representations to subject-object 'deep structures'.

The same notation as employed in (14) allows us also to relate as suppletive variants pairs like *die* and *kill* or *see* and *show*, the difference between which is attributable simply to a partial discrepancy in the array of cases they require, their CASE FRAME:

(15) a. *die* + [————— D]
          kill + [————— D (I)(A)]
      b. *see* + [————— O + D]
          show + [————— O + D + A]

where the interlocked parentheses in (15.a) indicate that at least one of the cases I and A must be present. However let us note at this point that it is not at all clear that the semantic difference between such transitive/intransitive pairs (or for that matter that between transitive and intransitive *open*) is adequately characterised simply in terms of absence versus presence of A,[5] so that the lexical entries will differ in other respects than the case frame. It may be that these further properties are at least in part specifiable by redundancy rules based on elements in the case frame, but this is not clear from Fillmore's discussion. It is plain too that the statement of the relationship between the members of such pairs will not involve a common lexical entry (as usually conceived), given the absence of (even partial) phonological identity, but rather intersection in the non-phonological content of the entries. But in this respect the case notation retains whatever merits it can be said to have with respect to the *open* example, i.e. in distinguishing in a straightforward manner (as A, and concomitant properties) what differentiates between the related entries, whatever the distribution into subjects and objects may be.

Predicates too may vary simply in which case is the unmarked subject choice, as perhaps in (16):

(16) a. The film pleased Roger
      b. Roger liked the film

However, examples like this present some problems for Fillmore's notion of a hierarchy of cases with regard to subject selection, in that each such pair necessarily involves an item that must be marked as exceptional in its selection of subject; and when for any two cases, say D and I, the exceptions (I as subject) are almost as numerous as the regular forms (cf. Fillmore's (1971c) discussion of 'psychological predicates'), then the need for some independent motivation for the hierarchy is made plain (cf. Mellema, 1974, 63-6). Moreover, it seems to me that it is in itself unilluminating simply to mark such an item as 'exceptional' without seeking to establish whether there is some independent principle which might account for its exceptional behaviour or whether the hierarchy is in need of revision or the assignment of cases requires reconsideration. Again, this topic will be resumed in the ensuing discussion.

Certain markers are according to Fillmore (1968a, 32) the unmarked realisations of the K dominated by particular cases, as *by* for an agentive K, or an instrumental (in the absence from the proposition of an A), *to* for datives, *with* for instrumentals (otherwise) and objectives, as in *The duchess presented Maria with the prize,* as compared with *The duchess presented the prize to Maria,* with the same array of cases but in which the objective rather than the dative has been objectivised. Locative and time prepositions are not fully determined (i.e. are lexical options) or are required by the associated noun phrase. And the distribution of some prepositions remains idiosyncratic to certain predicates, and this too must be included in the lexicon, as with the *on* which marks the dative in the case of *blame*. Once more these proposals have aroused a number of criticisms, some of which will figure in the succeeding discussion.

1.3.3. Rather than pursue here in any detail the lexical characterisations proposed by Fillmore for their own sake, however, I want now to focus our attention on what must be crucial to any case grammar proposal, viz. the empirical correlates of the CRS themselves. Leaving aside notional definitions of the kind listed in (10), which I return to below, we can divide the properties identifying cases into two main groups, those which are alleged to correlate with the presence (or absence) of a particular case, and those which simply indicate that instances of case phrases are either instances of the same case or otherwise. I shall label these, for reasons that I hope will soon become clear, IDENTIFICATORY *v*. DISCRIMINATORY correlates respectively.

As an instance of the former, consider Becker's (1971) description of the verbal prefix *be-* in German (though he himself concedes that his discussion does not strongly support case grammar over alternatives like the *Aspects* theory), which within a case grammar framework can be said to signal the presence of one CR rather than another. Or, to take a perhaps more familiar example, recall Fillmore's (1972, § 32 – see too § 5b) discussion of the adverb *personally,* which he suggests 'occurs only in sentences with subjective experience verbs and in connection with the NP identified as the Experiencer' (one subdivision of his former dative), and this 'independently of whether this NP is or is not the sentence subject'.

He adduces the examples in (17):

(17) a. Personally, I don't like roses
      b. Your proposal doesn't interest me, personally
      c.*Personally, you hit me
      d.*Personally, ontogeny recapitulates phylogeny

In so far as such a restriction correlates with other criteria distinctive of the particular case relation, we derive some support for the case analysis (particularly over an account whereby the first person pronoun in (17.a) and (17.b) shows a different underlying function). A number of such correlates for particular functions are also discussed by Gruber, 1965.

However, such identificatory criteria have in a number of proposed

instances proved somewhat elusive. Even the generalisation underlying
(17) is not as secure as Fillmore's discussion suggests. Observe in the
first place that the same generalisation can be associated simply with
the deep subjects of subjective experience verbs, provided that the
object in samples like (17.b) has been moved out of underlying
subject position by 'flip' or PSYCH-MOVEMENT (Postal, 1971).
However, Rogers (1974) objects to this that both of (18):

(18) a. Personally, I hate him
      b. He hates me personally

are viable. However (though Postal, for instance, does not draw this
distinction) only the former shares the relevant ('as for me', 'as far as
I'm concerned') interpretation with (17.a-.b); only under that
interpretation is the adverb appropriately set off with a comma. Under
the latter interpretation ('in person') the adverb is of course viable in a
wide range of situations not permitted to the other, as in e.g. *I wrote
to the director personally, The director personally took charge of the
project,* etc. However there are other counter-examples to Fillmore's
and Postal's generalisation; in particular sentences of the type:
Personally, that doesn't give me a kick. Interestingly, such a distribution
accords better with Fillmore's earlier (1968*a*) proposals, whereby this
me as well as *I* in (17.a) and *me* in (17.b), is a dative, than with the later
suggestions (1971*c*), whereby it is an allative. It is also consistent with
the framework developed below, in terms of which the relevant NPs are
all characterised as [loc, erg] . However, it is clear that still further
refinement is required, in that whereas most agentives do not permit
modification by *personally* (in this sense), this is overruled if the action
is linked to some inferred later state, as in *Personally, I gave it up
years ago.*

Consider too the problems connected with the notion of instrumental
discussed by Nilsen (1973). Or Fillmore's (1968*a*, 31) attempt to
correlate G. Lakoff's (1966, 1970*a*) distinction between 'stative' and
'non-stative' predicates with the absence *v.* the presence of A, such
that: 'No special features indicating stativity need be added to verbs
because . . . only those verbs which occur in P's containing A's will
show up in these sentences anyway'. Certainly, 'true imperatives' and
benefactive phrases (like *for Bill* in *John opened the door for Bill*)
seem to correlate quite well (with the presence of A) in this regard. It
seems to me that putative counter-examples of the *Die for your country*
variety (cf. Mellema, 1974, 60-3) merely show that some kind of

'agentive' interpretation can be imposed on the subject of many verbs
by appropriate contextualisation: crucial to the interpretation of such a
sentence is that (Cruse, 1973, 18) 'an act of Will is stated or implied.
Willing is a kind of doing, whether what is willed is a state, process or
action.' On some of the ways that agency can be indicated when it is not
marked by the verb, see e.g. Fischer and Marshall, 1969; Jackendoff,
1972*a*, § 5.12.

Unfortunately, however, Lakoff's criteria do not all define the same
set of predicates. For instance, a somewhat larger set of verbs can occur
in the progressive than permit 'true imperatives', as illustrated by (19):

> (19) a. 1. We are receiving lots of complaints
> 2.*Receive lots of complaints
> b. 1. That rock is toppling
> 2.*Topple (, rock)

and such progressives are in no way agentive otherwise. And on the
other hand, the avoidance of progressives is not limited to 'state' verbs
like *know,* etc., which also reject *do so,* but is also characteristic of
such 'achievement' verbs (Vendler, 1957) as *find.* Cf. the examples in
(20) (from Mellema, 1974):

> (20) a. Judy found a gem and Horace did so too
> b.*Judy is finding a gem

Fillmore himself (1968*a,* 31, note 40) sets aside the *do-so* evidence.[6]

Similar observations can be made with respect to Fillmore's proposal
to restrict what he terms 'outer locatives' to agentive propositions. The
'inner/outer locative' distinction concerns pairs like that in (21):

> (21) a. John keeps his car in the garage
> b. John washes his car in the garage

such that the locative in (21.a) is a necessary complement to its
predicate, whereas that in (21.b) is merely optional with certain verbs.
But 'outer locatives' no more require an agentive to be present than
do 'inner locatives'. Consider (22):

> (22) a. Fred died in his bed
> b. The butter in this dish has melted in that cupboard

However, whereas this proposal is apparently simply untenable, the problem with the stativity correlation is mainly due to the non-homogeneity of the sets delimited by Lakoff's criteria. Otherwise, if we take 'non-stative', or preferably, 'active', more narrowly, as reflected in imperativisation and the use of adverbials like *carefully*, ·the correlation seems just, though there remain problems with the 'preferably animate' requirement for agentives.

But, to my knowledge, it is the discriminatory criteria for cases proposed by Fillmore that have provoked most criticism; and we must now turn our attention to these and the objections to them, particularly since an attempt to meet these objections will lead us to what I suggest is a more adequate conception (on various points) of a grammar of case. However, we must return later to a consideration of the character and identification of individual cases, and the question of how the range of application of the term CR is to be limited in a principled way.

1.4 Some problems for case grammar 1: Multiple case relations per noun phrase

1.4.1. Fillmore (1968*a*) imposes or implies various constraints on combinations of cases within a proposition the consequence of which is to provide us with criteria for deciding whether two case phrases are or are not instances of the same CR. He invokes, in particular, something like the following:

(23) a. only one (possibly coordinate) token of each case is permitted per proposition (1968*a*, 22)
      b. only instances of the same case are coordinated (*ibid*).
      c. each NP is associated with only one case label, such that in any proposition there is a one-to-one matching of CRs and NPs (1968*a*, 24).

All of these have been challenged, or at least claimed to be in conflict with other aspects of Fillmore's analysis. But only (c), it seems to me, has been shown with any certainty to be in general too strong, and this in relation to a variety of phenomena.

In discussing (c) Huddleston (1970), for instance, points out that it is semantically insufficient to contrast, say, *see* and *look at* simply (as far as the CRs are concerned) in terms of the opposing case frames in (24):

(24) see   + [———— O D]
      look at + [———— O A]

In (25.b):

(25) a. Jimmy saw the Lotus Elan
      b. Jimmy looked at the Lotus Elan

Jimmy is as much 'affected by the state or action identified by the verb' (cf. (10)) as in (25.a), and as such is apparently both A and D (cf. too D. Lee, 1973).

Similarly, contrasting *John moved,* on an 'agentive' reading with *John moved the table* in terms of the absence versus the presence of an O (*the table* in the latter) involves attributing 'moving object' status to two different cases, A if there is no O, O otherwise. Contrast Gruber's (1965) 'theme' which uniquely designates the moving object in such movement predications. See again also Huddleston, 1970; 1971, 72-3.

Such considerations might lead us to reanalyse in either of two obvious ways: relax (c), so that the number of relations per proposition may be greater than the number of arguments (NPs) — which entails the introduction of some more complex mechanism for associating each NP with the appropriate CR or CRs (to which I return); or introduce lexical decomposition, whereby *look at* for instance can be derived from a complex structure consisting of an embedded predication of the *see*-type and a superordinate containing an agentive NP identical to the lower D. Fillmore himself (1971*a*, § 4; 1972, § 42) discusses the first possibility in the light of such motivations as we have considered, and the latter (1971*c*) with regard to some more general considerations. I shall argue below that both kinds of extension are necessary.

1.4.2. The necessity for allowing more than one CR per NP is also discussed by Gruber (1965), Jackendoff (1972, e.g. § 2.3) and Ruhl (1972). Indeed, this requirement is the major motivation offered by Jackendoff for preferring over 'case grammar' Gruber's proposal concerning what he terms 'thematic relations' on the grounds that 'in proposals on case grammar with which I am familiar, . . . each surface noun phrase is assumed to have exactly one deep structure case' (1972, 34). But, whatever their other deficiencies, some descriptions of case systems (e.g. Anderson, 1968*a*, *b*, 1969*a*, *b*, 1971*b*, etc.) have explicitly incorporated such a multiple-CR proposal. And it does not seem to be in itself a sufficient distinction to warrant positing a difference in kind between 'case grammar' and the theory of thematic relations. Both represent attempts to articulate the relationship between CRs and CFs and to characterise the set of CRs ('cases' or 'thematic relations').

Observe that Jackendoff provides no motivation, apart from the violation by 'case grammar' — specifically by subject-formation — of the putatively 'useful' structure-preserving constraint proposed by Emonds (1969, 1970), for electing to 'choose a more traditional deep structure' (1972, 37) *in addition to* the theory of thematic relations, or case grammar. And that objection has no force whatsoever with respect to a case grammar in which subject formation is a feature-changing rule applied to invariant or sequence-free representations (see below). We must therefore evaluate the theory of thematic relations as a variant of case grammar. So that more germane to our concerns at present is Jackendoff's further failure to provide adequate support for the theory of thematic relations as compared with other existent or imaginable variants of case grammar. Jackendoff offers (1972, 33-4) two sets of reasons for preferring the system of thematic relations which he adopts from Gruber: viz. (1) 'it provides a way of unifying various uses of the same morphological verb', i.e. it achieves lexical generalisations; (2) it 'is of crucial use in describing independent aspects of the language' (three of which aspects he goes on to consider). However, the benefits described under (1) follow from any case grammar analysis in which in particular multiple CRs per NP are permitted, and thus do not uniquely favour 'thematic relations'. To show this it would be necessary to demonstrate that other systems which are not notational variants do not permit an equally natural account of the appropriate lexical generalisations. And the evidence for (2) is similarly inconclusive, although evaluation is impeded by the vagueness of the characterisations provided for the different relations (Rosenberg, 1975).

1.4.3. Jackendoff discusses the relevance of thematic relations to the description of three apparently disparate sets of phenomena: (a) exceptions to the passive (§ 2.5), (b) the distribution of reflexives (§ 4.10), and (c) the identification of the controller (or antecedent) in complement subject deletion/interpretation (§ 5.11), henceforth EQUI. With respect to (c), he shows (cf. Postal, 1970, § V) that the controller for a particular verb cannot be specified simply with respect to grammatical relations or in terms of Rosenbaum's (1967, 1970) 'minimal distance principle'. *Get* in (26) illustrates the former point:

(26) a. John got to leave
      b. John got Bill to leave

in that *'get* switches controller position when an object is added' (1972*a*, 214); and *promise* in (27) the latter:

(27) a. John promised to leave
      b. John promised Bill to leave

such that the subject NP remains the controller in (b) even though it is now further from the complement than the object. Such a principle is also incompatible with the existence of sentences in which more than one or a double selection of controller is possible, as in *Harriet argued with Betty about visiting you* (Postal, 1970, §§ V. D.I, V.E; Jackendoff, 1972, § 5.10). With respect to such cases as this last, Jackendoff suggests (1972, 213) that 'if there is no network of co-reference imposed by the verb, selection of a controller should be free within the constraints imposed by pronominalization'. However, when a unique controller is specified by the verb, 'it is possible, using thematic relations, to explain the position of controller NP by means of a single marking' (1972, 217) Thus, the controller with *get* is always the 'theme' (in Gruber's (rather misleading) terms): *John* in (26.a) and *Bill* in (26.b), in which latter *John* is the 'agent'. Whereas for *promise* the controller is always the 'source'; *John* in both of (27). But the second of these examples ('the crucial cases' – Jackendoff, 1972, 217) is not decisive in the absence of a demonstration of the preferability of Jackendoff's account in terms of thematic relations to Postal's theory of modal constraints (1970, § V.D., and Appendix), whereby the controller with *promise* is again in accordance with restrictions on pronominalisation. And the first is compatible with the minimal distance principle, which thus with certain marked verbs can be interpreted as overriding the controller predictions deriving from pronominalisation. And once again, while (if correct) demonstrating the irrelevance of Chomskyan '(deep) grammatical relations' to a resolution of the control problem, Jackendoff's observations provide us with no motivation for selecting the theory of thematic relations over other versions of case grammar in which the subject and object of verbs like *get* share a CR. However, I shall not pursue this in any detail at this point, since we shall have to return to 'the control problem' with equi at rather greater length in ch.3.

Both of the other sets of phenomena brought forward by Jackendoff as providing support for this version of case grammar invoke the notion of a 'thematic hierarchy'. He claims (1972, § 2.5) that the five thematic relations he discusses (whose existence is established independently of the hierarchy) are hierarchised as in (28):

(28) 1. Agent
        2. Location, Source, Goal
        3. Theme

and that there hold the following two 'thematic hierarchy conditions':

(29) a. The passive *by*-phrase must be higher on the Thematic
           Hierarchy than the derived subject (1972, 43)
       b. A reflexive may not be higher on the Thematic Hierarchy
           than its antecedent (1972, 148)

Thus, for instance, whereas a sentence such as (30):

(30) John was touching the bookcase

is 'ambiguous between an agentive and nonagentive reading of *John'*
(1972, 44), in the passive only the agentive reading is present:

(31) The bookcase was being touched by John

'The absence of the nonagentive reading is predicted by the Thematic
Hierarchy Condition [(29.a)]: if *John* were only Theme, it would be
lower on the hierarchy than the derived subject, which is Location or
Goal' (*ibid.*).

However, the predictions made by (28) plus (29) are not as firmly
supported as one might desire. I do not wish to dwell on this, because
even if such a formulation were adequate, it would still not serve to
select the theory of thematic relations. But the phenomena are of some
intrinsic interest. It is not clear whether Jackendoff intends (29.a) to
serve as a sufficient or merely a necessary condition for passivisability.
Obviously, it would have a strong explanatory force if the former were
the case. Unfortunately, this does not appear to be so. Consider, for
example the sentences in (31):

(31) a. That trunk contains my books
      b. John has my books

These have no passive equivalent:

(32) a.*My books are contained by that trunk
      b.*My books are had by John

However, on the basis of the kind of evidence adduced by Gruber and subscribed to by Jackendoff, the subjects in (31) appear to be 'locations' and the objects 'themes'; compare, for instance, (33):

(33) a. My books are (contained) in that trunk
      b. My books are with John

Thus, the unacceptability of (32) is not predicted by (29.a), which accordingly does not constitute a sufficient condition.

A consideration of its status as a necessary condition is almost as discouraging. In the first place, the thematic assignments made are not always uncontroversial, and require more support before any conclusions concerning the validity of (29.a) can be drawn. Consider, for example, (34):

(34) *Two hundred pounds are weighed by Bill

Jackendoff (1972, 44) attributes the deviance of this to an infringement of (29.a), since 'the (deep) subject is theme, and the sentence specifies its location on the scale denoted by the measure phrase'. He compares (35):

(35) The Champ weighed in at 654 pounds

as support for the 'locational' analysis of 'two hundred pounds'. But we can paraphrase the active of (34) by (36):

(36) Bill has a weight of two hundred pounds

in which, if the 'various uses of the same morphological verb' are to be unified (Jackendoff, 1972, 33) we have a locational subject (cf. (31.b)). Notice that this accords with the observation that what is being given a 'location on the scale denoted by the measure phrase' is not the subject (*Bill*) but the weight which is attributed to him. In the light of such considerations it appears that Jackendoff's thematic assignments are at best doubtful. And if something more like the structure suggested by (36) is appropriate, then such examples as (34) must be added to the set of those whose deviance is not attributable to a failure to conform to (29.a).

Jackendoff (1972, 44-5) considers two other sets of anomalous passives whose deviance he claims is explicable on the basis of (29.a).

The actives from the first set are reproduced in (37):

(37)   a. John was touching the bookcase
         b. John hit the car with a crash

These are said to be 'ambiguous between an agentive and nonagentive reading of *John*', whereas the passives in (38):

(38)   a. The bookcase was being touched by John
         b. The car was hit by John (with a crash)

display only the agentive readings. This distinction between (37) and (38) I simply do not perceive. There is a reading for (37.a) which is not found with (38.a), namely in which *touching* is a 'locational adjective' like *near;* but in that case no passive equivalent is available for the same reason as with *near,* which, as an adjective, lacks a passive. But if we set aside this particular interpretation, we can associate either an 'agentive' or 'nonagentive' interpretation with both (37) and (38), given that 'the Agent NP is identified by a semantic reading which attributes to the NP will or volition toward the action expressed by the sentence' (Jackendoff, 1972, 32).

Moreover, if 'Agent' is defined in such a way, the acceptability of another large range of viable passives remains unaccounted for. These are examplified by (39.b):

(39)   a. A falling boulder hit his car
         b. His car was hit by a falling boulder

Further, if the 'deep subject' in (39), being excluded as an 'agent' on any reasonable interpretation of Jackendoff's definition, is taken to be a 'theme', (39.b) and the like (for a number of further examples, see Gee, 1974*a*, 304-5) constitute counter-examples to what is predicted by (28) and (29.a). In some such instances one might appeal to some notion like 'Instrument' or 'surrogate Agent' (Jackendoff, 1972, 150), but Jackendoff does not make clear how such a notion would participate in the 'thematic hierarchy'. And this is not true of another set of Gruberian 'themes' (Gruber, 1965, 33-7) that show straight-forward passives, indicated again by Gee (1974*a*, 305), such as (40):

(40)   a. The circle surrounds the dot
         b. The dot is surrounded by the circle

On the other hand, there is a large number of active transitive sentences with 'agent' subject which lack a well-formed passive (Gee, 1974a, 306). Compare e.g. (41):

(41) a. I meant what I said
      b. John found happiness

and (42):

(42) a.*What I said was meant by me
      b.*Happiness was found by John

These again reveal that (29.a) is not a sufficient condition for well-formed passives; (39.b) suggests that as formulated (29.a) makes erroneous predictions. On the other hand, the large number of examples that appear to support (29.a) do so trivially (cf. again Gee, 1974a, 306-7), as a consequence of there being a large number of agentive, and generally animate, 'deep subjects' (a point to which we return below).

Jackendoff's (1972, 45) final set of examples involve 'psychological predicates'. He attributes the deviance of (43.a) as compared with (43.b):

(43) a.*Harry is $\begin{Bmatrix} \text{struck} \\ \text{impressed} \end{Bmatrix}$ by Bill as pompous
      b. Bill is regarded by Harry as pompous

as passives of respectively (44.a) and (44.b):

(44) a. Bill $\begin{Bmatrix} \text{strikes} \\ \text{impresses} \end{Bmatrix}$ Harry as pompous
      b. Harry regards Bill as pompous

to the fact that *Harry* is a 'goal' and *Bill* a 'theme'. Cf. (45):

(45) Bill is striking to Harry

(Jackendoff cites *Harry is striking to Bill* as an 'alternative form' to (44.a), but this must be an error.) Thus in (43.a), but not (43.b), the NP in the *by*-phrase is lower on the thematic hierarchy ('theme') than the subject ('goal'); and the sentence is excluded by (29.a). Unfortunately as Gee (1974a, 305) observes, (46):

(46) Harry is impressed by Bill ('s mastery of the flute)

in which presumably once again *Harry* is a 'goal' and *Bill* a 'theme', is perfectly well-formed. The deviance of (43.b) seems to be independent of the 'thematic hierarchy'.

There is thus no firm support to be derived from the instances of anomalous passives invoked by Jackendoff for the 'thematic hierarchy' or derivatively the theory of thematic relations. And the same can be shown for the reflexivisation phenomena later adduced by Jackendoff (1972, § 4.10). However rather than pursue this further at this juncture – since even if correct, Jackendoff's observations would, as I have observed, provide no unique support for the 'thematic relations' version of case grammar – I leave the reader to follow out the consequences of the examples involving passives and reflexivisation noted by Gee (1974*a*, 307), or to reflect on such examples as those in (47):

(47) a. The road turns back on itself

b. John is $\begin{Bmatrix} \text{pissing} \\ \text{shitting} \end{Bmatrix}$ (on) himself ((with) laughing)

c. This theory contradicts itself (cf. is in contradiction with itself)

d. The bladder evacuates itself in 5 seconds

in the light of Jackendoff's: 'If there were an acceptable sentence with an inanimate (and therefore non-Agent) subject, but with a semantically plausible reflexive object, and with a verb like *touch,* which marks the subject as Theme, such a sentence would violate the [Thematic Hierarchy Condition] , since the reflexive would have to be higher on the Thematic Hierarchy than its antecedent' (1972, 149).

1.5 Some problems for case grammar 2: Multiple case tokens per proposition

1.5.1. Huddleston also discusses principle (a) in (23), which allows only one token of each case in any one proposition, in relation to certain sentences in which two NPs appear to differ only thematically (in a more traditional sense) rather than in terms of the CRs involved (cf. too Teng, 1970; Nilsen, 1972, 13-6; 1973, ch.1, § c), as in perhaps (48):

(48) a. John is similar to Paul
      b. Paul is similar to John

One superficially attractive solution in this instance is to derive both of

(48) from underlying NP-coordinations via conjunct movement (Lakoff and Peters, 1969). The two NPs would then share a single underlying CR as far as the main proposition is concerned. Unfortunately, for such sentences conjunct movement should almost certainly be abandoned,[7] eliminating the possibility of such a derivation for (48). And if this is so, (48) must contain two NPs with distinct underlying CRs if (23.a) is to be satisfied. Whereas, however, (48) can be plausibly related to underlying representations in which the CR of *John* is different from that for *Paul*, specifically in (48.a) Source *v*. Goal (as argued in Anderson, 1973a; see too Fillmore, 1971*c*), there do appear to be residual instances like the equatives in (49):

(49)   a.   The man by the window is the guy I want to marry
       b.   The guy I want to marry is the man by the window

which seem indeed to show two instances of the same CR thematically ordered. I shall argue below that there are further motivations for allowing in a single proposition just two of just one specific CR, what I shall term the ABSOLUTIVE (the 'nominative' of Anderson, 1968*a* etc; roughly Fillmore's objective).

1.5.2. A further problem for (a) is raised by Dougherty (1970*a*) in relation to another aspect of Fillmore's analysis. And this concerns sentences such as (50):

(50)   The car broke the window with its fender

which Fillmore argues (1968*a*, 23) does not involve two instrumentals (*the car* and *with its fender*) but rather derives from a structure in which *the car* is part of an underlying instrumental, as preserved superficially in (51):

(51)   The car's fender broke the window

(50) differs from (51) in showing extraction of an underlying adnominal phrase from the instrumental, which is 'promoted' to become an argument of the main verb. Fillmore elsewhere in the same work (1968*a*, § in discussing inalienable possession proposes that possessors of such originate in underlyingly adnominal case phrases, thus:

(52)

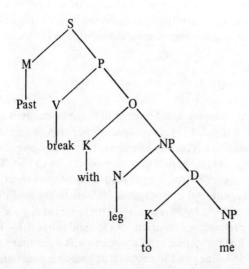

which underlies either (53.a) or one interpretation of (53.b):

(53) a. My leg broke
      b. I broke my leg

the latter again showing 'promotion' (to become a daughter of P) and
subjectivisation of the adnominal. Other readings for (53.b) depend
on the presence of an underlying agent (either intentional or accidental).
(54):

(54) I broke John's leg/the window

on the other hand, is unambiguous in this respect: only the agent
readings are present, in that the subject cannot have been derived by
promotion of an adnominal. Notice that correspondingly, in the present
case, *The car broke the window with the lampstandard* is unacceptable,
since, on Fillmore's account, *the car* cannot have been derived by
promotion in this instance.

Dougherty (1970*a*) points out that (55):

(55) Caruso broke the window with his voice

can also have such a source, i.e. in which *Caruso* originates as an
adnominal within the instrumental. But (55) could also within Fillmore's

framework be an instance involving an underlying A (with a co-referential adnominal within the instrumental). (55) thus has two possible underlying representations, abbreviated in (56):

(56)   a. M V O I
        b. M V O I A

But (55) is not ambiguous, at least not in the appropriate way. D. Lee (1972) points out that (55) is 'ambiguous', between an 'intentional' and an 'unintentional' reading. But this is true of any proposition containing an agent, as we noted in connexion with (53.b). There ought thus to be three possibilities for (55): with intentional agent, with unintentional agent, and non-agentive. Unfortunately for Fillmore's analysis only the first two are available. It appears as if we must abandon the promotion derivation for (55) and thus (50) — unless some non-ad hoc restriction can be invoked which disallows only sources like (55). One can formulate an appropriate constraint: viz. no promotion of dative adnominals from instrumentals, thus allowing (53.b) and (50) but not (55). But the promotion analysis becomes that much less plausible, in the absence of independent support for its associated constraint. If it is abandoned, then (50) and the like do constitute apparent exceptions to (a). We shall find in a moment that there are however further motivations for reviewing the status of instrumentals, such that (a) can be preserved in relation to underlying representations, with the exception I have noted in relation to (49). However, the determination of the general viability of the constraint depends on some independent definition of the notion 'single proposition', its scope (deep structure/surface structure), and the relation between deep and surface structures in this regard.

1.6 Some problems for case grammar 3: Coordinating cases

Dougherty (1970*a*) raises a further set of problems concerning, now, constraint (b). In particular, he points to the well-formedness of NP-coordinations like that in (57):

(57)   John and Mary gave and were given a book respectively

which links presumably an agentive (*John*) and a dative or recipient (*Mary*). But (57) represents one of the subset of cases of NP-conjunction which almost everyone agrees must be derived. Thus, (57) merely shows that (b) does not apply to derived NP-conjunctions. Admittedly this leaves the scope of the constraint somewhat uncertain, in view of the controversy concerning what range of NP-coordinations is derived (cf. Gleitman, 1965; Stockwell Schachter & Partee, 1973; Lakoff & Peters, 1969; Dougherty, 1970*b*, 1971; Anderson, 1974*a*). But that is an independent issue. And given a non-transformational view of most NP-coordinations (Dougherty, 1970*b*, etc.; Anderson, 1974*a*), the constraint retains some predictive value. However it must be conceded that given a transformational source for NP-coordinations (as Fillmore (1968*a*) seems to have in mind – even for 'phrasal conjunctions', in the sense that their source is in an adnominal comitative) and in view of the status of conjunction-reduction as a post-cyclic rule (e.g. Koutsoudas, 1971), it is unclear how such a constraint is to operate even in those instances where its predictions appear to be met. Quite simply it is not clear how the information concerning the CRs (which are removed by subject/object formation) is to be made available (save by a global rule) to a post-cyclic transformation. (On this and other problems, see Plank, 1974).

An apparently even more serious problem concerns the coordination of putative instrumentals like those in (58):

(58) *? The chisel and the wind broke the window

discussed by Huddleston (1970) and taken up by Fillmore (1971*c*), coordinations which are decidedly unnatural. Now, this is unproblematic if *the wind* is not an instrumental (and represents, say, Huddleston's 'Force' or Kirkwood's (1973) source/cause). But clearly not all such restrictions reflect differences in CR: i.e. the converse of constraint (b) does not hold, since coordinations can be anomalous for a variety of semantically and pragmatically conditioned reasons. However, the unnaturalness of (58) correlates with another restriction which appears to depend at least partially upon CRs, as illustrated by (59):

(59) a. John broke the window with the chisel
      b. John broke the window with the wind

the second of which requires for a natural interpretation that there is involved some mechanically contrived 'wind'. However, this in itself underlines the pragmatic basis for the instrument/force distinction. I shall pursue further below the question of whether (59) etc. do or do not involve a difference in case, and moreover whether 'forces' and many instances of instrumentals should perhaps be collapsed with A.

What does emerge from this situation, at this point, though, is that (b) is at best a much less coercive constraint in default of the tenability of the converse restriction.

1.7 Some Problems for Case Grammar 4: Preposition marking

1.7.1. Dougherty (1970*a*) and Stephen Anderson (1971) present arguments for the semantic and syntactic relevance of the deep subject and deep object configurations proposed by Chomsky (1965). Anderson claims in addition (1971, 396) that his data support the hypothesis that the level at which deep object may be defined also 'serves (a) as input to the transformational component; (b) for the statement of selectional and subcategorisation restrictions; and (c) as input to the semantic component, at least insofar as that component makes reference to formally defined grammatical relations', and thus his demonstration 'is a striking confirmation of the hypothesis about semantic interpretation made by the standard theory'. We examine this demonstration in some detail in § 1.8.

Dougherty's argument starts from the observation that within Fillmore's proposals there is one particular area in which a generalisation concerning the distribution of CFs is lost rather than gained. Fillmore (1968*a*) suggested that 'The rules for English prepositions may look something like this: the A preposition is *by*; the I preposition is *by* if there is no A, otherwise it is *with;* the O and F prepositions are typically *zero;* the B preposition is *for;* the D preposition is typically *to, . . .*'. It is already apparent from the first two statements that the distribution proposed is less than optimally natural, in so far as a unitary source is not provided for individual prepositions. But the situation is worse than that. For not only is *by*, as well as marking A, the marker under certain circumstances of an instrumental, as illustrated by Dougherty's:

(60)   Mary was killed by the poison

It can also be associated with certain other cases, like O and D, the latter illustrated by (61):

(61)   The book was known by many people

Moreover, there is a generalisation concerning the distribution of *by* which remains uncaptured by Fillmore's formulations. Notice that (60) and (61) possess certain characteristics, like a particular form of the main verb and the presence of *be,* together with that of the *by*-phrase, which we might label as 'passive'. Now, we can formulate a generalisation that these various NPs, whatever their case, can occur in the *by*-phrase in a 'passive' sentence if there also exists a corresponding 'active' sentence (i.e. one otherwise identical except in lacking these characteristics) in which the NP occurs in subject position (and the 'passive' subject is in object position), as in (62):

(62) The poison killed Mary

and (63):

(63) Many people knew that book

Observe that whereas both of (64):

(64) a. Mary was killed with the poison
b. Mary was tortured with a red-hot ice pick

(again Dougherty's examples), in which *with* marks an I in the underlying presence of a (subsequently deleted) A, are well-formed, neither of (65) is:

(65) a.*Mary was killed by a red-hot icepick
b.*A red-hot icepick killed Mary

And the kind of contextualisation that renders (65.a) more acceptable (via, say, imagining the icepick to have fallen from a great height) also improves (65.b). All this is in conformity with the generalisation just formulated. The question now arises: how is this generalisation to be captured?

In a grammar with a deep structure of the character advocated by Chomsky (1965), in which the CRs can be viewed as assigned by interpretative rules which take into account the underlying grammatical relations ('subject of', 'object of', etc.) and the semantic properties of the individual lexical items, the generalisation has an obvious embodiment: the passive transformation. (60) and (62) and (61) and (63) have respectively (at least partially) in common a deep structure in which the superficial subject and object of the active versions are the deep subject and object respectively. The deviance of (65.b) is thus predictable from that of (65.a). Whereas the *with*-phrases in (64) are underlying PPs, and their well-formedness is independent of the status

of (60) or (65.a). But the framework of 'The case for case' does not
include such deep structure configurations and such a passive
transformation. Unmodified as to levels of representation and
transformational apparatus, the case grammar must apparently involve
us in a rather complex formulation of this relationship, specifically in a
restriction having the power of a transderivational constraint. Fillmore
(1971*c*), indeed, reintroduces the passive, together with a device for
coding into case representations the relevant information provided by
Chomskyan deep structures.

1.7.2. But in fact such phenomena do not require for their explication
the presence in the grammar of either such deep structure configurations
or a transderivational constraint. For instance, in a grammar, either
specifically a case grammar (Starosta, 1973) or not (Freidin, 1972*a*,
1975), in which the passive transformation is rejected, such correlations
can be stated in terms of lexical redundancy rules. Notice too that,
even in the absence of such a possibility, the remote subject/object
representation cannot be regarded as a replacement for a representation
including CRs; rather, if Dougherty's conclusion were correct, both
would be required. It would be necessary, for example, to indicate
that the 'unmarked' value for 'deep subject' in a transitive clause, and
thus for *by*, is agentive, in view of the fact that whereas *by* is a possible
realisation for, say, datives, with agentives it is the primary marker
(cf. P.G. Lee, 1969). And this, I shall argue, as well as the phenomena
adduced by Dougherty, can be reflected directly by appropriate CRs,
without recourse to 'deep structure subjects', even in a grammar which
does not depend upon a lexicalist treatment of the active/passive
relationship, provided that we abandon assumption (c) in (23), whereby
'each NP is associated with only one case label.'

Let us, for example, introduce a CR the presence of which by itself
characterises agentives, so that the subject in (11.b), *John opened the
door,* displays this relation, with which we can associate the
imperativisation etc. phenomena discussed in § 1.3. Let us label this
relation, to avoid confusion, ERG(ATIVE). Suppose that the subject
of (63) is also associated with this underlying relation, but this time in
conjunction with some other CR. I shall argue below that this other case
is LOC(ATIVE), but this is unimportant for the present discussion: let
us simply assume that it is for the moment. Thus, the two subjects can
be characterised as to their respective underlying CRs as in (66):

(66) a. *open*   erg.

b. *know*   loc, erg.

Occurrence in a *by*-phrase in a 'passive' and subject-position in the corresponding 'active' can then be allowed for uniformly in terms of the occurrence of erg. But only erg in a non-locational proposition allows imperativisation. The subject of *open* is also less 'marked' in showing a simple CR. Further, we have now achieved another generalisation concerning the character of A and D. Fillmore (1968*a*, 26) introduces a rule 'which specifies that any N in an A or D phrase must contain the feature [+animate]'. If this is at all a viable observation, at least in linking A and D in some way, then we can now associate this restriction uniquely with erg.

We can allow for a similar distribution for certain objectives (subject in 'active', *by*-phrase in 'passive') in like manner, in terms of a conjunction of erg and what I have called an absolutive, again to avoid confusion. The 'typically animate' generalisation, however, if tenable, does not in this instance carry over, though it does seem to me that a conjunction of abs and erg tends to require a NP higher on the 'humanness hierarchy' than abs alone: i.e. there is a degree of 'personification' associated with erg. Compare the sentences in (67), for instance:

(67) a. The obelisk occupies the top of a hill

   b.?The $\begin{Bmatrix} \text{rock} \\ \text{pebble} \end{Bmatrix}$ occupies the top of a hill

where the subjects in (67.b) are felt to be unsuitable here as erg. However, the constraint is essentially pragmatic and subjective and the set of candidates for unsuitability will vary from instance to instance.[8]

The situation with the sentences, (60), (62), (64), (65), which on Fillmore's (1968*a*) analysis involve instrumentals, appears to be somewhat different. Recall too our problem in § 1.6 with 'instruments' *v.* 'forces', and with the analysis of such sentences as (50). I suspect that Fillmore's original position on instrumentals is irretrievable, and that 'instrumentals' in subject-position and in passives with *by* may be simply instances of A, or in the terminology just introduced, of erg. That is, the difference between, say, (11.b) and (11.c) has not to do with the CR involved but rather other semantic properties of the NPs. This would mean that the A/imperativisation correlation can no longer be observed: only some A's allow imperativisation. But this is not surprising in view of the pragmatic character of whatever determines both what can be an ergative and what can be imperativised.

Alternatively, in the spirit of the proposals we have just made, the 'Force' instances may represent a node with multiple CRs, specifically perhaps an ABL(ATIVE) (Kirkwood's source/cause) and an erg, which conjunction also seems appropriate with the subject of a verb like transitive *benefit,* and, if we follow a suggestion of Huddleston (1970), perhaps 'unintentional agents'. *By*-instrumentals could then be I (if there is such a distinct CR) or perhaps PATH (PROLATIVE, 'through' – Anderson, 1971*b* – on the assumption that *with*-instrumentals are paths – but see below) *plus* ergative. In this way, we could restrict imperativisation to subjects which are simple erg. But the cost is a considerable complication in the lexical entries of a large number of verbs. Where only erg was a possible CR, now we would have to specify [path, erg] and [abl, erg] as well. This could however perhaps be allowed for by a redundancy rule which specified that predicates taking erg also take [abl, erg] and [path, erg]. Whichever of these alternatives – or some other – is eventually to be preferred, it seems to me that Fillmore's original analysis cannot be retained.

Only *with*-instrumentals then remain, and I suspect that they are a realisation of path; at any rate, they now clearly have much more in common with 'manner adverbials' (like *easily, with difficulty*) than with the propositional cases we have been looking at, an observation we shall substantiate in ch.2. If my modification is just, then the problems associated with the present sentences have a semantic-pragmatic resolution, in that whereas both *the poison* and *a red-hot icepick* are generally reckoned to be equally suitable as instruments, *the poison* is much more susceptible to interpretation as an agentive. Similarly the subject of (50) can now be interpreted as an A and thus in conformity with principle (a) of (23) without our having to invoke the dubious derivation proposed by Fillmore.

1.7.3. Some further support for some such modification derives from another observation of Dougherty's (1970*a*) – cf. too Fletcher, 1971, 241-2. A non-subjective I can appear in three rather different structures with verbs like *open* and *lock,* as illustrated in (68):

> (68) a. The door was locked with a key
>   b. The door was locked by a key
>   c. The door locked with a key

Now, if, following Fillmore, we distinguish (68.a) and (68.b) as containing or lacking respectively an underlying A:

> (69) a. M V O I A
>   b. M V O I

then (68.c) appears to share its underlying structure with (68.b),
namely as abbreviated in (69.b). They differ in whether the verb has
been 'passivised' or not. These verbs must apparently be marked as not
requiring passivisation of the predicate if I and A fail to be
subjectivised. But whereas both an 'instance' and an 'iterative'
interpretation are available with (68.a) and (68.b), the 'non-passive'
sentence (68.c) allows only the 'iterative', and indeed seems to be
modally marked. Within Fillmore's framework, we must apparently
associate this semantic distinction with a rule-feature or the
application *v.* non-application of a transformational process. In terms
of the first revision proposed above only (68.a) and (68.c) contain an
instrumental, and both (68.a) and (68.b) are associated with an
agentive. Thus, the restriction pertains only to the sentence containing
an instrumental and no agentive.

Alternatively, if some motivation can be given for the position that
the *by*-phrase in (60) and the subject in (62) do show a distinct case
relation from John in *John opened the door,* then they can be marked
as I or path but also, in the spirit of the previous proposals, [erg] .
Whereas the *with*-phrases in (64) are merely instrumental (or path).
That is, the case arrays are as in (70):

> (70) a. John opened the door   [erg] [abs]
>   A   O
>   b. The poison killed Mary   } [erg, path] [abs]
>   c. Mary was killed by the poison   }   A, I   D
>   d. Mary was killed with a red-hot toothpick [erg] [path] [abs]
>   A   I   D

Under such an analysis the problem with the set in (68) has a natural
resolution, such that the *with*-phrase in (68.a) is simply I but there is a
deleted A, the *by*-phrase in (68.b) represents a conjunction of I and A
and the *with*-phrase in (68.c) is again simply I; the important
distinction being that only (68.c) lacks an A of some sort. Whether such
an analysis is to be preferred to the one that rejects I for (60) and (62)
depends upon whether there are sufficient arguments for suggesting
that such sentences display a CR distinct from that associated with a
simple A, and for identifying the other component (combined with A

in the case) with the I element we can associate with (64).[9]

1.8 Some Problems for Case Grammar 5: The *Spray paint* cases

1.8.1. Dougherty's argument against case grammar on the basis of the
distribution of *by* in passives is thus inconclusive, if condition (c) of (23)
is dropped, i.e. if a single NP can be marked as having more than one
CR. Indeed such a revision enables us to formulate some fresh
generalisations, e.g. what underlies the 'animacy' restriction on A and
D NPs. And for the expression of none of these do we need to invoke
Chomskyan syntactic 'deep structures'. Recall too that the imposition
of condition (c) was Jackendoff's (1972) main reason for rejecting
case grammar. We shall discover in the present section that once again
an abandonment of this condition enables us to provide for the
phenomena discussed by Stephen Anderson (1971). I shall argue
moreover that such phenomena would lead us to prefer a case grammar
lacking condition (c) to the framework that Anderson attempts to
provide support for.

His starting point is certain sets of sentences much discussed in the
recent literature and earlier.[10] Consider in this regard the pairs in (71):

(71) a. John smeared paint on the wall
      b. John smeared the wall with paint

and (72):

(72) a. John jammed pencils into the jar
      b. John jammed the jar with pencils

In both instances we have, in Fillmore's terms (1968*a*, 47-8), identical
case arrays, respectively perhaps as in (73):

(73) (M V) L I A

and (74):

(74) (M V) G(oal) I A

The members of each pair differ in showing either objectivisation of
the L/G phrase (b) or lack of it (a). But the members are not synonymous.
This is highlighted in a pair like that in (75):

(75) a. John jammed a pencil into the jar
      b. John jammed the jar with a pencil

where the (b) instance, with objectivisation of G, requires us to
conceive of there being, say, a giant pencil involved. In each of the (b)
instances the instrumental is construed as exhausting the relevant
dimensions of the L/G NP. Fraser (1971) notes other properties which
such pairs do not have in common, some of which we shall take into
account in a moment.

Similarly, a pair like that in (76):

(76) a. Bees are swarming in the garden
      b. The garden is swarming with bees

appear to share the case array (77):

(77) (M V) O L

and differ only in which case phrase is subjectivised. Once again,
there is a semantic difference, and of the same character: in (76.b)
'bees' fill 'the garden' space, but not necessarily in (76.a). The
distinction is also appropriate to other post-verbal PP/NP alternations,
either with the same verb (Anderson, 1971, 391) or not: cf. *The
statue occupies/stands on a plinth.* Anderson (1971, 389) labels the
exhaustive interpretation ((b) instances) 'holistic' and the (a) instances
'partitive', and I shall retain his terms in what immediately follows.

Fillmore also (1968*a*, 48, note 49) draws attention to such examples
and describes the difference as one of 'focussing'; he concedes that they
illustrate certain 'semantic difficulties in treating subject and object
transformationally' but concludes that he is 'inclined to tolerate the
reintroduction into grammatical theory of transformations that have
semantic import (of this highly restricted kind)'. But 'focussing' is
clearly, as he himself appears to feel, a rather inadequate label for the
distinction we have looked at. And, more substantially, it is the burden
of Anderson's argument that it is the deep object NP in (71.b), (72.b)
and (75.b) (whatever its case relation, L or G) that receives the
holistic reading; and Chomsky (1972*a*) likewise argues that it is the
choice of deep subject in (76) that correlates with the holistic/partitive
distinction.

Chomsky adduces a number of examples to illustrate that the effect
of various transformations is to destroy the relevant deep structure

configuration, but that in such circumstances the readings remain
constant and are not 'overruled' by derived loss or gain of subject
position. Compare, for example, the pair in (78):

(78) a. Bees were believed to be swarming in the garden
      b. The garden was believed to be swarming with bees

Likewise, in the case of (71), (72), (75), 'the structural level in
question must precede the application of more or less well-known
transformations' (Anderson, 1971, 390), as illustrated by (79):

(79) a. A pencil would be easy for John to jam into the jar
      b. A pencil is certain to be jammed into the jar by John

v. (80):

(80) a. It's the jar that John is certain to jam with pencils
      b. It's pencils that John is certain to jam the jar with

As Anderson observes: 'The sentences in [(79)] are synonymous with
[(75.a)] in the relevant respect, while those of [(80)] are like [(72.b)]
where the holistic reading is assigned to *the jar*'. Thus, we have
motivations for pre-transformational configurations with respect to
which the notions deep subject and object can be defined and which
contribute crucially to the rules of semantic interpretation. There is
thus claimed to exist a generalisation the statement of which requires
just the deep structure configurations proposed by Chomsky (1965).

Moreover, these configurations are associated with a level that
displays the other defining properties for 'deep structure'. Thus, while
there are verbs, like those in (71), (72), and (75), which allow either
the instrumental or the L/G to appear in object position, others select
only one variant:

(81) a. John spread/*covered jelly on the sandwich
      b. John spread/covered the sandwich with jelly
      c. John sprayed/threw paint on the canvas
      d. John sprayed/*threw the canvas with paint

Also, the prepositional phrase, and not the NP, is optional for both
variants if a verb permits both, or for the one that is permitted:

(82)   a. John sprayed the paint
      b. John threw the paint
      c. John sprayed the canvas
      d.*John threw (on) the canvas

((82.d.) is anomalous on the desired interpretation.) This can be allowed
for if the level at which deep object is defined is also the level at which
selectional restrictions are stated ((81)) and strict subcategorisation
relevant ((82)) — such that the verbs surveyed select the frame (83):

(83)   ——— NP (PP)

but whereas *spray* etc. have two possible readings for the 'NP (PP)'
sequence, *throw* has only one of these and *cover* the other. In this way
such a converging variety of phenomena can be taken to lend support
to the conception of deep structure proposed by Chomsky.

    Fraser (1971) lists some further selectional restrictions associated
with the holistic/partitive distinction. There are for instance various
adverbials which select one or the other:

(84)   a. The boy loaded the boards one by one on to the wagon
      b.*The boy loaded the wagon with the boards one by one

Prefixes like *over* are possible only with the holistic:

(85)   a. Harry overloaded the wagon with hay
      b.*Harry overloaded hay on to the wagon

Again this argues for a non-transformational relationship between the
members of holistic/partitive pairs, apparently of the character
suggested by Anderson, such that *load* is associated with two different
possible interpretations of the following 'NP PP' sequence. Thus, it is
not open to Fillmore that the difference between the members of
such pairs can be associated with a surface (or some derived) structure
interpretation rule, since a transformational relationship is excluded.
Rather it looks as if *Aspects*-like 'deep structures' must be incorporated
into a case grammar, such that the case structure is accorded at best
the status of a part of the semantic representation associated with deep
structures by the projection rules. (Cf. here Katz, 1972, ch.3; Mellema,
1974.) Very schematically, the situation in the present instance might
be envisaged as in (86):

(86)

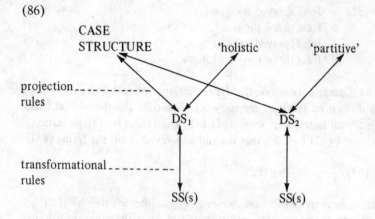

(DS = deep structure, SS = surface structure). The distinctness of case grammar from the *Aspects* theory, or vice versa, as far as claims concerning levels of representation are concerned, would in such circumstances be rather difficult to discern even despite the notational differences.

1.8.2. However, once more a natural account in terms of CRs is available for the phenomena discussed in § 1.8.1, even if we neglect the possibility of a lexicalist description, and provided we again drop the constraint on 1 CR per NP, i.e. (c) of (23). Indeed, we shall find that there are reasons for preferring the case grammar account, even apart from that deriving from the lack of independent motivation for the deep subject/ object configurations Anderson invokes.

Let us first of all discount one possibility that has some initial attraction but which must be deemed unsatisfactory as an account of the distinction under consideration. This is to withdraw from the claim that the pair in, say, (71) share the case array of (73), and to interpret only the *with*-phrase as an I, and the corresponding phrase in (71.a) as O simply. However, it is doubtful whether one can maintain even the position that the *with*-phrase in the (b) instances in (71) and (72) represents an instrumental. Observe that an instrumental phrase can be added to a sentence like (71.b), as well as to (71.a).

(87) a. John smeared the wall with paint with a large brush
      b. John smeared paint on the wall with a large brush

(though the succession of *with*'s renders (87.a) somewhat awkward).[11]
Such a source, then, is in Fillmore's terms (in the absence of a more
'abstract' analysis) in conflict with the contraint requiring 1 case per
Prop. i.e. of (23.a). Observe too that these particular *with*-phrases,
unlike other 'instrumentals', can occur in stative sentences like (88.a):

    (88) a. The wagon is loaded with hay
            b.*The wagon is loaded with a pitchfork

(88.b) can be interpreted as iterative (and non-stative), but a stative
interpretation is at all possible only if the pitchfork is thought of as the
load (like the hay in (88.a)) rather than the instrument of loading. Nor
(as Dave Roberts has pointed out to me) do these *with*-phrases allow
the *with* to drop optionally in such constructions with *use* as are
illustrated by *Fred used the hay to load the wagon with*. 'Instrumentals'
allow the *with* to drop: *Fred used the pitchfork to load the wagon
(with);* other phrases require retention of the preposition: *Fred used
the bench to lean the plank on.* Vestergaard (1973, 86; see too Fraser,
1971) also adduces further examples like those in (89):

    (89) a. The gardener stripped the bark off the tree
           b. The gardener stripped the tree of its bark

in which no *with* occurs and the corresponding phrase is even more
difficult to construe as an instrumental. He concludes that each of
these phrases 'is simply an Objective'. It certainly seems as if neither
the *with*-phrases nor the corresponding objects can plausibly be regarded
as simply instrumental.

    But there is a further, perhaps more important reason why such an
analysis, of the *with*-phrases as instrumental, is unhelpful in the present
context. It throws no light whatsoever on the source of the semantic
distinction between the members of the pairs in (71) etc., the
distinction that Anderson labelled as holistic *v.* partitive with respect
to the other (post-verbal) phrase in the sentence. And similar
considerations apply to the suggestion, within a grammar that allows
multiple CRs per NP (where constraint (c) of (23) is rejected), that
paint in (71.a) realises only O but *with paint* in (71.b) represents
O,I (see Vestergaard, 1973, 87). Within such a grammar, however, it is
conceivable that the other phrase, i.e. *(on) the wall* in (71) differs in
the CRs present in the (a) and (b) examples, specifically in that the
(b), holistic variant enters into an additional CR (Vestergaard, 1973,

§ 3). Let us now consider this possibility.

We have already observed that it may be necessary to relax condition (a) of (23) to allow up to two instances per proposition of just O, or abs; specifically to allow for equative sentences like *The guy in the corner is the man I want to marry*, wherein the NPs apparently differ thematically rather than in the CRs involved: cf. *The man I want to marry is the guy in the corner*. Suppose now that two of the NPs in (71.b) etc. are objective, but that one, the phrase which is overtly locative in the (a) instance, is also a L. That is, (71.a) and (71.b) show the case arrays in (90):

(90) a. [abs] [loc] [erg] :   John smeared paint on the wall
      b. [abs] [loc, abs] [erg] : John smeared the wall with paint

(maintaining the terminological innovations introduced earlier to characterise a grammar with multiple CRs per NP). Semantically, this accords well with how abs is normally interpreted, as exhaustive, as in (91):

(91) John read the book

unless, of course, 'over-ruled' as to the exhausting having been completed by, e.g., a progressive, as in (92):

(92) John was reading the book

Cf. (93):

(93) John was smearing the wall with paint

And the distribution of abs is as subject in passive and intransitive sentences and object in active, which accords with that of our holistic readings. All that we need add is a condition that in the (subject/object) hierarchy of cases [case, abs] outranks simple [abs], though it is outranked by [... erg ...]. So in (71.b) *the wall* becomes object, and is subject in the corresponding passive.

Such a proposal generalises to a sentence like (67.a), *The obelisk occupies the top of the hill*, where object position for the locative, and subjectivisation in the corresponding passive:

(94) The top of the hill is occupied by the obelisk

as well as its holistic character, is associated with a [loc, abs] specification, just as subject position in the active and presence in a *by*-phrase in the passive is associated with an erg in conjunction with the abs (cf. the discussion of (67) in § 1.7). Compare here Platt's (1971, § 3.1.2) discussion of *inhabit,* which requires a subject that exhausts, literally or metaphorically, the relevant dimensions of its object. More significantly still, such a proposal allows without extension for examples of the type illustrated by (76). (76.a) differs from (76.b), according to the current proposal, as in (95.a) *v.* (95.b)::

   (95) a. [abs] [loc]   : Bees are swarming in the garden
        b. [abs] [loc, abs] : The garden is swarming with bees

[loc, abs] outranks [abs] and thus becomes subject in (76.b), whereas of course in (76.a) the situation is reversed. Thus, in terms of the distribution of abs and reference to such a case-hierarchy, both the semantic distinction which initiated our discussion and the variation in subject- and object-formation can be allowed for.

1.9 Some problems for Subject-Object Grammar

1.9.1. There exists, accordingly, a plausible description in terms of CRs alone of the phenomena discussed by Anderson. Reference to 'deep subject' and 'deep object' is therefore unnecessary, and no support accrues therefrom for the proposals made by Chomsky (1965) in this regard. Moreover, not only are such notions redundant, but it is also the case that an account which attributes the holistic/partitive distinction to such configurations misses an important generalisation. For observe that there will have to be two rules of semantic interpretation involved; one which applies to deep subjects in instances like (76), another which is associated with the deep objects in (71) etc. In the case grammar account, on the other hand, the holistic interpretation is associated uniquely with the presence of abs. Thus, ascribing the determination of the holistic/partitive distinction to 'deep structure' configurations destroys the possibility of giving a unitary interpretation such as is provided by a case grammar which is like Fillmore's except for an independently motivated relaxation of two of the discriminatory constraints we discussed above.

But the situation is still worse for the subject-object grammar. Under Fillmore's analysis, verbs like *throw* will have to be marked as not permitting objectivisation of the locative (cf. (81)), whereas with *cover* and the like such objectivisation is obligatory. Anderson argues

(394-5) that it is an advantage of his account that it permits the elimination of this necessity. Rather, these verbs and *spread* etc. are all subcategorised as selecting the frame '——NP (PP)'. But

> verbs like *load, smear, spray* have two possible interpretations of the following PP . . . while those like *litter, cover* on the one hand, and *throw, pitch* on the other have only one possible interpretation of the PP which differs from one class to the other.

However, is it really an improvement to have to say, for this is what is involved, that selectionally there are two verbs *load* or *smear,* which both happen to appear in the same frame but which have their respective restrictions in reverse, PP in the one instance corresponding to NP in the other and vice versa?

In terms of the multiple-CR analysis we have arrived at, the three classes of verbs distinguished by Anderson are differentiated in terms of their case frames, as illustrated in the relevant respects in (96):

(96)   smear   + [——[abs] [loc (abs)] [erg]]
       cover   + [——[abs] [loc,abs] [erg]]
       throw   + [——[abs] [loc] [erg]]

The two possibilities for *smear* etc. are allowed for by the facultative presence of the abs in conjunction with loc, a presence which is required by *cover* and disallowed with *throw.*

Notice too with regard to Anderson's account that the subcategorisation proposed is observationally inadequate as far as a verb like *jam* is concerned: compare with (75.a) **John jammed a pencil* which is. (non-elliptically) deviant (see Fraser, 1971). Moreover the proposed optionality of the PP makes it somewhat paradoxical for Anderson to claim that 'verbs like *load, smear, spray* have two possible interpretations of the following PP . . .' However Anderson does not present any evidence for the claim that the PP is absent in deep structure even in instances like those in (82), and thus optional in frame (83). At any rate the point is not important in the present discussion, since Anderson's claim can be accommodated by making the simple abs optional in the frames for *smear* and *cover* in (96) whereas for *smear* and *throw* loc is optional. The anomalous *John smeared (on the wall)* which would correlate with the absence of both instances of abs, is ruled out by the constraint that every proposition must contain one absolutive (cf. ch.2 below). Similarly, the *jam* situation can be allowed for by making both instances of abs facultative, such that the presence of at least one of them is again ensured by the general constraint that each proposition contain at least one abs. See too Anderson, 1975*a*, 94-5.

However, the (non-elliptical) non-acceptability of **John jammed the pencils v. John jammed the jar* presents what seems to be a rather serious problem for Anderson. Notice that it is now misleading to say that *jam* is a verb that appears in the frame '——NP (PP)', since the PP is optional only on one interpretation. Of course, we can allow for the non-viability of the former by attributing it to some semantic projection rule, which rejects such 'deep structures' — but only with some verbs. But this now commits us to saying that the optionality of the PP in *John jammed the jar (with the pencils)* is a 'syntactic fact' captured by strict subcategorisation, whereas the non-optionality of the PP in *John jammed the pencils into the jar* is a 'semantic fact' expressed by the projection rules. I know of no basis for this particular distinction between 'syntactic facts' and 'semantic facts', which is apparently an artefact of Anderson's utilisation of the *Aspects* framework. Such an arbitrary distinction need not arise if lexical insertion is not made with respect to 'deep structure' configurations but in relation to case structure.

Accordingly, an examination of the phenomena adduced by both Dougherty and Anderson (§§ 1.7, 1.8, respectively) does not lead us necessarily to a rejection of case grammar or to an interpretation of case structure as simply part of the semantic representation provided by the projection rules on the basis of Chomskyan 'deep structures'. On the contrary, we find that lexical insertion and subcategorisation of verbs refer crucially to the case representation rather than to 'deep structure' configurations. And that the holistic/partitive distinction can be given a uniform description only with reference to CRs; attributing it to 'deep structure' destroys the unity of formulation. What we have gained for case grammar is, I think, a more adequate conception of the relation between NPs and CRs, specifically involving the abandonment of (c) of (23). We return in the following chapter to a consideration of how the assignment of CRs to NPs is otherwise to be constrained.

Let me make it plain that I do not consider that the account we have arrived at of the syntax and semantics of the *spray paint* phenomena is totally adequate. It is clearly lacking, particularly on semantic grounds: for discussion, see Jessen, 1974, ch.7. Moreover, it should be noted that the 'holistic/partitive' phenomena do not uniquely support the theory of case grammar, in that the 'holistic' generalisation is also expressible in a subject-object grammar in which the object in (71.b) etc. originates as the subject in an embedded clause. Such an analysis as I advocated in §1.8.2 also, when taken together with the discussion of 'instrumental *with*' in § 1.7, and its use as a 'comitative' marker, fails to provide a uniform account of the source of this preposition, despite the fact that there are semantic similarities between all three instances (cf. Seiler, 1973). A resolution of the discrepancy would seem to require a more abstract analysis, perhaps along the lines suggested by the paraphrases in (97.b):

(97) 1. a. Fred opened the window with a chisel
        b. Fred opened the window by using a chisel (on it)
     2. a. Fred loaded the wagon with hay
        b. Fred filled the wagon by loading hay (on it)
     3. a. Fred went to the party with Bill
        b. Fred went to the party by accompanying Bill (to it)

On the relation between (97.2.a) and (97.2.b) cf. again Jessen, 1974, ch.7. These and other *with's* are discussed in Roberts, forthcoming: ch.5.

My concern here, however, has been simply to show that an account incorporating CRs is preferable to one which invokes reference to 'deep structures'. This being so, we have clearly also not demonstrated that such 'deep structure' configurations as Chomsky proposed have no systematic status. The possibility of finding support for such a status is however considerably weakened if lexical insertion and subcategorisation invoke case structures rather than these configurations. In particular, the characterisation of 'deep structure' provided in Chomsky (1972*a*, § 2.2), viz. 'the level of representation . . . defined as the set of phrase markers that appear in derivations after all transformations of L <the set of lexical transformations> have applied', would select case representations as 'deep structures' rather than subject-object configurations. And the expression of the holistic/partitive distinction certainly provides no evidence in support of deep subject-object grammars, in that again it correlates crucially with case representations. Accordingly, since Chomsky's original discussion was provided with no empirical support for the postulating of subject-object 'deep structures', and since the predictions made there are disconfirmed by the phenomena we have looked at, the onus is very much upon the proponents of such a view to offer some more adequate proposals and some substantive evidence relative to the 'deep structure' hypothesis and to its subject-object character.

The prospects for such an enterprise are not encouraging. As far as I

am aware, and given the primitiveness of the discipline, the situation
with the 'holistic/partitive' distinction is typical. A number of further
semantic distinctions which correlate directly with a case representation
or a more 'abstract' analysis but cut across Chomskyan subject-object
'deep structures' are discussed by Jessen (1974, e.g. §§ 6.2.3, 6.3.4).
Consider, for example, Macaulay's (1971, vii) observation that
'inherently [−PERFECTIVE] verbs form part of a [+PERFECTIVE]
predication if the direct object is a singular [+SPECIFIC] noun phrase'.
Thus, whereas (98.a), with [−PERF] verb and [−SPEC] object and
thus [−PERF] VP is viable, i.e. the VP accepts such adverbials as *all
day*:

(98) a. John delivered notices to quit all day
      b.*John delivered the notice to quit all day

the [+SPEC] object in (98.b) renders the VP [+PERF] and thus
incompatible with such an adverbial. Now, whatever the adequacy of
Macaulay's formulation (for some problems, see Jessen, 1974, § 6.3.4.4),
the same restriction seems to apply with respect to the subjects of such
intransitive verbs as that in (99):

(99) a. Notices to quit arrived all day
      b.*The notice to quit arrived all day

As Jessen observes, 'this is simply a reflection of the ergative relationship
holding between such pairs' as (98.a) and (99.a). In a case grammar the
object in (98) and the subject in (99) share the CR abs; but in a deep
subject-object grammar the property is not associated with the same
deep relation.

Thus, as far as *Aspects*-type deep structures are concerned, it is
not merely the case that, as Bedell (1973, 23) concludes, 'there is no
generalization which will be lost, or explanation which cannot be made,
if deep structures . . . are not provided for in grammatical theory'.
Rather, the statement of some of those generalisations which are
criterial for deep structure − semantic rules which refer to grammatical
relations, strict subcategorisation, selectional restrictions (Anderson,
1971, 396) − is incompatible with a concept of deep structure whereby
it is distinct from case representations. This is of course not to claim that
there is necessarily a single level to which all these generalisations can
be referred; but simply that their formulation invokes case representations
rather than the information provided by Chomskyan 'deep structures'.

1.9.2. Moreover, I think it can be maintained that in so far as there are transformational rules that make reference to 'grammatical relations' (and this appears to be quite far), the relations involved are the CRs and the derived relations (like subject) rather than the 'deep subject' etc. of the *Aspects* theory. Let me try to illustrate this for one particular instance, anticipating the more general discussion of ch.3, though the characterisations must remain somewhat schematic in that we have not yet arrived in our exposition at more than an outline of a case grammar which will provide for the various phenomena discussed in the previous sections. The instance is the rule of RAISING.

Postal (1974) has recently devoted a lengthy work to an attempt to establish the existence of a rule which raises the subject of a complement sentence into object position in the main clause. It is not my concern here, and indeed it is unnecessary, to determine whether or not the existence of raising is incompatible (as Lightfoot (to appear) argues is not the case) with the recent framework outlined by Chomsky (1973), who rejects subject-to-object raising. This is because that framework retains the essential inadequacies, from the point of view of our present enquiry, to be found in Chomsky (1965), and is thus of no direct interest to us. I merely take it that there is a range of evidence supporting the view that there is such a rule. Of the three counter-arguments of Chomsky's discussed by Postal (1974, ch.5), Lightfoot attempts to defend two, that based on unexpected exceptions (given raising derivations) to *tough*-movement and that involving extraction from subject NPs. While it seems to me that the import of the full range of phenomena connected with the former remains unclear, and they are thus indecisive, the evidence relevant to the latter supports Postal's formulation, as I shall try to show in § 2.8.

Postal is mainly concerned with English examples like that in (100):

(100)   I expected John to like Fred

wherein the NP *John* originates in the complement sentence, as subject of *like,* and is moved by raising into the object slot in the upper sentence. However, he also provides some evidence (1974, § 12.2) which suggests that a rule with the same effect (stated, as above, in an informal way), and which shares various other properties with raising in English, has also applied in such sentences of Japanese as (101):

(101)   John wa Mary o baka da to omotte ita
                    'fool' 'is' 'thinking' 'was'

('John thought that Mary was a fool')

(cf. too Kuno, 1972). Here *o* marks *Mary,* which NP originates in the
lower clause, as object of the verb in the upper. He goes on to consider
the question of why these two unrelated languages should show such
similar rules, and concludes:

> The most direct, natural, and ultimately most interesting answer to
> this kind of question would be that the similarities are a function of
> the fact that, in effect, both languages *have the same rule,* this being
> an element of universal grammar, characterised in general linguistic
> theory.

But if English is an underlying VSO (McCawley, 1970) or SVO
language while Japanese is SOV the rule which expresses raising in
English cannot be collapsed with that expressing raising in Japanese,
given the usual practice of formulating transformations in terms of
constituents like NP etc. and their order: i.e. the universal rule of
raising cannot be given a uniform formulation. That this is so is
apparent from the structural descriptions offered by Postal (1974, 381):

(102)   a. *English* X, Verb, (NP) [$_{NP}$[$_S$ Verb, NP, Y$_S$] $_{NP}$],   Z
                      1   2   3   4   5   6   7
        b. *Japanese* X (NP), [$_{NP}$[$_S$ NP, Y, Verb$_S$] $_{NP}$] Verb, Z
                      1   2   3   4   5   6   7

Raising in English involves moving term 5 of (102.a) out of its S,
such that it intervenes between that S and terms 1-3 (including
the main verb); whereas in Japanese it is term 3 of (102.b) that is
extracted, and it comes to be separated from the main verb (term 6)
by the S it leaves behind. In the face of this, and for other reasons
we shall note in a moment, Postal proposes (1974, 385) that raising
be formulated 'in terms of grammatical relations, in terms making
crucial utilisation of the Functional Succession Principle.' Let us
now consider such a formulation, and, firstly, the latter
principle.

    Postal (1974, 287) expresses the functional succession principle,
which applies to all 'promotion rules' ('which have the effect of
extracting one NP from a larger containing NP'), as follows: 'when a
promotional rule extracts one NP, NP$_a$, from a containing NP, NP$_c$
in the output, NP$_a$ takes on the grammatical function manifested by

NP$_c$ in the input'. This principle, in effect, embodies a claim that certain properties of raising in English are not contingent but are design features of promotion rules. For instance, given a pre-raising representation of the shape (103):

(103)   [$_S$ believe I [$_{NP}$[$_S$ understand Sally herself$_S$] $_{NP}$]

(assuming again the VSO hypothesis), (104):

(104)   I believe Sally to understand herself

but not (105):

(105)   *Sally believes me to understand herself

is a possible output in terms of the principle, in that in (105) the NP *Sally* has been raised out of an object complement into subject position in the main clause. According to the principle the absence of such an output for raising is not an idiosyncratic feature of English, but a consequence of a property of general linguistic theory. Postal (1974, 385) suggests that, this being so, raising can be reduced to a formulation such as (106):

(106)   Promote the subject of a complement

and comments: 'If it is true that Raising is reducible to a statement of the form indicated in [(106)], with the output structure determined by the Functional Succession Principle, then under the assumption that the relevant grammatical relations can be defined independently of the position of the main verb of a clause, it would not matter whether a universal rule of Raising operated on verb-initial or verb-final structures'.

Now, whereas the relation in the complement S referred to in (106) is clearly the derived subject (cf. *I expected John to be thought disingenuous by Fred* and the like), it seems to be the case that, with raising at least, the relations in the main clause which are relevant are CRs rather than (deep) subject and object. Raising in (100) involves, as we have observed, movement of a NP out of an object complement S to occupy object position in the main clause, and in (107):

(107)   John happens to like Fred

movement of *John* out of the subject complement into subject position, both in accordance with the functional succession principle. But observe that a further generalisation is possible; in both instances the CR involved (whether the NP occupies the subject or object slot) is the absolutive (Fillmore's O). The main clause subject with verbs allowing raising into object position is either ergative (*cause,* or Postal's N-verbs — Postal, 1974, §4.13) or [erg, loc] (*believe, want* — cf. § 1.7 on *know*); the object is absolutive, is prepositionless and passivises. On the other hand, the subject of verbs that show raising into subject position, such as *happen* (Postal, 1974, § 2.2), is absolutive (specifically, it lacks any agentive characteristics). It is not accidental, given (despite Szamosi, 1973) the unity of raising (Roldán, 1972; Radford, 1975), that what is involved is the object in (100) and the subject in (107). Equi, on the other hand, never involves a marked controller which is a simple abs; indeed, in § 3.4 we shall find that it is perhaps even more constrained and with reference to CRs. Raising thus comprises the taking over of the absolutive function of (the NP containing) a complement S by the subject of that S. If subject and object are derived functions, and subject/object selection is cyclic, then this is what one would expect: the relations referred to in the main clause can be and are the CRs and those in the complement (where subject/object selection has already applied) must be the derived functions. In neither instance need the notion of a 'deep' subject, distinct from a derived one, be invoked. Thus, once again, and on this occasion in the formulation of the transformation raising, there exists a generalisation which is unexpressed if subject-object 'deep structures' are invoked in preference to CRs.

1.10 Postscript

1.10.1. In the preceding I have tried to sketch out some of the motivations underlying the development of case grammar and to indicate in a preliminary fashion some of its properties. We have also surveyed some of the major criticisms of Fillmore's earlier presentations, and have concluded that most of the phenomena invoked in such in fact support the theory of case grammar rather than the subject-object grammar of *Aspects.* One general feature of Fillmore's proposals (which however was not subscribed to in Anderson, 1968*a*, etc.) we have found reason to modify, namely the restriction of each NP to one CR. In the following chapter we must turn to the question of how such (multiple) CRs are to be assigned, and in general to a more careful characterisation of the form of the grammar.

Moreover, we have thus far had little to say concerning the character

of the cases themselves, and this too requires to be remedied. In
chapter 2 we consider this question in the light of a general
characterisation of the notion 'possible CR'. For this reason, too, I have
not pursued in the preceding the various modifications to the set of
cases which have been envisaged over the years by Fillmore and others.[12]
Some of these discussions will be important, however, for the development of the argument of chapter 2.

Moreover, there is clearly a vast number of proposals, made within
a variety of frameworks, which are more or less relevant to any
extended discussion of the character of a case grammar but which in the
present context I am unable for the most part to take account of
explicitly. I am thinking particularly of work on Valenztheorie[13] and
systemic grammar[14] and a variety of other enterprises.[15] Another time
and place (and probably another writer) will hopefully accomplish the
huge task of comparison, evaluation and synthesis that the range of
recent researches has created: for a step in that direction, see Hofmann,
1974.

1.10.2. As the ensuing discussion develops in the following chapter and
particularly thereafter we shall be led to propose underlying
representations which are increasingly 'abstract' in that they are linked
by a complex set of mappings to appropriate superficial structures. I
shall nevertheless maintain that such representations are NATURAL,
not only in providing in part for semantic properties of the sentences
concerned but also in determining details of surface structure. In
particular we shall be concerned to provide derivations which are
LEXICALLY NATURAL, in that, *ceteris paribus*, accounts which
assign a unitary source to a particular lexical form will be preferred to
those which require homonymy. (Cf. here Zwicky, 1968; Anderson,
1973*b*.) Moreover, the derivational mappings, local derivational
constraints, transformations or whatever assumed in the discussion
will belong to a small universal set, involving crucially raising and
SUPERIMPOSITION ('quantifying in' — Anderson, 1973*a*); and the
invoking in the analysis proposed of ad hoc transformational rules
is thus precluded. The notion 'possible transformation' is in principle
further constrained in terms of the requirements that they comply
with conditions of learnability and that they be relatable to some
communicative function; raising and superimposition, for instance,
serve simultaneously to abbreviate underlying structures and
foreground the basic propositional content (Langacker, 1974);
EXTRAPOSITION in a SVO language like English reduces

centre-embedding (Langendoen, 1970; Kuno, 1974).[16]

Nevertheless, we shall posit underlying representations which are related to the corresponding surface structures by derivations which are rather complex (or at least extended), no matter how simple or restricted the components. By contrast, the work of Starosta (e.g. 1971*b*, *c*, 1972, 1973*a*, *b*, *c*, 1974) has involved a retreat (or, if you prefer, advance) away from even the rather limited degree of discrepancy between corresponding underlying and surface structures characteristic of Fillmore, 1968*a*, etc. It thus behoves us to give some attention to the viability of such a development.

Starosta's work (e.g. 1973*a*) has moved towards a radical 'lexicalist' position, such that

> the role of transformations as devices for formalizing the speaker's knowledge of how sentences are related may be minimal, and most surface structures may be generated directly by phrase structure rules.

Starosta proposes to retain case-free constituent structure representations and suggest that CRs be interpreted as features on lexical items (verbs as well as nouns, prepositions, etc.) and that the relationship between, for instance, 'corresponding' actives and passives may be mediated by a lexical derivational rule of the character of (108):

$$(108) \quad \begin{bmatrix} + V \\ + AGT \end{bmatrix} \longrightarrow \begin{bmatrix} + Adj \\ + OBJ \\ + \underline{\quad} ([+AGT]) \end{bmatrix}$$

'which derives [+ OBJ] adjective predicates allowing agent complements from [+ AGT] verbs' (cf. again Freidin, 1972*a*, 1975). If all such relationships can be adequately characterised in terms of the formally simple derivational rules he proposes, then 'there is no longer any reason for having a separate deep structure at all'. Starosta, following Taylor (1972, 8), dubs such an approach a 'LEXICASE GRAMMAR'.[17]

The lexicase framework makes in principle a very strong claim concerning the degree of complexity of the relations that hold between sentences of the language. These are limited to derivational rules of the form of (108). However, it remains to be seen whether such a strong claim can be maintained with respect to the range of transformational relationships that have been argued for,[18] and whether the 'lexicase' syntactic representations provide a sufficient basis for

semantic interpretation. (For some discussion, see Seuren, 1973.) It
seems to me, moreover, that this strong claim may be being made at
the expense of strong claims (like the localist one we consider in ch.2)
concerning the notion possible CR and the relationship between CRs
and their expression. Since I can see no way whereby the phenomena
to be examined in the following chapters can be accommodated
within the 'lexicase' framework,[19] subsequent discussion will be cast
within the kind of framework whose major properties were sketched
out above and will be elaborated on in what follows, namely one
wherein derivational constraints mediate between corresponding
underlying (semantically relevant) and superficial structures and in
which CRs play a role throughout derivations: call it 'semanticase', if
you will.

1.10.3. However, before leaving this area, let us explore in a little more
detail one aspect of Starosta's proposals, viz. the relationship between
CRs and CFs, not merely in an attempt to substantiate the claim I have
just made concerning the weakness of Starosta's hypothesis concerning
such, but also because the discussion will serve to introduce what
seems to me an important restriction on the character of this
relationship.

Starosta (1973*a*) concludes, primarily as the result of a survey of
seven languages with rather different systems of case-expression, that
'the realization of two case relations by the same case form is not random'
and that 'the same pairs of case relations tend to share common
realisations in many different languages', and that 'to describe this
phenomenon properly, it becomes necessary to assign labels to case
forms'. Thus, two universal sets of 'case' features are proposed, firstly
a set of CRs of roughly the dimension and content advocated by
Fillmore, and secondly a set of case forms, which include the
following: ergative (in 'ergative languages'), nominative (in 'accusative
languages'), benefactive, dative, allative, instrumental, locative, accusative,
ablative. It then 'becomes possible', Starosta argues, 'to state the
systematic correlation between relations and forms where it occurs,
and to indicate which form-relation associations are universal'.

However, it can be observed that the set of 'case forms' just listed
bears a striking resemblance, with one or two exceptions, to the set of
CRs proposed by Fillmore. But since the CRs and CFs are two disjoint
sets, it is not entirely clear what this identity of labelling is intended
to betoken. Are the CFs simply labelled in the same way as the CR
which they 'most typically' manifest? If so, then the introduction of

such CFs is redundant, since this information is extractable from the rules specifying which phonological shapes go with which CRs – that is if the notion of 'typical manifestation' is to have any empirical content. In which case the introduction of CFs is an unnecessary complication. Moreover, their introduction does not in fact explain the character of the CR/CF correlations that Starosta establishes. He finds, for example, that 'all languages have a single case form that can realize [the CRs] DAT, DIR, and LOC'. But why is this so? On his account, it would be equally plausible to find that all languages had a single CF for 'Source', 'Benefactive' and 'Time'. If this is not so, it is unexplained by the positing of a set of universal CFs. Such a position offers no advance over a theory which lacks such CFs but simply says that in many (sometimes all) languages the cases X, Y, Z have an identical realisation. It does not help to ascribe the universal CF/CR correlations to an innate (or intrinsic) human language faculty, since that still leaves unexplained why those particular correlations are the ones that are universal/innate.

Starosta himself, quoting some suggestions of Fillmore's provoked by his paper, indicates the direction in which explanation might lie, such that 'certain cases do have some kinds of shared characteristics'. There exist semantically and syntactically natural explanations for the apparently haphazard syncretisms. In fact, the localist theory provides an explanation of why 'all languages have a single case form that can realise DAT, DIR, and LOC': they all involve the same case relation, locative (cf. Anderson, 1971*b*; and see too chapter 2). Of course, some of the 'natural' correlations are only historically so; and it appears that it is such instances that lead Starosta to adopt a very weak, i.e. unconstrained position vis-à-vis the CR/CF correlation. Thus, for instance, *to* marks not only 'DAT, DIR and LOC' in English but also acts as a complementiser (whatever the source of these). But, historically, the *to* + infinitive construction belongs naturally with a group that includes 'DIR'. The synchronically unnatural grouping is the result of the generalisation of the use of the *to* + infinitive construction outside its semantically natural province. But even synchronically this does not necessitate the introduction of a set of CFs of the kind envisaged by Starosta. It is a stronger hypothesis to maintain that the set of CRs is sufficient to describe the semantic and syntactic phenomena associated with case. In the present instance it is preferable to regard the use of *to* as a complementiser as a syntactic or lexical assimilation (of the complementiser to loc), and thereby explicitly mark it as the unnatural use, as compared with the others, which are not the result of

assimilation but are semantically and syntactically natural. Only if the
same set of primes (here CRs) is utilised throughout can we
differentiate in this way between the semantically natural and the
syntactically derived or lexically specified.[20]

There remains as apparently a CF with no CR analogue the
nominative. Starosta would add the 'accusative' and the 'ergative', but
these can be given a natural definition in terms of CRs. Thus the
'(objective) accusative' marks an abs phrase in an active proposition
that also contains a distinct erg; whereas the 'ergative' marks an erg
phrase in a proposition which also contains a distinct abs. (For some
refinements see §§ 3.5.-.6.) Even the use of the 'accusative' to mark both
an abs and an allative, as in the Latin examples discussed in § 1.1, is
natural with respect to a localist analysis of CRs: in both instances the
'accusative' marks the 'goal', i.e. a non-source CR in the presence (in
the same proposition) of the corresponding source (either locative or
non-locative) CR (cf. the componential analysis in Anderson, 1973*c*,
chapter 1; and see chapter 2). And even the 'subjective nominative' may
yield to an analysis in terms again of assimilation to erg (roughly,
agentive), i.e. subjects are either original erg phrases or phrases whose
CR assimilates to erg in the absence in that proposition of an original
erg. Subject-formation either applies vacuously (if the predication
already contains an erg) or it consists, in a predication lacking an
underlying erg phrase, of making some phrase into an erg: after
subject-formation, the phrase marked as erg is the subject. (See further
chapter 3.) If the Indo-European masculine singular nominative, for
example, is indeed historically derived from an ergative marker (on the
controversy, see Martinet, 1962, 49-52), an assimilation theory for
subjects would provide an explanation for such an evolution.

However that may be, it seems to me that we still lack compelling
evidence that it is necessary to posit such an independent universal set
of CFs as Starosta proposes (as opposed to the traditional
morphologically defined sets with more or less natural CR correlations).
Unfortunately, the two examples cited by Starosta (1973) to illustrate
'the fact that they [case forms] play an important role in various
rules of grammar' are given too brief a discussion to permit realistic
evaluation (particularly since the work of Manley's (1972) invoked was
not available to me at the time of writing). Notice too that the two
sets of case features are 'universal' in rather different senses. Only the
CRs (particularly within a localist theory) are contenders for 'strong'
universality, i.e. necessary inclusion in the grammar of a natural
language; the CFs of Starosta are 'weak', in that they constitute a set

from which languages select in various ways. My own impression is
that they can also be regarded as at most epiphenomenal with respect
to CRs and combinations of CRs.

1.11 PPS on Serialisation

1.11.1. Such a view of derived relations as was introduced above, i.e. as
assimilations of one CR to another, raises some intriguing possibilities,
possibilities to which we must now devote some attention. In the first
place it means that it becomes plausible to consider that all cyclic
'NP-movement' rules are framed in terms of CRs, either original (as with
the absolutive in the upper clause in the case of raising) or derived (the
'subject', i.e. ergative (either from an original erg or some other case),
in the lower clause with raising). Moreover, instead of Fillmore's hierarchy
of CRs with respect to subject-selection, we shall be able in ch.2 to
propose a much more restricted hierarchy of cases susceptible to
ERG-ASSIMILATION. Further, such rules, and perhaps cyclic rules
in general, can now refer to order-free representations: NPs are no
longer identified by sequence. The SEQUENCING constraints (cf.
Anderson, 1971*b*, ch.11) responsible for proper linearisation can then
be late, possibly post-cyclic; and the tenability of this last proposal is
then enhanced if those transformations whose formulation or indeed
whose presence in the grammar of a particular language is conditional
upon constituent ordering (Hankamer, 1974) or upon the word-order
type of the language (as e.g. extraposition — Kuno, 1974) are also
post-cyclic, and can thus refer in a straightforward way to sequenced
(rather than 'wild' (Staal, 1967*a*)) trees. (On the linear character
of post-cyclic syntax see e.g. Pullum, 1975*a*.) And significant constraints
are imposed by such a proposal — henceforth POST-CYCLIC
SERIALISATION (PCS) — on the character of underlying structures
and the content of transformations. For instance, if PCS is assumed
deep structures cannot include two identically labelled pre-lexical
nodes that differ only in relative sequence — provided that sequence
cannot be invoked — if these are to be assigned different functions or
be susceptible to different transformations. I formulate this consequence
of PCS, informally, as in (109):

(109)   *Monoparity constraint*
If in pre-shallow structure nodes N_i and N_j, bearing the same pre-
lexical label, are both immediately dominated by some N_k (i.e.
are sisters), then $N_i \equiv N_j$, N_i and N_j are the same node.

(In other words, twin nodes are excluded.) Thus, PCS requires that the (rather widely entertained) analysis of indirect objects presented in, for example, Jacobs & Rosenbaum (1968, 54-5) should be rejected. They propose a phrase structure rule of the form (110):

(110)   VP   →   VB (NP) (NP)

where the indirect object (the first of two NPs introduced by (110)) can be moved over the direct (by 'indirect object inversion') and thus retain its preposition, as in (111.b) *v.* (111.a):

(111)   a. A dispatcher handed the engineer a message
        b. A dispatcher handed a message to the engineer

There are other reasons for rejecting such an analysis (see e.g. Anderson, 1971*b*, ch.9; and §§ 2.6-.8 below). The principle of PCS predicts this; and it predicts that all such analyses are indefensible.

A similar constraint is imposed by Chomsky's (1965) requirement that grammatical functions be definable in terms of immediate dominance relations, which again requires that only one instance of any category be immediately dominated by a particular node. It is this which allows Chomsky to suggest that the definition of subject as [NP, S] is universal, even if languages may differ in their underlying word order. However, this requirement is immediately violated by, for example, the rule expanding VP in his 'illustrative fragment', which introduces (optionally) two PPs, unless it is intended that for some unstated reason no grammatical relations in fact hold here. And we have already seen (§ 1.2) that the treatment of functions in terms of configurations is unmotivated and inconsistently interpreted.

It is possible, of course, in the case of Jacobs & Rosenbaum's analysis of direct and indirect objects, to reformulate (110) so that reference to sequence in defining the functions is eliminated, if, for instance we substitute for (110) the rule in (112):

(112)   VP   →   VB ((NP) NP)

and the associated structures bear optionality diacritics; such that the indirect object is defined as the innermost NP, and serialisation and preposition deletion/retention is framed with reference to the functions 'indirect object' and 'direct object'. In which case, sequence is clearly irrelevant, as elsewhere, to the definition of the grammatical relations.

But even this formulation is excluded by (109), in that the two nodes retain their identical labelling and sisterhood status: thus, not only relative sequence but also relative optionality is excluded as an identificatory diacritic in pre-shallow structures. I conclude that PCS imposes significant constraints on pre-shallow representations and the rules that relate them. Thus, PCS is a significant empirical hypothesis; its import for our present discussion is this: in a grammar in which subject is a derived relation and NPs originate as (unordered) arguments of a predicate, PCS can be ensured only if the arguments bear labels (CRs); i.e. PCS entails labelled arguments (relations), but not vice versa. The viability of PCS is accordingly of some interest to the case grammarian.

1.11.2. In insisting that some decision on underlying order is required and determinate for any language, discussions rejecting late serialisation have generally failed to appreciate the empirical content of such a claim. In dismissing such 'set-systems' of base rules as have been proposed by Curry (1961) and Šaumjan & Soboleva (1963), Chomsky (1965, 125), for instance, claims that 'it has invariably been found that different sets (of syntactically related structures) in a single language lead to the *same* decision as to the abstract underlying order of elements'. Such a statement is quite at variance with the controversies over the word order of, say, German and Old English. It must be regarded as hypothetical only. Moreover, as far as I am aware, there is in fact no motivation offered by most discussions for selecting any particular order as opposed to no particular order for pre-shallow structures. And it transpires that the formulation of such universal rules as raising does not depend on ordering; indeed, reference to sequence is undesirable. Chomsky (1965, 125) merely confuses the issue by his unwarranted conclusion that

> presumably, the proposal that the categorial component should be a set-system entails that in a set of syntactically related structures with a single network of grammatical relations . . . , each member is directly related to the underlying abstract representation, and there is no internal organisation − that is, no order of derivation − within the set of structures.

But this follows only if transformations are formulated so as to require reference to relative order. Otherwise the questions of underlying linear order of elements (concatenation) and order of derivation are clearly distinct. It is only the necessity of making the former kind of decision that I am suggesting here has lacked motivation.

A more recent and, in some ways, rather more cautious defence of the ordered base hypothesis is offered by Bach (1975). However, as evidence on this particular issue none of his arguments are quite to the point. (One consideration he raises, nevertheless, is one of several which have led me to adopt in what follows a rather different view of pre-shallow structures than is required by PCS: see below.) Notice in the first place that Bach's evaluation of the relative strengths of various theories of the base (1975, § 1) is debatable at the very least. Let us distinguish three main possibilities: (a) unordered bases (UOB); (b) single order base – i.e. the hypothesis that there is a unique universal underlying order (SOB), determinate for all languages; (c) ordered bases, the particular order being a linguistic variable but determinate for a particular language (OB). Bach argues that UOB and OB are both weakenings, in contrary directions of SOB. Now, given his unexceptionable formulation whereby a hypothesis is stronger than another if it 'rules out more possible states of affairs within its domain of application' than the other, clearly OB is a weakening of SOB in that the former allows for there to be more possible deep structures than the latter. But it is not at all clear that UOB is simply a weakening of SOB. Both UOB and SOB embody a claim that languages cannot differ in their base order, either because order is not relevant to base structures or because it is not a linguistic variable. To be sure, SOB also embodies, if it is not to be vacuous, a claim that the evidence internal to any language will lead us to select a particular underlying order, and that this order will be the same for any language. This claim, of DEEP STRUCTURE DETERMINACY, UOB clearly fails to make (while for the OB hypothesis determinacy appertains, apparently idiosyncratically, to particular languages). But, as we have seen, UOB also embodies as a natural consequence a hypothesis that is not intrinsic to SOB, namely that formulated as (109), the monoparity constraint, which forbids identically labelled sisters, and, by extension to other pre-shallow structures, rules which move but do not reattach. It seems to me that we have here two different empirical hypotheses which are not to be compared simply in terms of some crude unidimensional measure of strength. I shall propose below a hypothesis which embraces both monoparity and deep structure determinacy of a degree intermediate between SOB and OB.

Bach (1975, § 4) presents 'a number of facts which seem to [be] best explicable on the basis of rules or constraints that are applicable to intermediate structures that differ in their order from surface structures'. But even if this were so, some variant of UOB could still be maintained. If, for instance, all order-dependent rules and constraints referred to post-shallow structures, then PCS is maintainable. Alternatively, sequence can be introduced as part of the cycle of transformations, perhaps at the end of each cycle (Pullum, 1975*c*). Again, these are empirical alternatives which Bach fails to consider. And once more his claim (p.318) that a grammar that introduces order in the course of derivations rather then in the base is weaker (in the sense introduced above) is contestable, to say the least. He argues that such UOB grammars 'make weaker assumptions about the class of possible grammars' in that in terms of such a system 'two languages could differ in their transformations and in their ordering rules, not merely in their transformations'. But we have already seen that the set of deep structures and the class of transformations are automatically more restricted within a system with UOB, which requires of necessity that the monoparity constraint hold. Further, even if this were not so, the extent to which Bach's observation is of significance is dependent upon the degree to which ordering rules can be shown to be universal (in the sense of being universally predictable from other aspects of structure).

This leads on to a further respect in which Bach's evaluation of competing hypotheses is misleading. He devotes a paragraph (p.324) to berating, with some justice, the proposition (which he fails to document) that 'set systems' (UOBs) are preferable to 'concatenation systems' because they are 'more abstract'. But in occupying himself solely with dismissing this as 'absurd', he misses, it seems to me, an important point. Namely this: a grammar which provides for the syntax of English without reference to precedence relations and in terms of which order is predictable from other properties is in Bach's own terms stronger than one which utilises both these other properties (like dominance relations) and ordering, i.e. in which ordering and dominance are semi-independent. The former excludes *ceteris paribus* more states of affairs than the latter. Thus, with respect to all of the general considerations which he raises, and in terms of the measure of strength that he himself introduces, Bach's assignments of relative strength to the hypotheses concerning the base that he considers seem to me to be questionable (at the very least).

1.11.3. I shall, however, in what follows not adopt the PCS hypothesis but rather what I shall call the SEQUENCE-PRESERVING HYPOTHESIS. In terms of this, serialisation is early in the cycle or,

more probably, precyclic, but throughout the cycle the relative order of
lexical categories is invariant. Thus, the only 'movement' possible is via
rules like subject-raising, whereby a subconfiguration is copied into an
'empty' slot and the original possibly deleted. However, reattachments
involving simply a change in the dominance or government (cf. ch.2)
relations are possible. But these reattachments must not infringe the
linearisation principles. More generally, at shallow structure,
linearisation must be in accord with the principles in terms of which
linearisation was imposed before the application of the cyclic
rules.

Linearisation is imposed on the basis of (a) modifier-head relations
and (b) grammatical relations. Modifier-head relations may be serialised
in either direction: modifier before head; modifier after head. This is a
linguistic variable: we may distinguish, utilising Tesnière's terminology,
centripetal (head last) from centrifugal (head first) languages. The viability
of such a generalisation depends upon an adequate characterisation of the
notion 'modifier-head'; and we return to this in ch.2. We also return, in chs.
2 and 3, to a consideration of the character of the relations invoked in
serialisation and of the principles of serialisation themselves. I merely
observe at this point that if serialisation is predictable (throughout the
cycle) from (a) and (b), then, as well as there being large classes of
derivation types excluded, the monoparity constraint (109) is still
maintained (even in the absence of PCS). Bach is thus mistaken in suggestin
that 'a theory in which base structures are unordered and in which the
ordering rules apply before transformations is obviously completely
equivalent to the standard theory' (1975, 332). Such a theory is (in his
own terms) stronger, even if the sequence-preserving constraint does not
apply, in that: it excludes twins in base structures; it claims that order
(apart from the centripetal/centrifugal distinction) is predictable from
other properties of base structures. Moreover, the present formulation also
claims, unlike UOB and like OB, that for a particular language underlying
orders are determinate (unless 'free word order' can be motivated in
certain languages).

I am proposing then, to sum up, that 'base structures' are unordered,
but serialisation is introduced cycle-initially or pre-cyclically and is
invariant throughout the application of the cyclic rules; and that with
respect to these rules of serialisation languages are either centripetal or
centrifugal. It remains here to outline my motivations for adopting the
sequence-preserving hypothesis rather than PCS. I shall, however, not
endeavour, as Bach attempts to some extent, to consider arguments for
and against PCS without commitment to a highly specific framework,

namely the one we are in the process of developing here. Thus some motivations will arise only as the conceptual framework becomes well enough established for arguments to be formulated: consider, for instance, the discussion of lexicalisation and serialisation in ch.2.

1.11.4. The difficulties of constructing arguments which outside some tightly controlled assumptions count against the principle of UOB, or even PCS, are illustrated by the discussion in Bach, 1975, § 4.1. He firstly (§ 4.1.1) points out, correctly, that many people would accede to the existence of phonological rules of metathesis. This does not, however, constitute an obviously compelling argument against UOB. He then discusses (§§ 4.1.2-.4) various rules and constraints (pronominalisation and extraposition, left-dislocation, etc.; *wh*-movement: and stress placement in questions; and stress in main and subordinate clauses in German) whose formulation is not obviously incompatible with PCS. (We return below to the status of extraposition, however.) The same seems to be true of the argument from pronominalisation in Chinese relative clauses (§ 4.1.5), though I have not sufficient grasp of the data to fully evaluate this. More promising is the final argument concerning the order-dependence of universal rules (§ 4.1.6), to which I return in a moment.

Even appeals to the order-dependent properties of rules whose cyclicity is relatively uncontroversial are difficult to make decisive (without making rather specific assumptions concerning other properties of the grammar), either against the sequence-preserving constraint or PCS. I suggest in ch.2 a (in this respect) rather conservative specification of the SD for ordinary reflexivisation (Postal, 1974, § 3.2) which includes crucially the requirement that the (unemphatic) NP to be reflexivised be to the right of its antecedent. Indeed, it is possible to impose this condition on all subsequent structures in the derivation up to shallow structure. So this excludes (113):

(113)   *Himself $\begin{cases} \text{impresses Bill} \\ \text{strikes Bill favourably} \end{cases}$

(differing from e.g. *Bill regards himself highly* by psych-movement) — Postal, 1971). Compare, however, post-cyclic *Himself, John never praises.* But it is not clear that this condition cannot be applied simply at shallow structure, by, say, incorporating the constraint on reflexives into the linearisation rules. I exclude, of course, on principle, a third possibility, namely exclusion of (113) by appeal to arbitrarily imposed extrinsic ordering of psych-movement prior to reflexivisation (Postal, 1971); however, this is not available anyway in a grammar incorporating PCS, in that its viability as an account of the deviance of (113) depends on an appeal to left-right order. Inclusion of the reflexive condition in the linearisation rules will also allow for the examples discussed by Pullum (1975c):

> (114)   a. I was told lies by a beautiful girl about herself
> b. I was told lies about herself by a beautiful girl

Pullum stars (114.b), and on the basis of this proposes that since this reveals that reflexivisation must invoke sequence, linearisation must be in the cycle (an end-of-cycle operation), ordered before reflexivisation. However, as I have indicated, the deviance of such sentences does not seem to me to constitute a strong argument against PCS. Moreover, in this particular instance, I am, in the first case, not of the opinion that (114.b) is bad (or at least any worse than (114.a)); and secondly it is not obvious that we have here an example of ordinary (rather than 'picture noun') reflexivisation (see further §§ 3.2-.3).

What we need as counter-evidence to PCS, on the basis of the reflexivisation condition, is to establish the existence of sentences which as a result of two 'movements' come to have the proper antecedent-reflexive order at shallow structure but remain deviant. Such a sentence is (115):

> (115)   *Bill is impressed by himself

which shows psych-movement followed by passive, and thus conforms to the reflexivisation condition at shallow structure, but which is nevertheles deviant. In § 3.2, I attempt to show that such phenomena cannot be accounted for adequately on the basis of the crossover principle (see too Jackendoff, 1972), but that since both passive and psych-movement are sequence-preserving rules, the deviance of both of (113) and (115) can be allowed for within a grammar incorporating the sequence-preserving constraint in terms of the condition on reflexivisation. However, unless (115) and the like can be excluded on the basis of some independently motivated principle, they constitute direct counter-evidence to the viability of PCS, as would any other such phenomenon.

Of course, if grammatical relations can be appealed to, such a conclusion does not necessarily follow on the basis of just (115). We can, for instance, impose the condition on reflexives that they may not be subjects. Since this condition does not refer to sequence it can operate pre-cyclically in a grammar incorporating PCS, indeed throughout a derivation. So both (113) and (115) can be excluded on account of the reflexive having been a subject at some point in their derivations. However, this would have to be an additional constraint; it would appear that the sequence constraint (imposed at shallow structure) is still required to account for the deviance of *I talked about himself to Bill v. I talked to Bill about himself,* unless this too is not an instance of 'ordinary reflexivisation' (cf. § 3.3). In a grammar which has pre-shallow structure ordering, all of these sentences are excluded by a single condition: that throughout the derivation, up to shallow structure, the antecedent must precede its reflexive. (See ch.3 however, for some refinements and qualifications.)

Another area where evidence concerning the viability of PCS can be sought includes cyclic rules whose very presence in the grammar of a particular language is associated with an order-dependent property. Here we return to Bach's discussion (§ 4.1.6). He suggests that only complement sentences with initial complementiser are eligible for extraposition, both within a particular language and as a universal condition; and Hindi (with initial complementisers) shows extraposition but Japanese (without) does not. If extraposition is cyclic (Grinder, 1970; Jakobson & Neubauer, 1974; Baltin, 1975), then within a grammar that incorporates PCS this can only be specified globally, thus reducing the plausibility of PCS.

Such a generalisation, on the other hand, is quite compatible with the sequence-preserving constraint. However, the rule of extraposition itself, if cyclic, is perhaps more problematical. For is it not non-sequence-preserving? In English, it moves a complement S to the right of its matrix sentence, thus altering its sequential relationship with any elements intervening between its original position and its new one. Two possibilities suggest themselves. Either cyclic extraposition involves simply a change in the dominance relations and no change of sequence, and a S that has undergone extraposition is moved to the right post-cyclically. Indeed this can constitute part of the shallow structure rules of serialisation: compare Pullum's (1975c) suggestion that complex NP shift be incorporated into the sequencing rules (though he regards these as cycle-final). However it may be that the sequence-preserving constraint must be weakened to the requirement that NPs may not change their precedence relations. Since it seems to me that the stronger structure-preserving constraint (Emonds, 1969) has the same scope, i.e. can be maintained only for NPs (in the sense described in ch.2), the sequence-preserving constraint can in that case be dropped as such, as predictable from the structure-preserving requirement.

1.11.5. I shall not pursue this question here, or the general issues connected with the place and character of serialisation; the resolution of these are not crucial to the aims of the present discussion. I adopt the position I have done with due tentativeness. Let me conclude, however, by indicating that it appears to me that these last considerations suggest that the centrifugal *v.* centripetal hypothesis concerning cycle-initial structures combined with some version of the invariance hypothesis represents the strongest ordering hypothesis that can at the moment be plausibly entertained. The only hypothesis concerning underlying structures that imposes in one respect a stronger constraint is SOB, which requires that a single underlying order can be motivated for all languages. SOB is weaker in not requiring monoparity; but the hypothesis itself would seem to be too strong, if there is indeed a correlation between order of constituents and the occurrence of certain transformations, unless it can be shown that the order differences are in all such cases derived. Consider, moreover, the import of the universals of word order discussed by Greenberg (1963). It will not be sufficient to say, for instance, that SOV languages differ from VSO by the presence of a rule of 'verb-final' (Bach, 1974, § 11.5), or vice versa (Koutsoudas & Sanders, 1974), since the position of the verb correlates significantly with order in other constructions: prepositions *v.* postpositions, etc. In such circumstances, rather than a transformational difference an underlying centrifugal/centripetal opposition seems appropriate.

Now, if this is so, other 'dominant' word orders must arise at shallow structure. English, for example, is a consistent centrifugal language (Anderson, 1975*a*) which I suggest has as part of the shallow structure conditions on serialisation a rule of subject-positioning which (possibly among other things) places a subject before its verb. In Zeneyze (Genoese), on the other hand, the subject is moved out to the right from between V and O, giving a 'dominant' VOS order (Pullum, 1975*e*, 4-5). Pullum argues that on the evidence available to us only these four orders need be allowed for: i.e. SOV, VSO, SVO, VOS. (On apparent OSV languages, see Pullum, 1975*e*, 17-8; and cf. § 3.5 below.) And the latter two both involve movement of an internal S to left or right (at shallow structure, within the present framework). He concludes by sketching out a functional explanation for this situation in terms of two principles favouring early and/or peripheral presentation of the 'grammatically significant' elements V and S.

The framework I have indicated is, I think, sufficient for the investigations which follow. However, it is worth indicating some problems and a possible refinement. Return to the controversy over the underlying orders of German or Old English. Modern English is, as I have noted, consistently centrifugal, and thus VSO (though, as Berman (1974) and Zeyer (1974) note, McCawley's (1970) arguments based on simplification/ generalisation of transformations are inconclusive in this regard). Germanic was apparently SOV. Old English has 'dominant' SVO in main clauses but SOV in subordinate. This situation seems to depend on pre-OE, a SOV language, having developed a (shallow-structure) rule moving the V to a position after S in main clauses (probably historically via a topicalisation structure: Vennemann, 1974). That is, such SVOs arise from underlying SOV. In the history of English the SVO order is reinterpreted as coming (as is usual) from VSO; i.e. English is restructured as centrifugal rather than centripetal. The ambivalence of SVO is thus a major factor in this kind of word order change. One crucial problem is: at what point in this development as far as underlying structures are concerned, is Old English, or German, or Dutch?

Resolution of such questions is by no means straightforward. Criteria are elusive or even contradictory. Observe in the first place that if Ross's (1970*b*) proposals concerning the applicability of GAPPINGS are correct, then no underlying SOV language can change (in the course of a derivation) to SVO, and the history I sketched out is impossible. At any rate, any SVO would be immediately reinterpreted as underlying VSO. However, Maling (1972) has shown that there is some doubt as to whether any typological conclusions concerning word order can be drawn from the gapping phenomena. But, on the other hand, Bach (1971) argues that since question-movement does not occur in (deep) SOV languages but does occur in German:

(116)   a. Ich fragte, wen Hans geküsst habe,
         b. Er weiss, dass ich, wen Hans geküsst habe, gefragt habe

it cannot be (underlying) SOV. Which would mean that Modern German is already centrifugal: VSO/SVO. Observe, however that underlying V-before-O order for German is incompatible with the structure-preserving constraint of Emonds, in that it apparently requires a non-root transformation permuting V and O. However the viability of the strong version of the hypothesis is doubtful, anyway. And it is contradicted by verb-raising in Dutch and German (Evers, 1975, § 2.4). But if weakened, as proposed in ch.2, to allow only verb-to-verb reattachments, then the constraint can still be deployed in favour of underlying a SOV order. Moreover the explanation of restrictions on verb-raising itself requires a deep SOV order for these languages (Evers, 1975, § 1.3).

2 LOCALIST CASE GRAMMAR

2.1 Predicate Subcategorisation and Multiple CRs

2.1.1. In §§ 1.4-1.9 we uncovered various motivations for allowing a single NP to be associated in underlying structure with more than one CR. It is clear that this must affect our conception of how case nodes are introduced, and in particular of how the appropriate NP is to be brought into association with the correct CR or CRs: the rules of Fillmore's which allow for the representations discussed in §1.3 depend on there existing for each NP only one CR. Let us therefore, as a basis for our discussion, review the range of possibilities that must be allowed for, given the discussion thus far.

We have found that there are verbs like *know* which appear in the frame in (1):

(1)   know + [——[abs] [loc, erg]]

(cf. the discussion of *(1.66)* above); others, like *occupy* take (2):

(2)   occupy + [——[loc, abs] [abs, erg]]

(cf. the discussion of *(1.67)* and *(1.94)*). We allowed for the phenomena discussed by Stephen Anderson (1971) in terms of frames like those in *(1.96)* for *smear, cover* and *throw,* and in *(1.95)* for *swarm,* collapsed as (3):

(3)   a. smear   + [——[abs] [loc (abs)] [erg]]
          b. swarm + [——[abs] [loc (abs)]]

We can also provide for some of the observations made by Huddleston (1970) in this regard (cf. § 1.4), if a verb like *move* has a frame that is, in the relevant respects, like (4):

(4)   move + [——[abs (erg)] [(erg)]]

which allows for three possibilities (that in which both ergs are present is excluded by the constraint requiring only one CR of each type (except abs) per proposition (constraint (a) of § 1.4)), as illustrated by

(5):

    (5)   a. The stone moved [abs]
             b. John moved [abs, erg] / [abs]
             c. John moved the stone [abs] [erg]

(I ignore here the question of possible other CRs required by *move* —
e.g. directional ones. We return to issues related to this below.) On the
other hand, abs is now (in terms of (4)) obligatory in the case frame for
move. And it seems to me that this is true in general. Henceforth I
assume a constraint on propositions requiring the presence of at least
one abs per proposition. Let us explore this a little further here.

2.1.2. All of the verbs we have just surveyed have an abs among the
cases they require. What I am now suggesting (following Anderson,
1971*b*, etc.) is that all verbs take at least an abs. This is, I propose, what
underlies the other respect in which abs differs from the other cases, viz.
in having the potential of appearing twice in a simple proposition, as in
(3) or in equative sentences. That is, there is both an abs which like any
other case is optional and one which is obligatory. In this way the
availability of two instances of abs per proposition is in part dependent
on the requirement that every predicate take at least one absolutive
phrase. Apart from this, such a requirement, if maintainable in a non-ad
hoc way, is in itself of some interest as a substantive constraint on case
arrays. However, there are certain further generalisations which appear
to correlate with the predictions following from such a proposal. And I
would now like to outline one of these.
    There are, as is well known and much discussed, verbs in English (etc.)
which have both a causative and a non-causative use, the 'ergative' verbs
of Lyons (1968*a*, § 8.2.3). The causative use is differentiated by showing
an ergative (agentive) relation lacking with the non-causative use. Such
'ergative' verbs share a number of redundancies, lexical constraints, one
of which depends upon the proposal we have been discussing. This
involves a constraint upon the character of the case arrays we can
associate with 'ergative' verbs in their non-causative use; i.e. it is part of
the answer to the question: what kind of verb can have a lexical
causative congener? In short, the constraint I have in mind is this: the
non-causative variant of an 'ergative' verb has an absolutive subject. Thus
causative *move* has such a non-causative congener, as has, say, causative
trip: (5.c) implies (5.a). The same implicational relation holds with
respect to corresponding sentences involving a suppletive pair like

kill/die; and once again the subject of the non-causative is an absolutive.

However *march,* for instance, is also an ergative verb:

(6) a. They marched around the square
     b. Fred marched them around the square

But the subject of (6.a) is already agentive, and (6) is reconcilable with the constraint I have proposed only if it is also absolutive. That this is so is again (cf. *move*) suggested by the fact that in both of (6) *they/them* is the object that moves, which is the role of absolutives in directional sentences (cf. § 1.4). So the subject of (6.a) is both erg and abs. Thus we have intransitive verbs with absolutive subjects (*fall,* say) and with [abs, erg] subjects (*march*). Must we then also allow for intransitive subjects which are simply erg? This is unnecessary if we extend an [abs, erg] interpretation to all agentive intransitives. It also enables us to maintain the constraint on the non-causative variant of an ergative verb, in that e.g. *work,* an agentive intransitive, has a causative congener:

(7) a. The team works very hard
     b. Fred works the team very hard

even though there is no 'moving object' motivation for the presence of abs with the subject of (7.a). I propose then that all agentive intransitives have [abs, erg] subjects, and it is the presence of abs which permits such causatives as are exemplified by (6.b) and (7.b). And it is the absence of abs with the subject (in active sentences) of e.g. *read* (simple ergative subject, absolutive object) which explains the absence of a causative use for *read.*

Now, the examples we have thus far considered are equally compatible with another constraint, one which does not depend on the proposal that agentive intransitives be so interpreted: viz. the proposal that non-causative 'ergative' verbs are intransitive (in a rather traditional sense), as in (5.a), (6.a) and (7.a). But this latter proposal is contradicted by such 'ergative' verbs as *occupy,* which displays the (non-causative and causative) uses exemplified by (8):

(8) a. He occupied an important position
     b. The army occupied the town

Here the causative does not introduce an extra argument; the non-causative variant or congener is already transitive. Rather, it requires that its subject be agentive, presumably a self-moving agent, as with *move* in (5.b). Such examples, then, support the formulation proposed above, that a verb with a causative use takes an absolutive subject in its non-causative use, if it has one. This is clearly a necessary rather than a sufficient condition for the existence of a causative variant: there are verbs with absolutive subjects (like, say, *faint*) which nevertheless have no normal causative use. However, if valid, it captures one important element in the characterisation of the notion 'ergative verb'.

2.1.3. The formulation of this condition on 'ergative verbs' is moreover to a considerable extent independent of the question of how precisely the relationship between such causative and non-causative variants is to be expressed. However, there is one consequence which raises a question which we shall have to return to at greater length below. And it demands something of our immediate attention also, in so far as it is relevant to the concerns of this section. Observe that if the causative variant is characterised lexically simply by the addition of an ergative CR (together with all that entails) to the array of cases required by the non-causative, then the causative *occupy* of (8.b) will presumably select the case frame of (9):

(9)   occupy + [——[loc, abs] [abs, erg]]

But this is exactly the frame we introduced for non-causative *occupy* in (2). From the point of view of lexical distinctness, that can simply be remedied by associating with causative verbs the feature 'causative'. And the erg of the case frame of *occupy* will be interpreted as a true agent only if the verb is causative. However, in relation to the characterisation of the CRs, we now have a situation where erg in a locational sentence is a true agent only if the verb is causative, as with *occupy*, or the examples involving *plant, load*, etc. discussed in ch.1 (cf. the frames in (3)). If the verb is non-causative and locational, as with *know* or non-causative *occupy*, then erg is not agentive. We return to a consideration of the basis for this asymmetry below, where it is concluded (following Anderson, 1971*b*, chapter 11, etc.) that causatives have a non-simplex source. The interest of this for our present concerns is this: if this is so, then the rules, constraints which specify the range of CRs that can be associated with a predicate need not allow directly for the wide range of possibilities required for lexical causatives. If these are complex, then the range of cases they require results from the collapse of the arrays associated with more than one predicate. Accordingly, we shall be concerned in what immediately follows to arrive at a specification of the range of CRs required by non-causative predicates.

2.1.4. We are confronted with the problems of specifying which cases can co-occur (a) within the same proposition and (b) in association with the same NP. Also, even if we leave aside causatives, the case frames have now become quite complex compared with the conception outlined in § 1.3; moreover, they nevertheless fail in themselves to capture certain generalisations. For example, observe that the conjunction [abs, erg] is possible in a proposition which also contains loc only if the loc is also abs (cf. (2)). (Of course, causatives, if treated as simplex, are again exceptional in this regard.) To indicate this and the like would apparently require some further, ad hoc, complication of the case frame notation. Some, at any rate, of these problems are resolved if the CRs are introduced in accordance with the subcategorisation of the predicate and not vice versa (see Anderson, 1968*a*, 1969*a*, *b*, 1971*b*). I.e. we have to formulate a set of constraints on the notion predicate, constraints which specify possible arrays of arguments.

Such constraints are captured in a straightforward way by the use of feature notation. Given the possibilities we have surveyed in (1), (2), (4), and including equatives, we can associate with predicates, Vs, the features shown in (10):

(10)

$$V \longrightarrow \begin{bmatrix} loc \\ erg \\ abs \end{bmatrix}$$

These are unary features or components (but are easily translated into the binary features of Anderson, 1968*a*, etc.):[21] rule (10) is to be interpreted as asserting that V may or may not be further subcategorised as each of loc, erg, abs. This allows for 8 possible predicate types. Each type, associated with a different set of CASE FEATURES, containing from none to all three, correlates with a different array of cases, as indicated in (11):

(11) i.   V $\longrightarrow$ abs

ii.   loc $\longrightarrow$ loc

iii. $\begin{bmatrix} \text{erg} \\ \text{<abs>} \end{bmatrix} \longrightarrow$ erg / $\left\{\begin{array}{l} \text{a.} \quad [\underset{-}{\text{loc}}] \\ \text{b.} \quad <[\underset{-}{\text{abs}}]> \\ \text{c.} \quad - \end{array}\right\}$

iv.   abs $\longrightarrow$ abs / $\left\{\begin{array}{l} \text{a.} \quad [\underset{-}{\text{loc}}] \\ \text{b.} \quad - \end{array}\right\}$

Each rule in (11) states that given a specification for a predicate that includes the component(s) on the left of the arrow, then an argument of the kind specified on the right is to be introduced.[22] The introduced element may, however, rather than involving a new argument, be added as another component to an argument introduced by prior application of another rule. Such an environment for introduction is specified to the right of the slash in (iii. a,b) and (iv.a). Notice too that in these rules V figures as just another component of the predicate segment. The subparts of (11) are unordered; but each case feature can be invoked on the lefthand-side in the application of only one rule per proposition, and indeed each feature introduced by application of (10) must be invoked in the application of (11).[23] Thus, in the first place, all the rules can at most apply only once per proposition; and secondly, and more particularly, if abs and erg and not loc co-occur as case features, then (iii) will apply, and no abs CR will be introduced (by (iv)). In other words, abs in association with erg as features merely results (in the absence of loc) in the CR erg being added to the CR abs introduced by (11.i) rather than there being a new CR abs inserted. (This underlies the intransitive agentives like *work* discussed above.) (11.i) and (11.ii) merely specify that every predicate respectively takes an abs argument and every locative predicate a loc argument. (11.iii) and (11.iv) indicate together that an absolutive ergative V adds an erg CR to an already present abs (the option within angles) and abs to a loc if there is one; and that an ergative V otherwise by (11.iii) takes an erg CR, added to a node already specified as loc, if there is one, or added as a new node. Both of the first two options for (11.iii) thus are associated with a multiple CR. Similarly, (11.iv) introduces an abs either in association with a loc introduced by (ii) or separately.

I leave the reader to verify that/if the sets of features listed in (12) correlate with the case arrays suggested:

(12)   a. $\begin{bmatrix} loc \\ erg \\ abs \end{bmatrix}$ V $\begin{bmatrix} loc \\ abs \end{bmatrix}$ $\begin{bmatrix} abs \\ erg \end{bmatrix}$ *occupy*

      b. $\begin{bmatrix} loc \\ abs \end{bmatrix}$ V   abs $\begin{bmatrix} loc \\ abs \end{bmatrix}$ (holistic) *swarm*

      c. $\begin{bmatrix} loc \\ erg \end{bmatrix}$ V   abs $\begin{bmatrix} loc \\ erg \end{bmatrix}$ *know*

      d. $\begin{bmatrix} erg \\ abs \end{bmatrix}$ V $\begin{bmatrix} abs \\ erg \end{bmatrix}$ *work*

      e.   loc   V   loc   abs   *be (at)*

      f.   erg   V   abs   erg   *read*

      g.   abs   V   abs   abs   *be* (equative)

      h.   —   V   abs   *faint*

and that subject- and object-formation in sentences containing these verbs are in conformity with the hierarchy of cases proposed in § 1.9 and reproduced in (13):

(13) $\begin{bmatrix} erg \\ (case) \end{bmatrix} > \begin{bmatrix} case \\ abs \end{bmatrix} >$ abs

such that in active sentences a node labelled with erg (whatever else) is preferred as subject, and lacking that a node labelled with abs and some other CR, and finally by default a simple abs. In the presence of an erg (or in passives) a [case, abs] or in its absence an abs, if anything, becomes object (or subject, respectively). The hierarchy need reach no lower, in that, on the proposal made above, there will always be at least one abs in any proposition. (We return below to the status of such a hierarchy.)

Another consequence of such a proposal is that the complex case frames that had evolved out of the discussion in § 1.9 can be eliminated. Rather predicates can simply be subcategorised lexically in terms of the features loc, erg and abs. The arrays of cases (which of them label a single node, etc.) are specified by the formulation in (11). Thus *know*, for instance, is a V which is also, as indicated in (12), [loc, erg], and therefore takes the array of cases shown there; and even *move* is simply [V (erg (abs))] (if we again ignore, apart from its causativity, the problem of its optional directional arguments).

Obviously (10) and (11) must be modified as further CRs are

introduced. However it is my own view that the number of CRs over and above those we have considered, abs, erg and loc, is very small; indeed is limited to one, viz. abl(ative) (cf. Fillmore's Source case). Thus, the modification to (10/11), not just with respect to English, but as a universal base, is slight; in fact involves simply an extension. So that, in particular, predicates can still be characterised with respect to the array of cases they require in terms of a simple bundle of case features. Further, even causatives, which we have thus far excluded, can be allowed for in this respect by a combination of more than one bundle of just this range of features. However, this is to anticipate in a number of ways some of the discussion of section § 2.3.

2.1.5. What I want to conclude this section with is an attempt to define the role of CRs in the grammar, as a prelude to the brief description in § 2.2 of one kind of proposal for providing case grammars with an appropriate formal basis. Before quite leaving the present topic, however, observe that one further consequence of the position we have arrived at is that subject/object selection is determined simply by the CRs present in any particular proposition, in particular by the distribution of erg and abs. If this is correct, then pairs like *like/please* (cf. § 1.3.2) must after all differ in the case arrays with which they are associated, since they show distinct subject/object selection. And there appear indeed to be some independent motivation for supposing this. Both Daneš (1968) and Kirkwood (1973) argue that the object of *like* is objective whereas the subject of *please* is a source (ablative). Kirkwood points to ablative *please*-paraphrases like those in (14):

(14) a. The work pleases John
      b. The work gives John pleasure
      c. John derives pleasure from the work

(on *give* as an ablative-subject verb, see further below) and non-ablative *like*-paraphrases such as (15):

(15) a. He likes the work
      b. He has a liking for the work

and comments on the pair in (16):

(16) a. I liked the play immensely
      b. The play pleased me immensely

as follows: 'in [(16.a)] I would suggest that the adverb *immensely*
refers to the manner in which I reacted to the play, as opposed to
[(16.b.)] which refers to the manner in which the play affected me'.
The case arrays in (17) might therefore be appropriate:

(17) like + [—— [abs] [loc, erg]]
      please + [—— [loc, abs] [abl, erg]]

i.e. *like,* as *know, own,* has a [loc, erg] subject, and *please* a [abl, erg].

There are also of course active/passive pairs. Unless passives are given
a lexicalist interpretation, the alternation appears to contradict the
conclusion attempted above, that subject/object are determinate, given
the case structure. Anderson (1971*b*) allows for passives in terms of a
feature on the predicate which in certain circumstances is reflected in
the presence of the copula with an adjectival form and in the case of
passives also overrules the subject-hierarchy by removing erg from
consideration. However, such a suggestion encounters various semantic
and syntactic difficulties (as conceded by the discussion in Anderson,
1971*b*). And I would now favour a source for passives which involves a
complex structure (Anderson, 1972, 1973*d*; Dillon, 1974; § 3.3 below).
However that may be, a purely simplex, transformational account of
passives has to date received little support (cf. the discussion in ch.1). If
it can be supported, it provides no motivation for the Chomskyan view
of deep structure, as we have seen, but merely represents one instance
where subject-selection is facultative after all.

2.1.6. Another apparent exception of a rather different kind is
represented by the equative sentence. According to the rules of (10)/
(11), these are characterised as containing two absolutives (cf. (12)),
either of which can appear in subject position. The subject-forming
hierarchy obviously will rank them equally, and choice of one or the
other is apparently arbitrary. I suggest that, as far as these clause-internal
rules are concerned, this is indeed the case. Subject-formation is not
determinate. Clearly, however, subject position in this instance
correlates quite directly with topicalisation. (Elsewhere the identity of
the subject, as we have seen, is determined by the case array: it
constitutes merely an unmarked topic slot rather than being
necessarily topical.) What I suggest, then, is this: while subject-formation
in equatives is in terms of the case array arbitrary, the grammar will
throw out subject selections in which the subject of an equative is not
coreferential with the topic.

Clearly this can be formulated in various ways. Let me sketch out how I see the derivation as possibly proceeding, a derivation which though the evidence available does not necessarily select it uniquely, is at least consistent with the formulation of some other generalisations. There have been a number of proposals that the topic of a sentence be characterised by the presence of a NP which originates outside the S which 'comments' on that NP, and is at some point sister to the S. Compare Gundel's proposal (1975, 73) reproduced (18):

(18)

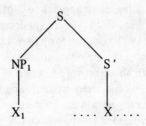

(cf. e.g Hofmann, 1974, §§ 3.3, 8). She argues (Part I) on various grounds that sentences showing LEFT DISLOCATION, as exemplified by (19):

(19) a. This room, it really depresses me
      b. Those slacks I gave you for your birthday, can you still fit into them?

do not involve a movement-rule that takes a NP to the left of the whole sentence (leaving behind a pronominal place-holder), as formulated by Ross (1967), but rather that the NP occupies pre-sentential position throughout the derivation: 'the dislocated NP exists as such, i.e., as an adjunct to the main sentence, in logical structure' (p.73). She points out, for instance, that dislocated pronouns are always objective whatever the form of the 'corresponding' pronoun:

(20) a. Me, I never drink beer
      b. Him, he never does anything right

And she notes: that (§ 4) restrictions on the specificity of the dislocated NP that are apparently accidental on a movement analysis follow naturally from a proposal embodying (18) as the source for left-dislocation sentence; that (§ 5), under an extraction analysis for left-dislocated NPs, sentences such as (21):

> (21) a. As for fruit, Jim likes cantelopes best
> b. As for Paris, the Eiffel Tower is really spectacular

despite many similarities, must be provided with a quite different derivation from (19) and (20); that (§ 6) the phenomena that motivated Ross's coordinate structure constraint, as well as some that were resistant to such an explanation, can be alternatively accounted for in terms of a reanalysis which incorporates the positing of such a structure for left-dislocation, and as a component in the structures underlying sentences showing clefting and *wh*-movement (both in questions and relative clauses).

Part II of Gundel's paper is concerned to make a case for such a structure as (18) as the basis for topicalisation in general. The derivation of superficially simple (un-dislocated) sentences thus involves a rule which copies the topic into the position occupied by the corresponding variable (cf. (18)) in the sister S´. This is the same kind of process as the superimposition which I have claimed is crucial to the derivation of quantified and contrastive NPs (cf. e.g. Anderson, 1974a); however I shall not pursue here the details of such derivations. My intention here is simply to refer to the kind of derivation which is compatible with the suggestion that I have made concerning equatives. I shall also not pursue here a further possible elaboration indicated by Gundel (1975, 77), namely that the topical NP of (18) originates as a component in the superordinate performative, though this seems to me a promising proposal. Nor shall I follow up one item of disagreement with Gundel's account, the obligatory presence of a topic which she claims: part II of her paper is subtitled 'On deriving all sentences from underlying left dislocated sentences'. Observe finally, at this point, however, that if such a non-movement source is generalisable to Y-movement etc., then the invariance hypothesis may be extensible to post-cyclic syntax also: i.e. there is no reordering (of NPs at least) throughout the syntax.

2.1.7. If both passives and equatives are complex, then the notion that subject-formation is fully determined by the case array has some considerable plausibility. And the array of cases is uniquely specified by the subcategorisation of the verb plus (11). The role of the CRs, on such a view, has become quite clearly simply to label which argument (NP) correlates with the presence of (a) particular feature(s) in the componential structure of the predicate and thereby to define its (the NP's function(s). [24] The arguments could alternatively be identified in underlying structure by sequence alone: but an ordering of arguments independent of the case labelling is arbitrary (cf. the problems conceded by Kilby, 1973*b*); and identification of arguments in surface structure in many instances clearly depends on case labels rather than sequence; sequence is invoked principally when the labelling (or its distinctiveness) is destroyed, as under subject/object formation in English or French. Moreover, we have also seen (§§ 1.9-.11) that it is the underlying and derived CRs that are crucially involved in the formulation of such transformations as raising, rather than there being direct reference to relative sequence.

We have also observed that the sequence-preserving constraint and the associated centrifugal/centripetal distinction (in underlying structures) can be maintained only in a grammar which includes relational labels. Even apart from these hypotheses, such generalisations concerning 'word order' as have been observed by e.g. Greenberg (1963) and Bartsch & Vennemann (1972) depend crucially on the notion 'head of a construction' (see further § 2.2; and cf. 1975*a*). And, in particular in such generalisations, the markers of CRs like prepositions and post-positions function as heads of the constructions they are part of. Thus, for instance (Greenberg Universal 3): 'Languages with dominant VSO order are always prepositional'. And (Universal 4): 'With overwhelmingly greater than chance frequency, languages with normal SOV order are postpositional'. That is, there is a direct correlation between position of the predicate (head of the proposition) and that of the CF. Now if serialisation is postcyclic, such an observation might seem to have no great significance for the underlying status of CRs. However, even if PCS rather than the invariance hypothesis is adopted, it does mean that if CRs are not present in underlying structures, we must postulate transformations which introduce them as the heads of a new construction type; i.e. there must be 'construction creating' transformations.

2.2 Dependency Case Grammars

2.2.1. The effect of the proposals I have outlined in the previous section is to emphasise the central role of the predicate in the proposition, in this instance as 'controller' of the case arrays. This and other properties of case grammar receive a very natural interpretation in terms of the notion of DEPENDENCY. And various proposals along these lines have recently been advanced (cf. e.g. Robinson, 1970*a*; Vater, 1973; Anderson, 1971*a*, *b*, *c*). The present section is concerned to explicate informally such aspects of the dependency characterisation as are most relevant to our ongoing discussion.

The formalism of a phrase structure grammar does not, unsupplemented, give expression to the notion 'head of a construction'. Such a grammar specifies as well-formed a set of terminal strings, i.e. strings constructed out of the (terminal) vocabulary of a language, and associates with each string one or more bracketings into constructions, each bracket bearing a label to indicate its construction type, as, schematically, in (22):

$$(22) \quad [_\gamma \; [_\alpha \; [_V \; a] \; _V \; [_W \; b] \; _W \;]_\alpha \; [_X \; c] \; _X \; [_\beta \; [_Y \; d] \; _Y \; [_Z \; e] \; _Z]_\beta]_\gamma$$

where 'a, b, . . .' are lexical items (terminal vocabulary) of the language, and 'V, W, . . .' are lexical categories (on brackets enclosing only one lexical item and no brackets) and '$\alpha, \beta, \ldots$' are prelexical categories (and mark 'higher level' constructions). Within the construction $[_\alpha \; \cdots]_\alpha$ the V and W elements are equipollent immediate constituents. Say, however, there exist criteria whereby one member of each construction is determinately selected as 'head', and that there exist motivations for supposing such a notion, or representations embodying such a notion, to be relevant to the formulation of certain other grammatical generalisation(s). Say, for example, our criteria select b, i.e. the W element, as head of α, d as head of β, and c (i.e. the item belonging to category X) as head of the total syntagm γ. How is this to be represented?

Let us adopt as a means of indicating that 'α' is a 'W'-phrase, i.e. a phrase which has 'W' as head, the notational modification of substituting for every occurrence of 'α' the symbol 'W'; 'W' then indicates both the lexical category that is the head of the construction and the construction itself. We can specify lexical occurrences by an auxiliary symbol '*', as in (23):

$$(23) \quad [_X \; [_W \; [_V \; a] \; _V \; [_{W*} \; b] \; _{W*}] \; _W \; [_{X*} \; c] \; _{X*}$$
$$[_Y \; [_{Y*} \; d] \; _{Y*} \; [_Z \; e] \; _Z] \; _Y \;] \; _X$$

But, given a proper bracketing such as (23), the distribution of '*' is sufficient to specify both the head and the construction it is head of, as in (24) (on the assumption that a category can be head of only the least inclusive construction that contains it), from which all pre-terminal category symbols have been dropped:

(24) $[[[_V a]_V [_{W*} b]_{W*}] [_{X*} c]_{X*}$
      $[[_{Y*} d]_{Y*} [_Z e]_Z]]$

Equivalently, this structural information can be represented in tree-form; compare (25):

(25)

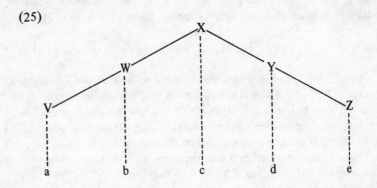

where the head of each construction labels a node from which diverge in a downward direction branches which terminate in the modifiers of the head. The head is said to GOVERN or be the governor of the modifiers, which in turn DEPEND on, are the dependents of, the head. Thus X governs W and Y; they are dependent on X. Y and Z, however, are both SUBORDINATE to X, as are W and V, in that they either depend on X or are connected (possibly via a succession of dependent nodes) by dependency to a node which depends on X. The discontinuous lines attach lexical items to lexical categories (which are now the only categories). They are the reflex of a category-assignment function which maps categories on to lexical items. The character of the rules which specify dependencies is in principle quite straightforward: they simply have to specify for any head its permissible dependents (and if appropriate the relative sequence of the members of the construction). I shall not elaborate on this here;[25] rather, let us concentrate on the empirical claims made by a grammar which assigns dependency structures

Consider again representation (22). If, say, 'e', i.e. the 'Z' element, is selected as the head of B, then the appropriate dependency representation is as in (26):

(26)

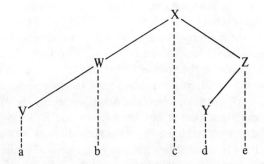

(or the corresponding bracketing). The phrase structure representation in (22) is indeterminate between (25) and (26). If there are then criteria which lead to the specification of a unique head for any construction, dependency representations are *ceteris paribus* preferable to phrase structure characterisations in incorporating this restrictive structural property.

Such a position is further supported, as we have noted, if there exist independent reasons for preferring representations of this sort. Robinson (1970*b*), for instance, has argued that this is indeed the case, in that: (a) there appear to be generalisations which require reference to the heads of certain constructions, and (b) dependency representations eliminate the necessity of special pruning rules whose function is to remove unwanted and misleading pre-lexical categories stranded by the operation of rules deleting most of the constituents they dominate. Elsewhere, it has been argued that the principles governing serialisation (Bartsch & Vennemann, 1972; Anderson, 1975*a*) must invoke the modifier-head (operator-operand) relation. Bartsch & Vennemann's 'Principle of Natural Serialisation', which offers a generalisation that allows for a large proportion of the implicational universals observed by Greenberg (1963), is couched, informally, as follows: 'The natural way of serializing the operator-operand relationship of all complex expressions is from right to left in OV languages and from left to right in VO languages' (1972, 136). This expresses the correlation between VO and the occurrence of prepositions, post-nominal relatives, pre-verbal auxiliaries, etc.[26] And it depends upon verbs, prepositions, nouns, etc. sharing a property: headship of a construction. Rather than pursue this generalisation directly, however, let us in the present context give our attention to the selection of heads, specifically within a case grammar.

2.2.2. We arrive at an intuitively plausible delimitation of the heads of
various constructions if we require of a head or governor that it be an
obligatory lexical category that is CHARACTERISTIC of the
construction in question. By 'characteristic' is meant simply that it
serves to differentiate that construction from others. Thus, the K of
Fillmore's case phrases is the head of that construction: it is obligatory,
lexical and crucially distinguishes a case phrase from a noun phrase. The
case phrase is an exocentric construction; nevertheless only one of the obligatory constituents meets the other criteria for a head. NPs are most often
analysed as endocentric, with the N thus as the obligatory lexical,
characteristic head (for a qualification, see Anderson, 1975*a*; §§ 6-7).
The head of the proposition is the predicate: there is no other lexical
category available. Robinson (1970*b*; §§ 3,5) argues that the head of the
sentence is an element T(ype) 'which bears the tense feature and a
feature which determines whether the sentence is declarative or
interrogative'. It thus might be possible to identify Fillmore's Modality
in part with T, but since both the status and composition of the
modality constituent are unclear, this must remain undecided. For my
part, I think it unlikely that the presence of such a constituent (or of
anything corresponding to T) can be supported. T is clearly not a
lexical category in anything like the sense that N and V are; and the
arguments for its presence in the grammar are unpersuasive. The
assignment of 'declarative' and 'interrogative' as features to T, for
instance, is arbitrary. A treatment of tense etc. in the absence of such
a constituent, is provided in e.g. Anderson, 1972, 1975*a*, § 3;
Anderson & Jessen, 1973.

Robinson (1970*a*, 10) thus arrives at representations for case
constructions of the character of (27):

(27)

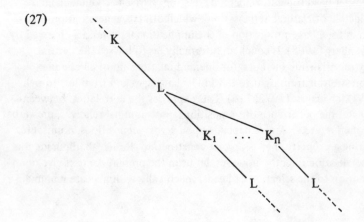

where L = N, V or A(djective). In such representations the category K
appears instead of O, A, . . . etc., which are redefined 'as positively
specified INHERENT FEATURES of the HEADS of the complement
constituents [case phrases], the Ks — in English, the prepositions'
(1970*a*: 71). Thus, information concerning strict subcategorisation is
separated out from the selectional — case frames being interpreted as
selectional features. A verb like *open* might then be said to take as
complements one obligatory and two optional case phrases (strict
subcategorisation) and be marked as selecting Ks which are specified
inherently as [+O] and (optionally) [+A] and [+I]; just as a
K which is [+A] or [+D] selects a NP head which is [+animate].

However, Robinson chooses to formulate the latter restriction as 'a
syntactic redundancy rule, which says in effect that a sentence is deviant
if an inanimate noun occurs after a preposition that is positively
specified as Agentive or Dative' (1970*a*, 73). It is not clear why some
such treatment is not extended to the characterisation of predicate/K
restrictions. This would in effect bring the formulation closer to that
we developed above, whereby the array of case relations is specified
by the subcategorisation of the verb (cf. (10)/(11)).

There are, moreover, problems with a separation of 'case
information' into strict subcategorisational *v* selectional. Notice, for
instance, that the strict subcategorisation frame is entirely predictable
from the selectional: if a verb selects a [+O] and optionally [+A] and
[+I] Ks, then it necessarily takes one obligatory and two facultative case
phrases. The information about optionality must be incorporated into
both frames since otherwise we would require some further constraint
to make certain that the selectionally 'wrong' case phrase is not
associated with optionality. Also, as Robinson herself observes (1970*a*,
72), either the rules adding case features to Ks 'are context sensitive, or
else there is a general convention to insure that no two Ks in the same
construction P are positively specified for the same case feature'. In the
framework outlined above, this is ensured by rule (10). One further
characteristic of the distinction between strict subcategorisation and
selection drawn by Chomsky (1965) was a difference in domain.
Lexical items were strictly subcategorised in terms of the categories
which were sisters to the category immediately dominating the item:
thus an item which was inserted under the immediate domination of
V was subcategorised with respect to the immediate constituents of VP.
Whereas V entered into selectional restrictions with the (deep) subject
of the sentence, which lies outside the VP construction. 'But in
Fillmore's analysis, there is no subject in the deep structure, and any NP

which may become the subject is dominated by the P which immediately dominates V. As we have said, it is one of the complements of V . . . Then selection and sub-categorisation operate in the same domain.' (Robinson, 1970*a*, 71). The distinction, it seems, is difficult to maintain in its classical form. If, however, strict subcategorisation is simply dropped as such from lexical entries, then the selectional restrictions must be extended formally to include information about optionality of modifying constituents. And the character of the constituents in the 'frame' of an item must be formally identifiable from the selectional features required of them; otherwise, the item imposing the selectional restrictions may be inserted in what is (in terms of 'strict subcategorisation') the wrong environment. This is most readily ensured if the categories themselves are either given the status of features or defined by a conjunction of features. Such an approach fits naturally with the proposal made in § 2.1 for coping with multiple CRs per NP, whereby the array of cases is determined by the specification of the predicate.

We can regard the rules in (11), for instance, as dependency rules which are sensitive to different component features in the complex symbol which labels the predicate node. That is, they specify the character of the dependents that different kinds of predicate require. Similarly, all nodes which depend immediately on a predicate, which can be specified by redundancy rule as 'cases', require a dependent N; and there may be certain kinds of cases, i.e. case nodes labelled with certain features, that require that the N node be in addition labelled in a certain way (if, for instance, we want to incorporate some kind of animacy restriction). Also, predicates impose constraints on the Ns which are their arguments, i.e. which depend on cases dependent on the predicate,[27] and on subordinate predicates.

We arrive at a view of the grammar wherein constraints are uniformly required of dependents by their (immediate or non-immediate) governors, and wherein each node is associated with a complex label such that selectional constraints can be formulated as restrictions on the components of the labels for dependent (or more generally, subordinate) nodes. Casehood, on the other hand, is an automatic concomitant of dependence on a predicate: cases are the dependents of predicates and have Ns as their dependents (or vice versa). It is moreover likely that 'verb', 'noun', 'adjective' are not among the components which label nodes: rather, these are classes defined by the intersection of certain other features (see Anderson, 1973*a*, 1973*c*). I shall not pursue this further at this point, but it does bring us to one aspect of

Robinson's account which involves an issue that we have so far skirted. However, since a decision in this area is relatively independent of the arguments for and against case grammars, I shall also not dwell on this at any length.

2.2.3. Fillmore (1968*a*, 27, note 36) affirms that 'I am adhering, in this discussion, to the Postal--Lakoff doctrine, which I find thoroughly convincing, that adjectives constitute a subset of verbs'.[26] Clearly too nouns in predicative function share some of the properties ascribed to the 'class' verb/adjective (Chomsky, 1970*a*; Schachter, 1973*a*). There are various ways of accommodating this, depending on in part unresolved empirical questions. Nouns, verbs and adjectives may belong to a class of PREDICATE, and differ only relatively superficially (cf. Bach, 1968); they may be categorially distinct and share certain features (Chomsky, 1970); or in a featurised base of the kind we have sketched out in the present section, they may be cross-classified in such a way as to share certain properties, such as 'predicative', the V of (10), while others are appropriate only to a subgroup (say, verbs and adjectives).[29]

Robinson (1970*a*), following Chomsky (1970*a*), maintains the categorial distinctness of N, V and A, and adopts a 'lexicalist' position regarding derived nominals, such that 'a great many items appear in the lexicon with fixed selectional and strict subcategorization features, but with a choice as to the features associated with the lexical categories noun, verb, adjective'. Thus (28.b) does not include in its underlying structure a sentential structure that would otherwise be realised as (28.a):

(28) a. The enemy destroyed the city
      b. The enemy's destruction of the city

Rather, the head noun itself takes the same range of complements. However, if non-predicative nouns in general are 'introduced into English sentences by way of relative clauses' (Bach, 1968; see too Anderson, 1973*a*, *b*, *c*, *d*), then the difference between the 'lexicalist' and the 'transformationalist' positions in this instance, within a grammar with a featurised base of the kind we are envisaging here, consists in simply whether the predicate in the relative clause included in the NP in (28.b) is marked from the beginning as 'nominal' or whether such a specification is derived as the result of some transformational operation. No other independent difference in underlying structure is necessarily involved. The resolution of this question, while not without empirical interest,[30] is in principle distinct from the central issues in the debate concerning case grammar.

2.3 On Ablatives

In discussing the subcategorisation of predicates with respect to their
case potential, as embodied in (10), I anticipated that (10) and (11)
need be complicated, once a wider range of sentence types is invoked,
only to the extent of adding one further CR to the set deployed at that
point: namely, the CR ablative. The following section will in the main
be concerned with the wider motivations for and the consequences of
such a limitation. As a preliminary, however, we must give some
consideration, in the present section, to the status of this further (and
final) CR.

2.3.1. Let us consider the consequences of simply adding abl to the set
of features with which, in terms of (10), a V is subcategorised – i.e. let
us replace (10) by (29):

(29)

$$V \longrightarrow \begin{bmatrix} \text{loc} \\ \text{abl} \\ \text{erg} \\ \text{abs} \end{bmatrix}$$

And let us add to (11) a rule which introduces such a dependent CR if a
V bears the feature abl. For the moment, consider only instances where
the CR abl labels a separate node; in other words, where it is not part of
a multiple CR labelling. If a V is subcategorised as, say, [loc, abl], then
we are involved with a simple DIRECTIONAL sentence, like (30):

(30)   The ball rolled from the door to the window

where *from* identifies the abl NP and *to* the loc; *the ball* is absolutive.
Various comments are in order at this point. Such an analysis, in the
first place, identifies 'Place' and 'Goal'; the potential CR 'allative' is
analysed as a loc which is dependent on a predicate which is also abl.
There are a number of motivations for such a proposal. It is lexically
natural, in that the markers of loc and allatives are frequently identical:
in and *on* in English, for instance, may mark either. Moreover, certain
syntactic possibilities chracterise loc and allative as against ablative. For
example, the preposition is absent under the same circumstances,
circumstances in which it must be retained with abl (Vestergaard, 1973).
Compare (31):

(31) a. He stops over at Bordeaux
      b. He flies to Bordeaux
      c. He flies from Bordeaux

with (32):

(32) a. He stops over (*at) there/here
      b. He flies (*to) there/here
      c. He flies from there/here

There is also a semantic affinity, such as is revealed by examples like:

(33) a. John has gone to San Francisco
      b. John is in San Francisco

where (a), with 'San Francisco' as Goal, implies (b), with 'San Francisco'
as Location (Lyons, 1968*a*, 398). Thus, the association of Goal and
Location required by the analysis sketched out above has, I suggest,
some plausibility, though as Bennett (1975, 26-8) points out, the
evidence of (33) at least is not decisive for an analysis involving
identification.

2.3.2. However, as it stands, there are other relationships which the
proposed identification of loc and goal casts no light on. For instance,
just as (33.a) implies (33.b), so (34.a) implies (34.b):

(34) a. John has gone from San Francisco
      b. John is not in San Francisco

In order to provide a transparent characterisation of both of these
relationships, an analysis would seem preferable whereby (33.a) and
(34.b) involve the embedding of a (positive or negative) locational
predication in a 'happen' predication, after the fashion of (35):

(35) John has come (not) to be in San Francisco

(For an analysis along these lines see e.g. Frajzyngier, 1975.) Sentences
like (30) which involve overtly both a Goal and a Source, are then
reduced from a coordinate structure:

(36) The ball has come (by rolling) to be not at the door and at the

window

We can provide some support for such a proposal by pointing out that although (37):

(37) *The ball rolled from the door and to the window

is unacceptable, other prepositions provide viable coordinations:

(38)   The ball rolled out of the house and into the garage

Only *from* and *to* require deletion of the conjunction. This would mean that the addition of even abl to the set of CRs is unnecessary (for such sentences at least), in that the properties which characterise it can be allowed for in terms of such an embedding of a negated locational predication.

Such a reduction, however, encounters a number of serious obstacles. The deletion of the conjunction with *from/to* remains totally ad hoc, an anomaly which is absent from an account whereby *from/to* do not involve a coordination. Observe that (38) is most obviously interpretable as specifically an 'and then' coordination. Presumably, if *from/to* sentences are reduced coordinations, they too are of this character: something that would eventuate as (39) underlies (30):

(39) *The ball rolled from the door and then to the window

But this seems to me to obscure the fact that (30) but not (38) or (39) refers to a single 'journey' (in the sense of Jessen, 1973, 1974). (38), for instance, involves one journey from inside the house to outside and a second from outside the garage to inside. If the exit to the house is the entrance to the garage, then not only does the Goal area of the first journey include the Goal of the second (the area outside the house includes the garage), and the Source area of the second include the Source of the first (the area outside the garage includes the house), but it will also be the case that no part of the journey will be outside the house or garage, and the journeys are simultaneous. But this latter needn't be the case, in that the Goal of the first journey and the Source of the second may lie outside both the house and the garage; and the journeys are necessarily successive. On the other hand, the suggestion that (30) doesn't involve a single journey will involve us in an infinite regress. If (30) is decomposed into, say, 'The ball rolled from at the door

to not at the door and from not at the window to at the window', we
can then decompose 'from at the door to not at the door' into 'from
at the door to (not at the door)$_1$ and from (not at the door)$_1$ to (not at
the door)'$_2$, where '(not at the door)$_1$, refers to an area intermediate
between 'at the door' and '(not at the door)$_2$'. Once we invoke
unprincipled reductions from coordination, it is difficult to motivate a
stopping point. At any rate, it is clear that the underlying structure of
(38) (or (39)) is more complex than that of (30), and that the viability
of (38) provides no support for deriving (30) from a coordinate
structure (cf. Gruber, 1965, § 5.1), a source which moreover fails to
reflect the status of Source and Goal as essential components of the
'journey' which is denoted by all directional predicates.

Such a derivation is even less plausible with STATIC directionals
such as (40):

(40) The fog stretches from Edinburgh to Stirling

or EXTENSION directionals like (41):

(41) The fog spread from Edinburgh to Stirling

In neither instance is a conjunct like 'The fog comes not to be at
Edinburgh' appropriate as part of the source. The difference between
these and between them and the DISPLACEMENT directionals
considered so far lies mainly in the relative tensing of the locations
specified as Source and Goal. With a displacement directional like (30),
the time at/for which the ball is at the door necessarily precedes the
times at which it is rolling, which necessarily precede that at/for which it is
at the window. The extensive directional is characterised by the fact that,
in this instance (41), the fog continues to include the Source in the area
it occupies when this extends to encompass the Goal. (The 'area
occupied', however, need not be continuous – as in, say, *The fever
spread from person to person/from town to town.*) Both of these types
are MOTIONAL, in that the occupancy of the Goal location follows the
occupancy of the Source. There is no such discrepancy with 'static'
directionals such as (40). And it is this which serves to distinguish them
as a class rather than their being semantically 'stative', as proposed in
Anderson, 1971*b*. They are no more stative than such static
LOCATIONALS as (42):

(42)   The fog lies over that valley

Both of (43) are well-formed (and not merely under a motional interpretation):

(43)   a.   The fog is stretching from Edinburgh to Stirling ⎫   at the
      b.   The fog is lying over that valley   ⎬   moment

and they involve the same semantic limitation over their respective non-progressive congeners.

And if we turn to Frajzyngier's argument (1975) for a de-coordinative analysis for the Kwa language Awutu, it turns out similarly to be rather insubstantial. Awutu seems to be a language with a paucity of case markers, argument-types being identified in terms of the associated predicate and their sequence with respect to it. Frajzyngier observes in particular that overt source and goal co-occur only via coordination; any single predicate takes overtly either a source or a goal. He concludes that this reflects a restriction in underlying structure, such that source and goal are simply the locative sub-types associated with certain verbs. If my conclusions concerning English are correct, then the two languages would then differ in the set of CRs they require. However it is clear that such a conclusion is unwarranted. The distribution could on the evidence he presents equally well be, for example, a reflexion of a surface constraint associated with the lack of case markers. There may be involved, indeed, a much wider constraint on expression, of which the complementarity of source and goal represents merely one instance. Certainly more evidence is required, and alternatives need to be discounted, before such a far-reaching typological distinction (involving distinctness in the set of CRs) can be set up.

2.3.3. If then we have no support for a de-coordination analysis of directionals (such as embodied in (36)), we have nevertheless found various properties associated with the relationship between directionals and corresponding locationals and with the difference between various types of directional which are rendered more transparent if the Goal and Source arguments of a directional predication contain embedded locationals. It is, in particular, the tense characteristics of these locationals which then make the difference between static and motional directional sentences, and, within motionals, between extension and displacement. The analysis for directionals like (30) envisaged above should thus be extended after the fashion indicated in (44):

(44)

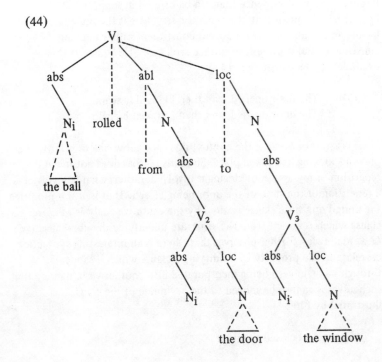

such that the relevant tense relationships, however they are introduced,
are to be associated with V_2 and V_3, the embedded locationals.
The abs nodes on which V_2 and V_3 depend embody the assumption
that the V and N nodes are universally separated in underlying
representations by functional labels. Some support for such a position
comes from the fact that such nodes (separating N and a subordinate V)
provide a plausible source for complementisers, given that these often
have the same shape as case markers (in English, *to* and the possessive
inflexion), and particularly if complementiser nodes have a status in
underlying structures rather than being derived (Bresnan, 1970).[31]

   Further support for some such (i.e. embedded locative) source for
Goals and Sources is provided if we extend some observations of
McCawley's concerning the structure of causative predications to the

present case of simple directionals. McCawley (1971*a*) argues that 'one important type of evidence that can be offered in support of a hypothesised constituent of a semantic structure is the possibility of having an adverb that modifies that constituent rather than any constituent that is present in surface structure'. He contrasts (his examples (8)) a pair such as (45):

(45) a. The door opened, and then I clósed it agàin
      b.*The door opened, and then I kícked it agàin

(45.b) is strange because the context does not allow one to infer that a previous kicking had taken place. Similarly, (45.a) does not mean that a repetition of my action of closing is involved; rather, what is involved is a repetition of the state of the door being closed. That is, *again* modifies the underlying state clause posited by the causative analysis of *close,* a clause which is absent from the structure underlying the non-causative *kick.* McCawley further observes that 'there is an interesting syntactic correlate to the property of modifying a clause which disappears through its main verb being incorporated into another verb, namely that such adverbs cannot be moved to the beginning of the clause', as illustrated by (46):

(46) Again I closed the door

which 'can only refer to a second action of closing the door, not to merely the door's being again closed'. Likewise although (47):

(47) The sheriff of Nottingham jailed Robin Hood for four years

is ambiguous (repeated jailings over a period of four years *v.* confinement lasting four years) only the one ('repeated jailings') interpretation is available with (48):

(48) For four years the sheriff of Nottingham jailed Robin Hood

(For some speakers (e.g. Roger Lass) the 'non-repetitive' reading is available if the preposed adverbial is emphatic). The relevance of these considerations to our present concerns depends on the fact that while sentences like (49):

(49) a. The water rose to this point for several days
      b. Algernon flew to London for four months

display the same kind of ambiguity as (47), (50), like (48), are
unambiguous:

(50)   a. For several days the water rose to this point
       b. For four months Algernon flew to London

and again the reading which associates the adverbial with the main
clause rather than the putative embedded one is preferred. Consider
too the scope ambiguity in a sentence like *The girl almost fell to the
bottom of the cliff,* such that on one interpretation the girl didn't fall,
whereas on the other she fell to a spot which was almost at the bottom
of the cliff. The former interpretation is excluded in this case if the
adverb is postposed to the verb: *The girl fell almost to the bottom of
the cliff.* Notice too that a simple locational like *The girl is almost at
the bottom of the cliff* is not ambiguous in this way. If simple
directional sentences, as well as causatives (the analysis of which we
return to below), involve embedding, in the instance of a locational
predication, then such phenomena can be allowed for in the same terms
as envisaged by McCawley.

2.3.4. What we have been concerned with is establishing the plausibility
of one of the predictions made by (29), namely that there are predications
characterised by the co-selection of loc and abl. However, what if abl
alone in (29) is selected? The most plausible candidate for such a
characterisation would be the sentence type (51):

(51)   Mary was $\begin{Bmatrix} \text{absent} \\ \text{missing} \end{Bmatrix}$ from the meeting

with overt abs (*Mary*) and abl (*the meeting*) arguments; and no
particular motivation for a derivation (by reduction) from a directional
predication. Again, however, the possibility of a negative locational
source arises. Such a course we discounted for *from* in directional
sentences, and thus lexical naturalness would argue against it in this
instance. Moreover, I have argued elsewhere (Anderson, 1973*d*, 1974*a*)
that the negative element (of sentence negation) itself is not simplex,
and may in fact include in its underlying structure an ablative component.
I shall therefore in what follows assume such a source for (51) as I have
indicated. And similarly (52) (if we now consider the role of abl as part
of a multiple case label):

(52) His paper was devoid of interest

can realise co-selection of abl and abs (*his paper* is [abl, abs] and *interest* [abs]) while erg and abl are perhaps realised by the subject of (53), with the object as abs:

(53) Fred failed the exam

or by the corresponding phrase in the equivalent passive. Co-selection of erg, loc and abl underlies both of (54):

(54) a. The local government officer received a crate of whisky from the businessman
      b. His interpretation of the 'Titan' afforded much pleasure to the audience

but whereas in (54.a) the subject is [loc, erg] in (54.b) it is [abl, erg] . (*a crate of whisky* and *much pleasure* are both absolutive, whereas *from the businessman* is of course ablative and *to the audience* locative (allative). We return in the succeeding sections to the analysis of other 'abstract' directionals.) The erg phrase in both instances occurs marked with *by* in the corresponding passives. (55), however, lack passives:

(55) a. The bank got the money from my agent
      b. We owe this discovery to Newton

and are accordingly realisations of the co-selection of abs, abl and loc, in which respectively abs is associated with loc (*the bank*) and with abl (*we*). (*Resemble* is similar to *owe* if we allow the analysis of similarity predicates as directional which is proposed in Anderson, 1973*a*.)

The members of (54) and (55) show the same selections of case features: respectively loc, abl and erg and loc, abl and abs. But the CRs are distributed differently in the (a) and (b) instances. We must add to (29) to allow for this. And the dependency rules of (12) must also be extended to provide for the introduction of abl and for its association with erg ((53), (54.b)) and abs ((52), (55.b)). Perhaps (56) will suffice:

(56) i.

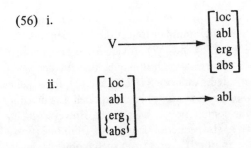

$$V \longrightarrow \begin{bmatrix} loc \\ abl \\ erg \\ abs \end{bmatrix}$$

ii.

$$\begin{bmatrix} loc \\ abl \\ \{ {erg \atop abs} \} \end{bmatrix} \longrightarrow abl$$

for subcategorisation, and for dependency, (57):

(57) i. $V \longrightarrow abs$
ii. $loc \longrightarrow loc$
iii. $abl \longrightarrow abl$
iv.

$$\begin{bmatrix} erg \\ \langle abs \rangle_1 \\ \langle abl \rangle_2 \end{bmatrix} \longrightarrow erg \ / \quad \begin{cases} \text{a.} \ \ \langle [{abl \atop \_}] \rangle_2 \\ \text{b,} \ \ [{loc \atop \_}] \\ \text{c.} \ \ \langle [{abs \atop \_}] \rangle_1 \\ \text{d.} \ \ - \end{cases}$$

v.

$$\begin{bmatrix} abs \\ \langle abl \rangle \end{bmatrix} \longrightarrow abs \ / \quad \begin{cases} \text{a.} \ \ \langle [{abl \atop \_}] \rangle \\ \text{b.} \ \ [{loc \atop \_}] \\ \text{c.} \ \ - \end{cases}$$

(56.ii) introduces a second ablative feature the effect of which is to serve as a condition on dependency rules (iv) and (v), such that if after the operation of (iii) there is still an abl feature around, erg or abs is associated with the abl phrase introduced by (iii) rather than with loc etc. Observe that if by (56.i) all of loc, abl, erg and abs are selected, then the effect will be to attach erg to abl by (57.iv.a) and abs to loc by (57.iv.b), realised as (58):

(58) His interpretation of the 'Titan' afforded the audience much pleasure

(cf. (54.b) in which abs is not selected). The form of rules set up to allow for the predication types considered above thus predicts the existence of the type exemplified by (58).

We turn in the next section to the significance of a hypothesis concerning CRs which limits their number to just the four deployed in (56) and (57). It may be that (56) and (57) provide for as basic more combinations of CRs than is necessary. Or it may be that further combinations can be motivated. Anderson (1971*b*, § 1.11), for instance, suggests that 'Path' (*through, across, along*) be interpreted as a multiply labelled node involving the conjunction of loc and abl. However, such a combination may be derived (by reduction from, say, 'from one (possibly extreme) point in/on X to another'). Apart from such modifications to (56) and (57), it is envisaged that no additions, specifically of further CRs, will be required. That is, all sentences in a language can plausibly be described in terms of representations which incorporate just the predication types allowed for by (56)–(57) (give or take one or two combinations). Moreover, generalisations will be obscured, I suggest, if further distinct types are admitted. In the sections that follow I shall endeavour to clarify the character of the hypothesis being advanced, and shall explore in some detail its consequences in one particular area.

2.4 Localist Case Grammar 1: A brief history

2.4.1. If the position (concerning the number of CRs) outlined at the end of the previous section can be given some support, the question arises as to whether this is a quite adventitious generalisation or whether it is to be expected of a case system that it should be so. Specifically, might such a limitation on the set of CRs follow from the intrinsic content of the notion case? Certainly the number of case markers in different languages would not suggest such a limitation, since even if we confine ourselves to inflexional systems the number of these can amount to several dozen. Nor have most theories of case, whether this was accorded only a superficial (morphological) status (Jespersen, 1924, ch.13; Chomsky, 1965) or equated with CRs in the sense invoked here (Fillmore, 1968*a*, etc.), provided any attempt at a principled limitation on the members of, or the distinctions appropriate to the category of case. We have seen that the 'external' criteria proposed by Fillmore are only partially successful in eliminating pseudo-CRs (see again Fletcher, 1971; Marino, 1972) — though we shall find below that a more radical deployment of his principles of contrast and complementarity than he undertakes leads to an inventory of CRs compatible with that I am proposing here. There is, on the other hand, a theory of the content of CRs that, appropriately constrained, requires just such a limitation as we have envisaged. This is the LOCALIST theory of case.

The earliest attempts at a localist theory of case are due to the

Byzantine Maximus Planudes and, a century later Theodorus Gaza, of whom Hjelmslev (1935, 13), in summing up their contribution, says:
'[Ils] ont établi judicieusement la théorie casuelle dite localiste en mettant à la base des définitions la notion abstraite de la DIRECTION, applicable à la fois aux rapports concrets ou locaux et aux rapports abstraits ou grammaticaux.'[32] A localist theory holds that the members of the category of case are opposed to each other in terms of (combinations of) the directional notions 'source', 'goal' and 'resting-point'. So that not only are the 'concrete' uses of case markers to be so interpreted but also the 'abstract'; and indeed even those markers (like the nominative in many languages) which are entirely or almost entirely 'abstract' or 'grammatical' in use are opposed to the other markers in such terms.

The former position, that the notion of 'goal', for example, is as appropriate to 'abstract' uses of, say, a preposition like *to* in English as to 'concrete', has been espoused by a number of scholars unaware of (or not caring to acknowledge) the localist tradition (as outlined by, in particular, Hjelmslev, 1935) or its relevance. Consider among recent work that of Gruber (1965, 1967), Ikegami (1970, 1973), Fillmore (1971*c*), Talmy (1973), or Robin Lakoff (1974). A number of people have proposed, for instance, to interpret a large range of rather 'abstract' predicates as 'verbs of motion'. As instances within earlier traditions, cf. Laurie (1959), who avers: 'We must consequently look for the primary ideas of the various cases in the relations subsisting between objects in space' (8); or the discussion of the Basque conjugation offered in Darrigol, 1829. (See further Anderson, 1973*b, c, e.*)

The latter proposal, that even predominantly 'abstract' case markers belong to the system of directionality, has been responsible for some ingenious but ultimately rather implausible or at best a prioristic analyses. Consider for example Hjelmslev's (1935, 124-5) description of the Turkish nominative:

C'est le cas du sujet et du prédicat, indiquant ainsi, sans distinction formelle, l'éloignement et le rapprochement. Souvent il est complexe ou neutre, comportant la signification dite "adverbiale", comme lorsque *dün* signifie à la fois "nuit" et "hier", lorsque *erte* signifie à la fois "matin" et "demain", etc. Le nominatif turc est à ce point un *casus generalis* qu'il joue aussi le rôle de *casus adverbialis.*

We gain no explanation of why such a 'casus generalis' should embrace in many languages the subject and predicate functions, or why even the subject function is uniquely one of 'éloignement', given the range of functions that seemed appropriate in (1) in § 1.1. In part such problems stem from a failure to recognise that a case marker may realise a case node which bears a multiple label: the nominative in many languages realises various combinations of erg with other CRs; the DATIVE often realises a combination of loc and erg. In part problems arise from a failure to recognise that such markers as nominative and genitive realise neutralised CRs; i.e. they do not always reflect the underlying status of the case node. I am not of course advocating the recognition of massive neutralisations, which would be quite unexplanatory. The amount of neutralisation involved with subject case markers will, on the view advocated in the previous sections, be strictly limited; we return to this in ch.3. Rather, it is mainly the recognition of multiple CRs, together with an extended concept of case marker that includes prepositions etc., that will enable us to maintain a plausible localist analysis for individual cases. However it seems to me that the main stumbling block in the establishment of a localist theory of case has not been a theoretical one. As we shall see, Hjelmslev, for instance, was aware of the complex nature of the relations marked by individual case markers; and he recognised in principle the 'equivalence' in some respects of inflexions, prepositions and word order. What is mainly lacking is the provision of adequate motivation for the analyses proposed as appropriate to particular cases. For the most part argumentation has remained on an intuitive notional plane, though the observations made were often extremely insightful.

2.4.2. The number of CRs allowed for by a localist analysis depends on how the articulation of CRs with respect to the dimension of direction is conceived. In Hjelmslev's proposals, the articulation is rather complex; and the number of terms in the system varies from language to language. At most, Hjelmslev's dimension of direction permits six distinct terms (1935, 125-6). However, according to Hjelmslev, 'le système casuel peut comporter plus d'une seule dimension et le fait souvent.' He envisages two further dimensions, 'cohérence-incohérence', which presupposes direction, and 'subjectivité-objectivité', which in turn presupposes 'cohérence-incohérence'. Latin '*in* + accusative', for example (13Q), realises 'rapprochement' cumulated with 'cohérence', whereas *ad* is 'incohérent'. As to the last opposition, 'une relation entre deux objets peut être pensée *objectivement,* c'est-à-dire, sans égard à l'individu pensant, et elle peut être pensée *subjectivement,* c'est-à-dire par rapport à l'individu pensant.'

This distinction opposes French *au-dessus/au-dessous* ('objectivité')
and *devant/derrière* ('subjectivité'). Since each of these further dimensions
can accommodate six terms,'le *maximum théorique* du système casuel
est 6^3 = 216.' However, in terms of Hjelmslev's own analysis (1935,
§ II.C.a), the largest inventory of cases he encounters is 52 for
Tabassaranian. Admittedly, Hjelmslev had available to him only Dirr's
(1905) work, which did not provide him with the full range of material.
But even if we supplement the inventory of cases he suggests for
Tabassaranian in the light of subsequent research on the language, in
terms of which the number (despite Žirkov (1948)) appears to surpass
Hjelmslev's total (Hanmagomedov, 1958), the 'maximum empirique'
represented by Tabassaranian still falls far short of the 'maximum
théorique'. This particular localist theory, then, provides a rather
inclusive definition of the content of the notion case, both in respect of
the 'maximum théorique' and the actual maximum encountered; and it
provides no explanation of the discrepancy between the two, if this
discrepancy represents, as Hjelmslev himself appears to intend, an
accurate picture of the situation as conceived of by him. He at least
envisages for any category a 'maximum absolu' which will be
encountered in a language, which is distinct from the 'maximum
théorique'.

However, Hjelmslev's additional dimensions are clearly quite distinct
in semantic character from the first. What he has provided, it seems to
me, rather than a definition of the notion case, is a typology (albeit
still under-restricted) of those elements apart from gender and number
(Latin) and definiteness (Basque) that can be cumulated in their
realisation with CRs. Thus a case marker like *devant* also incorporates
an element of deictic orientation, either with respect to the location of
the speaker or in relation to some conventional face of the entity which
is the reference object for the predication of location; while *in* in Latin
incorporates an element which relates to the dimensionality of the
reference object.[33] These different sources are morphologically rather
transparent even in Tabassaranian. For instance, the 'ablatif-postessif'
$-q^C an$ (Hjelmslev, 1935: 153) divides into $-q^C-$ ('behind' – cf. $-q^C$ *indi*,
'towards the rear of') and $-an$ ('from' – cf. $-\exists$ *an,* out of ', where
$-\exists-$ = 'in(side)').

Accordingly it seems just to regard only Hjelmslev's first dimension as
articulating CRs proper; this is certainly more in line with current
understanding of the scope of the notion CR, and thus makes
comparison with non-localist case grammars like Fillmore's possible. In
comparison with these, Hjelmslev's theory, divested of the notions

of 'cohérence' and 'subjectivité', makes a strong claim concerning the
number of CRs available to a language, viz. a maximum of six. And he
provides an intrinsic definition of the category of case: its content is
directionality; and the range of CRs depends upon the set of oppositions
which can be associated with this dimension.

Hjelmslev illustrates a six term (unidimensional) system by a discussion
of Turkish (1935, 121-5). The terms are distinguished in accordance
with the segments or cells they occupy relative to each other in the
'zone sémantique' of directionality, which is represented as in (59):

(59)   + (rapprochement)
                0 (repos)
                − (éloignement)

A term is intensive with respect to another or others if relative to them
it is concentrated say in a single cell. Thus the Turkish dative is intensive,
in that '[il] désigne toujours un rapprochement bien marqué et
exclusif', and '[il] est le seul cas qui recouvre une seule case de la zone
sémantique.' The + cell of (59) is thus intensive, and the system is said
to have a positive orientation. The Turkish nominative, in contrast to
the dative, 'est . . . un cas entièrement vague', and it occupies the entire
'zone sémantique'. The ablative 'insiste sur l'éloignement', but it can
also be used for 'rapprochement' of both, or for 'repos'. And the
accusative, on the other hand, 'sert uniquement à marquer l'objet
direct d'une action'; and is thus intensive with respect to the ablative,
but weaker than the dative ('il ne comporte pas l'acceptation concrète
contenue dans le datif'). The genitive marks 'le complément d'un nom'
whether the relation is one of 'rapprochement' or 'éloignement', and is
intensive with respect to the locative, which is a neutral ('repos') term
that can 'glisse insensiblement dans l'acceptation complexe'.

Turkish represents the maximal (unidimensional) system; the
theoretical minimum is a two case system, which Hjelmslev illustrates
from English (if no account is taken of word order − 1935, 114-5). In
this respect, Hjelmslev's proposal is not the strongest variant of a localist
hypothesis that one can envisage, in that the number of terms in the
case system is a linguistic variable; and moreover the definition of each
term is dependent on the number in the system. Hjelmslev strengthens
the hypothesis in terms of the 'lois de solidarité', whereby certain
term-types presuppose each other (1935, 125). Thus an intensive and
extensive pair of the type of the Turkish dative and nominative are
mutually presupposing. However, it is worth investigating whether the

hypothesis can be made stronger still, by requiring the presence of a specific number of CRs in any language, CRs which are again opposed in terms of directionality. Such a proposal, of course, is at all plausible (despite Hjelmslev: 'Il n'y a pas de cas *universels'* (70)) only if we recognise the functional equivalence of prepositions, postpositions, inflexions and, to an extent we shall consider below, word order. The failure to implement this (despite his recognition of Bernhardi's, Pott's and Wundt's contributions in this respect – 1935, 24, 41-3, 68-70), together with the neglect of neutralisation, is what leads Hjelmslev to attribute different sets of CRs to, say, English (118-20), German (120-1) and Turkish, whereas the difference lies, it seems to me, in the manner in which the case distinctions are assigned to (realisation by) inflexions, function words and word order.

2.5 Localist Case Grammar 2: A proposal

2.5.1. Let us label a localist theory of the kind advocated by Hjelmslev MINIMAL, in view of the fact that (in terms of the framework developed here) it claims no universality for the CRs themselves (but only for the category of case), though the set of oppositions whereby they are distinguished constitute a finite set from which a particular language selects in such a way as to allow for a maximum of six CRs. It is possible to envisage a slightly stronger variant in which a specific number of CRs is designated as universal, but in terms of which the groupings within the set are a linguistic variable: there are no natural sub-groupings. The theory is NON-NATURAL in this respect. For example, if there are four (universal) CRs, w,x,y,z, it is possible for language A to group w with x and y with z and for language B to associate w with y and x with z.

A still stronger localist claim is made in Anderson, 1973c, where it is proposed, as in the preceding discussion, that the inventory of CRs be limited to four; and further that these four are universally distinguished in terms of the distribution of two directional components, which I shall label here PLACE and SOURCE, as indicated in (60):

(60)

abs	loc	erg	abl
	place		place
		source	source

The CR labels are then abbreviations for the specifications in (61), which impose SEMANTICALLY NATURAL sub-groupings:

$$(61)\quad abs = \begin{bmatrix} case \end{bmatrix} ,\quad loc = \begin{bmatrix} case \\ place \end{bmatrix} ,\quad erg = \begin{bmatrix} case \\ source \end{bmatrix} abl = \begin{bmatrix} case \\ place \\ source \end{bmatrix}$$

That is, loc and abl are grouped together as place relations and erg and abl are sources, respectively the source of an action and the source of a spatial trajectory. The non-sources abs and loc are complex in something like Hjelmslev's sense in that they are goals only in the presence of erg and abl respectively, as the goal of the action and the spatial goal. This correlation between 'transitivity' and 'movement' is expressed rather vividly by Laurie (1859, 11), when he says:

> If we contemplate for a moment two things as distinct and standing absolutely, as *vir* and *canis,* and then perceive one extend its individuality over the other, *e.g., vir canem verberat,* we shall find that the idea of extension or continuity is realised, motion having been effected from one to the other, so as to unite the two. The same is true where the predicate does not indicate activity, but *sensation, e.g., Ægrotus sonum audit* or *dolorem sentit.* In the one instance the object is embraced *by* the activity, in the other it is absorbed *into* the consciousness, of the subject . . .

These latter verbs are those we characterised above (§§ 1,7, 1.9, 2.1) as taking subjects which are at once erg and loc: in Laurie's terms, as both source of the 'sensation' and the location into which the other argument is 'absorbed'. (See further ch.3.)

The use of 'spatial' in describing loc and abl is not meant to commit us to the view that the place CRs are only concrete; we shall find, on the contrary, that all of the CRs apparently manifest varying degrees of abstractness, depending crucially on the character of the predicate on which they depend and the arguments subordinate to them. In fact, abstractness/concreteness is irrelevant to the characterisation of the CRs as such. Though, again, the priority of the concrete uses, in the acquisition of language by the child and as a source for the renewal of the abstract (cf. e.g. Kuryłowicz's (1964) discussion of the origins of the Indo-European case inflexions), would tend to support the proposal that the elements of underlying representations as well as the constraints on the derivations associated with them (cf. § 1.10), have a cognitive basis, specifically in this instance in our perception of relations between objects in space. Compare in this regard an earlier statement (though it is perhaps rather more confident about ultimate origins than we might be), again by Laurie (1859, 8):

> (62) Language has its basis in external nature; and words, whether employed to denote an existence, an affection, or a relation, and however abstract may be their present use, originally denoted (it may be safely assumed) only external phenomena and external relations. We must consequently look for the primary ideas of the various cases in the relations subsisting between objects in space. On these original material or spatial relations, all the more abstract relations are built.

with such more recent discussions as are provided by Clark (1973), Traugott (1974), Stewart (1975), Washabaugh (1975).

2.5.2. In various languages such a system of CRs as is posited in (60)/(61) is realised rather transparently in the markers of case. Consider, for example, the situation in Colville (Mattina, 1973, § 4.32), which opposes to an un-marked absolutive a locational in $//1//$ (§ 4.323) and an agent in $//t//$ (§4.324). In terms of the scheme in (60), the loc CR incorporates a place component and the erg a source component. Abl includes both place (like loc) and source (like erg): in Colville the ablative marker is $//t1//$, which patently unites the source marker $//t//$ and the place marker $//1//$. However, the system of markers is even more interesting in the light of the discussion in the immediately preceding section in this chapter.

There I suggested that allatives involve the embedding of a locational predication under the locational argument of a directional verb, as represented in outline in (44). Now, the Colville allative marker is apparently (Mattina, 1973, § 4.323) $//\acute{k}l//$. Again the place marker $//l//$ is presumably included here. However the rest of the allative marker is identical to the element which Mattina (§ 4.325) translates by 'towards' i.e. the marker of incomplete extension, which can be appropriately represented by simply dropping V_3 of (44), the locational predication that characterises the final location in a directional structure. Observe that, in comparison with (49.b), (63) is not ambiguous in the appropriate way:

> (63) Algernon drove towards London for several days

(63) is ambiguous only between iterative and non-iterative readings

where the adverbial is associated in both cases with the *drive* predication and not an embedded locational. Of course both these readings are retained under preposing:

(64)   For several days Algernon drove towards London

Cf. (50.b). This is accounted for if (63)/(64) lack a locational predication embedded under the locative node in the directional to which the adverbial can alternatively be attached. In terms of the markers in Colville, this means that $//1//$ represents a non-directional locational (i.e. one in a predication that isn't also ablative, $//\overset{\text{!}}{k}//$ a directional locational and $//\overset{\text{!}}{k}l//$ a directional locational with a non-directional subordinate to it. With ablatives, there is no such contrast as is represented by $//\overset{\text{!}}{k}l//v.$ $//k//$ in Colville, and the representation is thus uniquely $//t1//$.

The localist theory we have arrived at here claims that the distribution of $//1//$, $//t//$ and $//\overset{\text{!}}{k}//$ in Colville is not fortuitous. Considerations of lexical naturalness would favour an account whereby this is the case. More strongly, the localist theory predicts that other conceivable distributions are not to be expected. (Of course, such a distribution of markers does not, conversely, uniquely select this variant of the localist theory.) However, in general, localist predictions can be tested only to a limited extent in terms of lexical naturalness. This is because of the neutralisation effected in many languages by, in particular, subject-formation (on which § 2.8), and on account of the fact that in terms of the framework we are developing here sentences typically represent reductions from complexes of predications, reductions which involve the application of rules like raising, such that an underlying ergative NP, say, can come to be associated superficially with some quite other CR. Perhaps, however, one can maintain at least the RESTRICTED LEXICAL HYPOTHESIS in relation to such a localist theory as we have been envisaging — i.e. roughly:

(65)   *restricted lexical hypothesis for a localist theory:* in the
       structurally least complex sentences in which a NP in a
       particular CR can appear, the character of the CF that
       manifests the CR will not be in conflict with the predictions of
       the localist hypothesis of (60)/(61), given the assumption of
       lexical naturalness

This claims, for instance, that in the simplest sentences in which they occur agents will not share a marker with locatives which does not also represent ablatives. As far as I can tell, the distribution of CFs in Colville strongly supports the predictions of (60)/(61) rather than merely not being in conflict with them. But as I anticipated above, in most languages only the more restricted hypothesis of (65) can be maintained, as a result of neutralisations, raisings or merely the absence of an overt marker in the simplest instances.

2.5.3. We are also now in a position, primarily on the basis of the discussion in § 2.3.3, to propose an even more radical theory than that embodied in (66). In § 2.3.3 I argued that goals and sources included an embedded locational predication (as represented in (44)). In the present section we have distinguished goals of incomplete (or not necessarily complete) extension from those implying completion in terms of the absence *v.* the presence of this embedded locational. However ablatives in directional predications (sources) apparently always contain an embedded locational: there is no parallel to the distinction between incomplete extension with goals. And this seems to be equally maintainable with respect to ablatives in non-directional predications like that in (51) with *absent.* This means that we can quite simply perform the identification tentatively advocated in Anderson (1971*b*) whereby erg and abl are 'collapsed', but retain the necessary distinctiveness: erg is simply an abl which lacks an embedded locational of the character of that in (44). Thus only three fundamental CRs need be envisaged, a locational, a source and abs (which is neither). And just as goals are differentiated from locatives on the basis of the governing predicate (it is directional with goals) and 'incomplete' and 'complete' goals can be distinguished in terms of the absence *v.* the presence of an embedded locational predication, so ergatives are distinguished from other sources simply in this latter manner. However, I shall not pursue the consequences of this further at this point, in that, in particular, in the discussion of case *v.* other grammars that follows we shall be much concerned with the distinctive role of erg as such.

We have already associated with erg (cf. § 1.7) the property of selecting an argument that is higher on the 'humanness hierarchy' than would otherwise be the case. When not associated with a locational CR, erg indeed introduces an agent, the quintessential human (and higher) role. Thus, if the localist theory embodies a claim about the basicness of spatial relations to the cognitive structures realised in language, the character and function of erg embodies what seems to me to be another major characteristic of linguistic expressions, viz. their 'anthropocentricity' (cf. e.g. Skalička, 1962; Jessen, 1974). And my formulation of subject-formation as erg-assimilation is intended to assert the status of (underlying) ergative predications as a model for derived structures. Thus, though subjects (in many instances at least) may originate (historically) in topics, the prevalence of ergative topics results in a reinterpretation of such topics as 'subjects', i.e. derived ergs, which constitute the unmarked topic slot. Such a history would underly the alleged development, alluded to above, of Indo-European from an earlier 'ergative language' by extension of the ergative marker to all subjects. For a recent statement, cf. Haudry: 'La plus ancienne structure que nous puissions restituer est la liaison d'un nominatif d'origine, d'un accusatif de but et d'un instrumental signifiant "entre, à travers" ' (1970, 83). On this view, subject-formation is but a further extension of anthropocentricity (cf. again Skalička, 1962).

2.5.4. One consequence of adopting a semantically natural case theory of the kind embodied in (60)/(61) is that other putative CRs must represent contextually determined variants of the four CRs allowed for by (60) or combinations of some of the four or combinations of a CR with other elements. With respect to the last possibility, I have, for instance, already suggested that the second two of Hjelmslev's (1935/7) 'dimensions' involve cumulation of a CR with other substructures. Specifically, a marker like *in* or *on* realises a CR plus a substructure embodying the dimensionality of the locational reference object. (See too e.g. Langacker, 1973.)

As an instance of the first possibility, on the other hand, one can make rather a good case for the factitive or object of result being the absolutive in a causative existential structure. Compare with (33), for example, the pair in (66):

(66)   a. Someone has built a filling station on that site
       b. There is a filling station on that site

where once again the (a) example, with an object of result (*a filling station*), implies the (b), an existential sentence. In (33) the absolutive phrase designated the object that moved or was located. Here it is the phrase *a filling station* which moves (into existence — (66.a)) or is located (in existence — (66.b)): see further Anderson, 1970. If this is a just parallel, then it begins to look as if factitives are appropriately to be reduced to (contextually determined variants of) absolutives, specifically absolutives in positively oriented ('into existence') 'existential causatives'.

Paths (*along, across, through*) are an example of a putative function
which is most plausibly interpreted as a combination of two others,
specifically allative and ablative (as proposed in Anderson, 1971*b*, § 11.1).
This accounts, for instance, for the fact that paths are permissible only
with verbs that take allatives and ablatives, i.e. directional verbs.
However, in this instance, we should note again, the combination of
allative and ablative may be derived (from an overt *from . . . to . . .*
structure). But, in any case, there is (despite Bennett, 1975, 28) no
need to posit a distinct atomic CR path.

Similarly, as anticipated in § 1.7, experiencer NPs like the subject in
(67):

(67) Many people know French

share crucial properties with locatives, some of which we shall return
to in the section that follows; but, as argued in § 1.7, and reaffirmed in
the preceding paragraphs, such a NP also shares properties with agents.
It is this dual aspect which prompted the [loc, erg] assignment proposed
in § 1.7. And it would, indeed, seem quite plausible to extend the
restricted lexical hypothesis of (65) to such combinations of CRs (as
well as simple CRs), in that overt markers of 'experiencers' are either
also locative/allative (though sometimes only historically), as in the
Indo-European languages (Kuryłowicz, 1964, 190-5) or also agentive,
as in Basque, where the ergative suffix marks the relevant (non-absolutive)
argument of both agentive and experiencer verbs, as in, say, (68):

(68) a. Amak besartatzen nu   '(my) mother kisses me'
      b. Amak maitatzen nu   '(my) mother loves me'

where the *-k* suffixed to *ama* ('mother') is the ergative marker.

However, when possibly more complex combinations of CRs are
putatively involved, the need to invoke considerations of lexical
naturalness only against a background of independent evidence
concerning the character of the construction concerned becomes
rather strikingly apparent. Each localist reduction of a construction-type
obviously requires extended consideration of the viability of non-localist
alternatives given the range of available evidence. One such reduction is
attempted, as an illustration, in the section that follows: specifically, the
elimination of 'indirect objects'/'datives' as a distinct function. However,
consider at this point, as an example of a function whose status (as far as
I am aware) awaits the presentation of crucial evidence, the much-debated

notion of 'instrumental'.

2.5.5. In ch.1 we were able to avoid some of the problems attendant on
Fillmore's (1968*a*) analysis by eliminating from the scope of the notion
'simple instrumental', NPs in subject position or in passive *by*-phrases,
i.e. examples like (*1*.60), (*1*.62) or those involving 'natural forces', as
opposed to (*1*.64), where an instrumental phrase marked by *with*
co-occurs with an agent. (We return below to the dependence of
instrumentality on agency.) Let us identify such instances as (*1*.64) or,
say, (69) here:

> (69)   Fred tortured Mary with a red-hot icepick

as involving an 'instrumental' construction (realised as the *with*-phrase);
and let as assume that we can identify at least the notionally 'cardinal'
or 'canonical' instances of instrumental constructions cross-linguistically.
In a cardinal instance such as (69) an agent wields the instrumental
entity and that entity serves as a tool in carrying out the action. If we
survey the case forms that mark such a construction in various languages
of the world there emerge, as far as I am aware, three main sub-types (if
we exclude those languages which possess a marker more or less unique
to this construction): (a) the *with*-type, illustrated, of course, by English,
where the marker is that also used for the comitative; (b) the *durch*-type
(German), in which a 'path' form is used; (c) the *-ta*-type (Chukchee,
Koryak – Bogoras, 1922, § 37), in which the agent and instrumental
share the same marker. If we look outside the cardinal instance, the
situation is usually more complex. English uses the *by*-form also found
with agents (in the passive) with non-cardinal instrumentals, specifically
those involving sententially specified instruments such as in *Fred
tortured Mary by boiling her in oil* and those involving vehicular
instruments such as *by car, by plane* etc. Moreover we also find *by*,
apart from as a locational, with such path-expressions as *by way of . . .*
(cf. the (b) type), parallel to the instrumental *by means of . . .* Consider
the syncretism of question form in (70):

> (70)   How did you go to London? $\begin{cases} \text{By car} \\ \text{By way of Birmingham} \end{cases}$

Even if we assume lexical naturalness, this situation (i.e. the diversity of
markers) is explicable in a number of ways, some of which are
compatible with variants of a localist theory. Clearly, other considerations

than lexical naturalness will be decisive here, but such an assumption at least allows us to rank these alternatives in terms of the interest of the predictions made.

Least interesting, and unnatural, is the hypothesis that instrumentals represent a unique, atomic CR or function. In terms of such a hypothesis the distribution of markers we have noted is inexplicable. If it is the case that instrumentals do 'syncretise' uniquely or even almost uniquely with these three other functions then this must simply be stated as an independent generalisation which is quite unexpected on any other grounds, after the fashion proposed by Starosta (1973*a*). More interesting is the proposition that these syncretisms are natural; that, for instance, the instrumental shares some property with path. This allows of various interpretations each of which is compatible, more or less strongly, with the localist hypothesis we have been developing. We can distinguish in particular between a strong localist interpretation and a weak one. In terms of the weak one, it is hypothesised that in any language the instrumental construction can and should be given *some* kind of localist analysis. The strong localist interpretation requires that all languages provide instrumentals with the same localist analysis.

In terms of the weak hypothesis we might take the use of *with* in English as an indication that in English instrumentals are positional variants of comitatives (which clearly incorporate a locative CR), such that they are the variant associated with agentive rather than locational or directional structures. Alternatively they are like comitatives but incorporate some extra component (realised as *help* in *with the help of*, say). Vehicular instruments occupy an intermediate position between instrumental/comitative and simple locational (*go by car/ in the car.*) In a (b)-type language, on the other hand, instrumentals are the form of path that is associated with actions rather than directions. And with type (c) the distribution of forms might be taken to reflect the status of instrumentals as 'demoted' or subordinate agents. In terms of the weak hypothesis, some non-canonical instrumentals, phrases which in some languages pattern with canonical instrumentals (as described above), may in a particular language syncretise differently and have a different source from the canonical group: cf. again the sentential and vehicular instrumentals of English.

The strong hypothesis, on the other hand, asserts a common source for at least the canonical instrumentals in all languages. There are then certain well defined ways in which the diversity of overt markers can be accounted for. At one extreme, one might claim that the occurrence of markers of all three types is lexically, and specifically semantically natural: all three are possible because the underlying representation for instrumental constructions contains subparts ('comitative', 'path', 'agent') which are naturally realised in that way. Alternatively, the use of these particular markers is natural but only on syntactic grounds; they are a reflex of some syntactic properties that the derivation of instrumentals shares with these other constructions. Intermediate positions combine these alternatives, a semantic explanation for one syncretism, a syntactic for another. For instance, whereas a semantic basis for the (c)-type syncretism, based on instruments as subordinated agents, seems most likely, the occurrence of *with* in English may have a syntactic motivation. We have already seen (in our discussion of 'the *spray paint* cases' in § 1.8) the use of *with* as a marker of a simple absolutive phrase that has been 'displaced' from object position by a complex absolutive. It is conceivable that such an interpretation can be extended to *with*-instrumentals. In this instance, *with* marks an absolutive which otherwise turns up as the object of a verb such as *use,* but is 'displaced' from object position by loss of its predicate. (This, so far as it goes, does not commit us to either a superordinate source for the predicate (G. Lakoff, 1968) or a subordinate (Chomsky, 1970*b*, 65, note 16). Now, if such an analysis is also appropriate to at least some comitatives, such that *with* in their case marks the 'displaced' abs object of an 'accompaniment' predicate, then the use of *with* in instrumentals is to that extent natural.

The preceding discussion is speculative and inconclusive, and intentionally so. My purpose has been simply to expose the ranking imposed on various interpretations of instrumental constructions by the assumption of lexical naturalness. Even if in this instance the assumption should be held to be valid only historically, it still imposes some constraint on our analysis of instrumentals. It poses the question, even if instrumentals are not to be characterised synchronically in terms of comitatives, paths or demoted agents or all three: what do they share with these which accounts for the adoption over time by instrumentals of markers associated with these others? It seems to me that at present all these questions are quite open. In this circumstance, an interpretation of instrumentals which embodies both a localist reduction and a unitary source for instrumentals whereby the (a), (b) and (c) markers are natural poses the most interesting hypothesis of those we have considered. It is one which needs to be investigated and disconfirmed before a retreat to weaker and possibly non-localist hypotheses becomes appropriate.

In all but the simplest cases, then, the existence of prevalent syncretisms is clearly insufficient to establish a localist analysis for a

construction or, more particularly in the last instance, to select from
competing localist interpretations. It is, as I have indicated, not my
intention, in the present context, to try to motivate localist analyses for
a range of construction-types. I merely offer the hypothesis that
localist analyses of the strong type will prove to be more compatible
than non-localist with the establishable characteristics of any natural
language construction; and I attempt to illustrate below (in § 3.2-.3)
that this is indeed the case with respect to a particular construction.
However, it is also worth inquiring whether there exist apparently
independent generalisations concerning case in general which can be
shown to depend on a localist hypothesis of the kind I have outlined,
and which thus constitute evidence against a theory which does not
incorporate such a hypothesis. Let me now try to establish the
existence of one such generalisation.

2.6 The localist hypothesis and the complementarity criterion

2.6.1. In ch.1 we encountered a number of problems in deploying the
discriminatory criteria for cases proposed by Fillmore (1968*a*). And
elsewhere (Fillmore, 1971*c*) he himself concedes that the results
obtained from their application are far from clearcut. However it seems
to me that this latter discussion of Fillmore's offers a conceptual
advance which has not been fully exploited. Specifically, to begin with,
he points out that the 1-instance-per-proposition constraint is one facet
of CONTRASTIVENESS, and he outlines another respect in which this
may be revealed. For instance, the subject of a predicate like *warm* can
be related, intuitively, in a number of different ways to its predicate, as
exemplified in (71):

(71) a. I am warm
      b. This jacket is warm

Whereas (71.b) can be understood in the same way as the most obvious
interpretation for (71.a), there is a further (more salient) possibility
wherein its role is that of warmth-giver rather than warmth-possessor
(and indeed the former reading is a secondary possibility with (71.a)).
If a similar distinction can be shown for a number of predicates, then
we have a basis for claiming that with such predicates subject position
neutralises a case distinction; and we can go on to seek syntactic
reflexes of this alleged distinction. Conversely, if a putative case
distinction can be attributed rather to other elements in the proposition,
say the class of the predicate itself, then the putative cases are in

COMPLEMENTARY distribution, i.e. are the same CR. Fillmore
illustrates this for change-of-place versus change-of-class predications like
the pair in (72):

> (72) a. The marble rolled from the door to the window
>   b. The house changed from a mansion into a ruin

wherein post-verbally we have a source and a goal, and the difference
in interpretation is attributable to the predicates (cf. too Anderson,
1970).

The contrastiveness criterion remains problematic in Fillmore's
discussion. For example, as well as the sentences in (71) he distinguishes
those in (73):

> (73) a. Summer is warm
>   b. The room is warm

However it is not obvious that these should be distinguished as to the
CR involved from (71.a): that is, (71.a) and (73) all involve warmth-
possessors (or possibly warmth-givers), distinguished by one being
human, one denoting a (repeated) temporal interval and the last a
spatial enclosure. In order to begin to establish contrastiveness the class
of the subject must be invariant (as with (71.b)). However I do not wish
to pursue the question of establishing contrastiveness in this way.
Rather, my concern is with the consequence of applying the notion of
complementarity consistently in determining the maximum number of
cases which are non-complementary. As far as I am aware, Fillmore's
contrastiveness criteria will not lead us to a larger number of distinctions
than we can arrive at via complementarity.

2.6.2. Fillmore (1971*c*) recognises seven CRs. One of these, path, I
argued above, can be regarded as a variant of a source-goal construction.
Another, time, is distinguished from place in terms of the NP involved
rather than the CR: however this does not entail that sentences
containing both place and time must be taken as representing a further
relaxation of the 1-instance-per-proposition constraint, provided the
source of time phrases is always extra-propositional; that is, if time
phrases are always CIRCUMSTANTIALS rather than PARTICIPANTS
(to use Halliday's (1967/8) terminology). For the moment, we can
consider as participants (i.e. propositional rather than modality or
adverbial CRs) those putative case phrases which are distinctive for a

class of predicates. Thus, for instance, we can distinguish a subclass of verbs that take an agent, whereas there is no class that is distinguished by a time CR (though there are verbs like *elapse* which require that their absolutive argument denote a period of time, just as there are agentive verbs that demand various properties of the agent – that e.g. it be male in the case of the sexist use of transitive *fuck* (Bang-Bang 1974)). I return in more detail to the motivation for this distinction below; for now, I simply assume we can leave time out of account in a discussion of propositional CRs (participants). There remain then in the Fillmorean inventory: agentive, experiencer, instrumental, objective, source, goal, place.

Stockwell *et al.* (1973, ch.12) invoke almost the same set in formulating the lexical entries for predicates in their sample lexicon. I now would like to examine this lexicon in the light of the complementarity criterion, in the anticipation that such a sample should bring to light potential contrasts. Observe, however, that they do differ, in the first place, in also including an essive. The essive, 'a case restricted to copulatives' (1973, 9) is, according to the subject index, mentioned only in one other place in their work, viz. p.29, where it is defined rather more explicitly as 'the case for predicate nominals'. It thus provides for the kind of equatives for which we have allowed an extra absolutive. Stockwell *et al.* offer no arguments in support of the inclusion of essive. Indeed, it is apparently purely accidental that within the grammar they propose, embedding of a complement or nominalised S is possible only through an absolutive (their neutral case) or essive (1973, 29). Moreover, the inclusion of essive necessitates the incorporation into the lexicon (1973, 748) of two complex and, worse, unparalleled redundancy rules governing the distribution of CRs, those in (74):

(74) a.
$$\begin{bmatrix} +V \\ \begin{Bmatrix} +NEUT \\ +DAT \\ +LOC \\ +INS \\ +AGT \end{Bmatrix} \end{bmatrix} \longrightarrow [-ESS]$$

b.
$$\begin{bmatrix} +V \\ +ESS \end{bmatrix} \longrightarrow [+NEUT\ -DAT\ -LOC\ -INS\ -AGT]$$

It further appears to be the case that the only verb in the sample lexicon, unless I am mistaken, which requires an essive is *be*, to which is assigned the case frame '+[——+ESS]'. This assignment is in itself strange, in that surely *be* can, in these terms, take either an essive or a locational as well as an absolutive/neutral. (*That village is in Switzerland?*) I'm not sure how this situation (involving the only lexical entry including essive) is to be expressed, given the redundancy rules in (74), except by having two lexical entries for *be*. However that may be, I feel that we can safely ignore the concept essive in the discussion which follows.

Stockwell *et al.* also subsume source and goal under place, labelled by them location. As far as complementarity is concerned this is unexceptionable, except that the co-occurrence of source and goal in the same simple proposition is unaccounted for (in the absence of a de-coordinative derivation − § 2.3). It is source and goal together that are mutually exclusive with location. We return to this below.

The remaining four CRs invoked by Stockwell *et al.* are agentive, neutral, dative and instrumental. I claim here in terms of our rough criterion that instrumentals, once we eliminate those in subject position in actives and in a *by*-phrase in passives as a kind of agent, with which as inanimates they are in complementary distribution, are again universally circumstantials. Instrumentals in this narrow sense are in principle permissible with any agentive verb and thus do not distinguish a (further) subclass of predicates. It is of course not possible to substantiate fully such a claim within the confines of the present discussion. But observe for instance that none of the verbs that Stockwell *et al.* list as '+[——. . . +INS −AGT]' (i.e. as requiring an instrumental but rejecting an agentive − see below) involve a *with* instrumental, but rather a subjective one, except for one or two inexplicable assignments like that for *hit,* which apparently for Stockwell *et al.* cannot be agentive. The only exception I can think of is the use of verbs like *open* or *lock* illustrated by (*1*.68.c), unless the subject there is [abs, erg] ; or unless some more complex source is to be preferred, specifically one that incorporates the modal and aspectual limitations (as well as possibly an agent) that are associated with such sentences (cf. Chvany, 1974). Conversely, almost all of the agentive verbs that they claim fail to take an instrumental fall into three well-defined semantic classes; verbs of communication (the majority of non-instrumental verbs), verbs of movement, and 'aspectual' verbs. It seems to me that there is no need to mark such verbs as *tell* as '−INS' in that any difficulty in construing these along with an instrumental phrase follows from their semantics, which specifies that the characterisation of the verb incorporates as instrumental the vocal apparatus, in the unmarked instance. Moreover, the difficulty is

alleviated with communicative verbs that are more neutral with respect
to medium: *We communicate by radio/by letter/with megaphones.*
Similarly many verbs of motion incorporate a component specifying
the instrument/means of locomotion, as *walk, drive, motor.* But consider
travel by car etc. Certainly too agentive aspectual verbs like *continue*
permit a rather limited range of instrumentals, but they do allow
sentential instruments (indicators of means) or the. . .*with the help
of*. . . variety. And, again, in this whole set (non-instrumental agentives)
there are also inexplicable assignments like, say, *give.*

2.6.3. However, my concern at this point must be with datives, which
cannot plausibly be deprived of their propositional status. The dative of
Stockwell *et al.* follows Fillmore's earlier (1968*a*) usage, and thus
includes both the active subject of *like* etc. and the 'indirect objects'
with verbs like *give.* A localist theory (e.g. that of (60)/(61)) predicts
that there exists no such distinct, abstract, non-local CR as dative (or
the narrower experiencer of Fillmore, 1971*c*). It thus predicts that
dative will be in complementary distribution with some local CR(s).
And this is indeed the case, it would appear, at least for the sample of
entries included in the Stockwell *et al.* lexicon.

The case frames for the entries in the lexicon take the following
form. If an item requires an argument of a particular kind, say of
$CASE_i$, this is indicated by including in the entry the specification
'+[——+$CASE_i$] '; if such an argument is incompatible with the item,
we have '+[—— –$CASE_i$] '; if this argument is compatible but not
necessary then $CASE_i$ does not appear in the case frame. Thus, the
relevant part of the entry for *smear* is as in (75):

(75) + [—— +NEUT –DAT +LOC +AGT]

which is to be interpreted as requiring neutral and locational and
agentive arguments for the verb and disallowing a dative; an
instrumental is optional, but an essive is ruled out by rule (74.a). This
means that for two putative cases to be in complementary distribution
each case frame in the lexicon must contain a minus specification for
at least one of the two cases. Otherwise they will co-occur in the same
proposition either optionally (if one or both are omitted from a case
frame) or obligatorily (if they both have a plus value in a particular
entry).

A scrutiny of the sample lexicon reveals that there are no items
that require the co-occurrence of +DAT and +LOC. And there are none

wherein +LOC appears but —DAT doesn't (i.e. where dative is optional
and locative obligatory). There are, according to Stockwell *et al.*, two
items which require a dative and for which a locational is optional,
namely *imprison* and *receive*[1]. The latter is so specified, I think, to
allow for sentences like (76):

(76)   Beppo received a present from Australia

wherein *Beppo* is dative, *a present* neutral, and *from Australia*
presumably locational. However this last assignment is simply a
consequence of the failure to distinguish source and goal from location.
Stockwell *et al.* themselves concede that the failure to include source
poses some problems for them, particularly in the analysis of sentences
like those in (77):

(77)   a.   John bought a car from Peter
      b.   John borrowed ten dollars from Bill

Imprison, on the other hand, is specified as in (78):

(78)   + [—— —NEUT +DAT +AGT]

However, in this instance, the motivation for assigning the object in,
say, (79):

(79)   Fred imprisoned his cousins in a big black tower

to dative rather than neutral is unclear, except that the object of
imprison is often animate. This is a rather slim basis on which to require
a distinction in case relation between (79) and (80):

(80)   Fred locked his socks in a big black cupboard

Stockwell *et al.* elsewhere (1973, 732) observe that 'there is . . . an
interesting constraint on verbs such as *find* which can take a
[+ABSTRACT] locative only with a [+ABSTRACT] object', which
they illustrate by (81):

(81)   a.   He found the pencil in a drawer
      b.*He found the idea in a drawer
      c.*He found the pencil in a footnote

    d. He found the idea in a footnote

Lock also obeys this constraint:

(82) a. Fred locked his insights in a cage of rhetoric
      b.*Fred locked his insights in a big black cupboard
      c.*Fred locked his socks in a cage of rhetoric

But then so does *imprison:*

(83) a. Fred imprisoned his insights in a cage of rhetoric
      b.*Fred imprisoned his insights in a big black tower
      c.*Fred imprisoned his cousins in a cage of rhetoric

This is natural if the object of both *lock* and *imprison* is simply
absolutive (neutral). There thus seem to be no firm examples in the
lexicon of an item whose case frame includes one of dative and location
obligatorily and either optionally or obligatorily the other.

    There remains the possibility, which scarcely constitutes a very
strong motivation for casehood for datives, that there are items for
which both dative and location are optional arguments. As far as I am
aware, four items are accorded this status by Stockwell *et al.* One of
these is *bearer,* for which is given the frame (84):

(84) + [—— −INS −AGT]

Another is *available,* for which they suggest the frame in (85):

(85) + [—— +NEUT −INS −AGT]

Thirdly we have *happen*[2] (the *happen* that doesn't take a complement
S), with the same case frame, i.e. again (85). The final example is *send:*

(86) + [—— +NEUT −INS +AGT]

Again all of these are doubtful candidates for non-complementariness.
Let us begin with a consideration of the last.

    Certainly both a sentence like that in (86):

(87) Coco sent a parcel to Australia

(with the locational *to Australia*) and one like that in (87):

(88)   Coco sent a parcel to his uncle

(with the dative *to his Uncle*) are well-formed. But according to (86) these two types of case phrase should also co-occur freely in propositions containing such a verb. However this is at best only marginally possible, and in one order only:

(89)   Coco sent a parcel $\left\{ \begin{array}{l} \text{*to his uncle to Australia} \\ \text{?*to Australia to his Uncle} \end{array} \right.$

and in this case moreover an interpretation involving apposition appears to be more appropriate. What this situation reveals is not a counter-example to the alleged complementarity of locational and dative but rather an inadequacy of the notation utilised in the lexicon, which is unable to represent mutual exclusiveness of optional arguments, or indeed of arguments in general, except (in the case of 'obligatory' arguments) by separate lexical entries. For instance, the only difference between *explain*[a] and *explain*[b] is that whereas (a) is '−INS +AGT' (b) is '+INS −AGT', i.e. instruments and agentives are mutually exclusive. (Admittedly in this particular instance I don't think their description is accurate.) Similarly, let us note in passing that, in eschewing Fillmore's linked parentheses convention (partly on the basis of the dubious requirement within their framework that 'the order of cases is fixed' − Stockwell *et al.,* 1973, 724), the notation compels the lexicon to offer two separate entries for *kill,* one with obligatory agentive and optional instrumental, the other with obligatory instrumental and no agentive. They do not, incidentally, justify this division over an entry with optional agentive and obligatory instrumental versus one with obligatory agentive and no instrumental. The former division is intuitively preferable in that, in the terms I advocated above, a *with*-instrumental depends on the presence of an agentive, but it is in the framework adopted in the lexicon quite unmotivated.

Send, then, even for Stockwell *et al.,* takes presumably mutually exclusive optional dative and locational arguments, though this cannot be reflected by their notation. (However, this is of course unnecessary if dative and locative do not otherwise contrast; indeed, we shall return to the complementarity of dative/locative in the case of *send* in §§ 2.6-.8.) The non-complementarity implied by the entries for *available* and *happen*[2] , on the other hand, does not appear to be simply an artefact of the notation. (That for *bearer* I am uncertain about (in the absence of explanation of the form of the entry in (84)); however, the verb *bear* seems to fall into the same class as *send* in being compatible with complementarity.) Let us then look more closely at what appear to be the only two obstacles (as far as the Stockwell *et al.* lexicon is concerned) to proposing that dative lacks a distinctive distribution, as represented by the case frame in (85), which they share.

According to (85) both location and dative are possible with *happen* and *available,* as presumably in examples like, respectively, (90):

(90) a. Nothing ever happens in Edinburgh
      b. Nothing is ever available in Edinburgh

and (91):

(91) a. Nothing ever happens to Charlie
      b. Nothing is ever available to Charlie

And, moreover, unlike in the case of *send,* they can be selected together:

(92) a. Nothing ever happens to Charlie in Edinburgh
      b. Nothing is ever available to Charlie in Edinburgh

However, the locational at least in such sentences can be argued to be circumstantial rather than participant. That is, the co-occurrence of *to Charlie* and *in Edinburgh* in (92) is no more an argument for distinguishing the two phrases as to CR than is the co-occurrence of the two prepositional phrases in sentences in (93):

(93) People keep their cars in garages in Edinburgh

In all these instances *in Edinburgh* is an outer, circumstantial locative.
    Vestergaard, (1975, § 2.2.1) points out the relevance of what he calls the '*do what*' test to the circumstantial/participant distinction. This depends, under one interpretation, upon *what happen* or *what X do* being substitutable only for a complete proposition and not part of one. Thus whereas the interchange in (94) is well-formed:

(94) What do people do in garages? They wash their cars

as is (95):

(95) What happens in Edinburgh? People keep their cars in garages

(though the responses are not the most exciting one could imagine), those in (96) are deviant:

(96) What do people do in garages?⎱
      What happens in garages?   ⎰
            *People keep their cars

With *keep* one locational is a participant and therefore cannot be excluded from the '*do what*' substitution as in (96); with *wash* locationals are circumstantial. Now, clearly the coherence of the test depends upon the locational (and the dative) in a sentence like (90.a) (and (91.a)) and (92.a) being extra-propositional.

Further, only the circumstantials are readily preposed:

(97) a. In Edinburgh people ⎰keep ⎱ their cars in garages
                              ⎱wash⎰
      b. In garages people wash their cars
      c.*In garages people keep their cars

The locational with *happen* and *available* is by such a criterion also circumstantial:

(98) a. In Edinburgh nothing ever happens
      b. In Edinburgh nothing is ever available

If the locationals in sentences involving *happen* and *available* are circumstantials and therefore not part of the case frame for these items, then on grounds of complementarity, as evidenced by Stockwell *et al.*'s own lexicon, the putative CR dative can be dispensed with.

The preceding argument is somewhat inconclusive in two respects. In the first place the lexicon offered is only a sample. However, it seems to me quite plausible that the inclusion of further entries will not reveal crucial instances of non-complementariness for datives. (Indeed, Fillmore (1971c), for reasons we shall return to below, has argued for a much more restricted scope for 'dative', relabelled 'experiencer', such that many former instances are lost to absolutive or allative.) Secondly, and more generally, we have shown complementarity for only one putative CR. Let me take this up in a moment, after formulating what seems an appropriate conclusion to the discussion this far. Of the original set of

CRs proposed by Stockwell *et al.*, if my argument is sound, there remain only agentive, neutral and locational. If we add a source CR, on account of the difficulties noted above which we otherwise encounter, then the set of distinctive CRs, of participants, is precisely the set predicted by the localist hypothesis of (60)/(61). We can now also confirm our earlier assignments.

2.6.4. In terms of the *'do-what'* test we excluded 'outer locatives' as participants. Within the limits of its applicability (it cannot for instance apply at all to statives) the *'do what'* criterion gives results in agreement with our earlier divisions based on the relevance of an argument's CR to verb subclassification. Clearly, time, for example, is thereby also excluded, as is the *with*-instrumental:

(99)   a.   What $\begin{Bmatrix} \text{did Fred do} \\ \text{happened} \end{Bmatrix}$ on Tuesday? $\begin{Bmatrix} \text{Fred} \\ \text{He} \end{Bmatrix}$ washed his car

         b.   What did Fred do with this sponge? He washed his car

and benefactives, and manner and other adverbials. Such phrases also prepose freely:

(100)   a.   On Tuesday Fred washed his car
          b.   With this sponge Fred washed his car

Neither property can be associated with allatives and ablatives:

(101)   a.*What $\begin{Bmatrix} \text{did Fred do} \\ \text{happened} \end{Bmatrix}$ (from Stirling) (to Falkirk)?

              Fred went

          b.*To Falkirk
            *From Stirling $\Big\}$ Fred went

(Of course, when a motional verb also incorporates an instrumental activity component (and in this respect is non-simplex), the external (circumstantial) source of the directional arguments with respect to the activity predicate which incorporates the instrumental renders marginally possible interchanges like: *?What did Fred do from Stirling to Falkirk? He hitch-hiked.*)

The conjoinability of question words in English leads to the same division into participant *v.* circumstantial. Wayles Browne (1972) observes that in English, which is also highly constrained with respect to the deletability of participants, only question words which are circumstantials ('free' parts of the sentence) can be conjoined:

(102)   1. a. When and where did you see them?
        b. Where and with what did he damage it?
        c. When and for what reason did Beppo build it?
     2. a.*How long and where do you keep the car?
        b.*Where and what did you see?
        c. *What and with what did he damage?

Browne suggests that the deviance of (102.2) etc. is dependent upon the restriction on deletability of participants in English, in that 'the conjunction of two question words is no longer a constituent of the same type as either one separately'. Thus (102.2.c), for instance lacks an object constituent. However that may be, the formulation of the restriction seems to require just the division into participant and circumstantial which we have invoked on other grounds.

Finally, we should note that although the '*do what*' test applies only imperfectly with directional sentences, it is possible on other grounds to exclude as circumstantial, paths in sentences also containing a distinct source or goal, as in *Fred travelled from Edinburgh to Glasgow by way of Stirling.* Specifically, such paths behave like other clear circumstantials as constituting a viable answer to questions like *How did Fred travel from Edinburgh to Glasgow? Cf. By car.* This accords with an interpretation of paths as collapsed source-goal predications, such that in the presence of a distinct directional CR, they constitute an 'outer directional'. (Cf. the discussion of 'outer locatives' above.)

Thus the second respect in which our discussion might be said to be inconclusive – namely the possible substantiation of further putative cases – is unlikely to prove relevant, in that the possible candidates that I am aware of (some of which are noted in passing by Stockwell *et al.,* 1973, 743-6) fall into the class of circumstantials. So, our conclusion seems to be sound, that within the set of participants, the only putative CR not amenable to a localist interpretation (as restricted to animates) does not show a contrastive distribution. (And we take up further arguments against dative as a CR in the section that follows.) That is, deployment of Fillmore's complementarity principle, together with the distinction between participant and circumstantial, leads us to select a set of participants congruent with the CRs required by the localist theory outlined above and motivated on quite other grounds.

2.6.5. The precise significance within a grammar of the generalisation that the number of participants in the proposition is at most four (and the same four are always involved) depends in part on how the role of lexical insertion is envisaged. I shall here take the view that lexical insertion is cyclic (see § 2.8) and that a lexical item is inserted with respect to a possibly complex label attached to a node in a tree, not with respect to a sub-tree which includes nodes distinguished in precedence/order. However, the label may be complex in including labelled nodes in dependency relation to each other though not differing in precedence. Thus, the substructure which in (103):

(103)   Fred usually travels by car

is realised as *by car*, is incorporated into the verb in (104):

(104)   Fred usually motors

This is achieved by a rule which removes the precedence but not the dependency relation between the predicate and its argument, as, schematically, in (105):

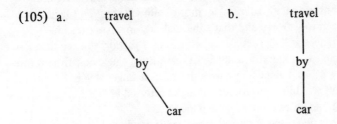

(105) a.   travel   b.   travel

                 \by |
                                             by
                   \ |
                    \car   car

(where the lexical items are, for illustration, utilised to abbreviate the relevant labels). *By* in (105.a) is said to be ADJOINED to *Travel*: it depends on the verb and differs in precedence from it, specifically, is ordered to its right. Similarly *car* is adjoined to *by*. In (105.b), on the other hand, *car* is SUBJOINED to *by* and the latter to *travel* ; all three nodes are equivalent in precedence, they are separated by the dependency relation alone. That the dependency relation remains is required by the fact that the complex retains the category of the original governor: *motor* in (104), for example, is a verb. (For discussion, see Anderson, 1971c; Anderson & Jones, 1974.) Let us call the configuration in (105.b) a subjunction tree. I am suggesting that lexical insertion involves attachment to just such objects rather than non-subjunction trees. In the present instance, *motor* can be inserted as a phonological label for a subjunction tree which includes the structure abbreviated in (105.b). Lexicalisation then comprises the two steps: subjunction of a dependent, lexical insertion.

The notion of subjunction imposes the constraint on the formation of lexical items that only direct dependents (and their direct dependents) can be incorporated. However, such a constraint can also be imposed without formulating lexical insertion in terms of subjunction if we require that lexical items be substituted for continuous (connected) subtrees. Either version is of interest only if the continuous subtrees arise through independently motivated processes. (Hence the controversy over predicate lifting.) Indeed, the requirement that substitution is for an uninterrupted subtree imposes a rather stronger constraint, namely that the dependent involved (in being lexicalised together with its governor) be contiguous. Gruber (1965) requires contiguity but not dependency. Of course we can incorporate this into the account involving subjunction by requiring that only a contiguous dependent can be subjoined, thus, making a stronger constraint than ones involving simply either dependency or contiguity. It is uncertain to what extent this stronger requirement can be maintained. However, the derivations proposed for *buy* etc. in the following section suggest that it is indeed too strong, and that subjoinability involves (in some circumstances at least) simply dependency. *A fortiori* this requires that lexicalisable configurations need not comprise a single constituent (see further § 3). In dependency terms this even stronger single-constituent constraint would require that an item be inserted in relation to a governor and all or none of its dependents.

There is one respect, on the other hand, in which the subjunction hypothesis concerning lexical insertion is stronger than any of these other possibilities, even the single-constituent variant. The formulation of lexical insertion in terms of prior subjunction explicitly embodies a claim that the relative sequence of the elements in a structure to be lexicalised is not relevant to lexical insertion. It is predicted that there will be no distinct lexical items which are inserted with respect to structures that differ solely in the order of sub-components.

One phenomenon which supports the subjunction interpretation over the view that lexical items be attached to non-subjunction trees is that the original adjoined configurations may be left behind. For instance, the verb *come* can quite plausibly be associated with a pre-subjunction configuration like that abbreviated in (106):

(106)

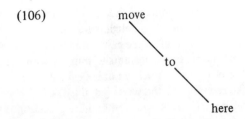

(Of course *here* is not a very good abbreviation for the content of the locational, which may also be realised as *there*; but this does not affect the issue.) As in the derivation of *motor,* the argument is subjoined to the predicate. However, in this instance, the original adjoined structure may be retained. So we get either . . . *come* or . . . *come here,* . . . *come there.* Thus *come* is not attached to a subtree such as (106) but to a subjunction tree that contains a copy of the allative phrase, or rather that part which is in common between *here and there* in sentences containing *come here/there.* Compare Green's (1974*a,* App. III) discussion of instrumental verb formation, where she points out that 'when instrumental verbs occur with "generic" or semantically predictable instrumental phrases [as in *she painted the woodwork with paint*], they are unacceptably redundant, but when the instrumental phrases describe some noteworthy aspect of the instrument, means, manner, material, etc. [as in *She painted the woodwork with red/latex/ Dutch/old paint*], they are not felt to be so redundant.' Here the original instrumental phrase is retained if needed to support an unincorporated modifier. In other instances, the original must be deleted, even if modified: *Ethelred decapitated Axelrod v. *Ethelred decapitated Axelrod's ugly/only/third/bloody head* (Green, 1974*a,* 222-3, n.1). (Obligatory deletion apparently correlates with argument-type, but I shall not pursue this here.)

Thus, as we have seen, lexicalisation via subjunction makes the claim that those aspects of a predicate's context which are relevant to lexical distinctiveness can be represented as a subjunction tree, i.e. as unordered. Subjunction establishes a distinction between predicate-internal and unordered *v.* predicate-external and ordered. If subjunction is a necessary preliminary to lexical insertion, then serialisation must indeed precede lexical insertion in the cycle, if the latter is cyclic (§ 2.8). This is strengthened further if the contiguity requirement on subjoinable dependents can be maintained, though in general this latter, as noted, seems unlikely.

The interest of this for our present concerns, however, is that whereas arguments that originate as circumstantials are eligible for subjunction, as in (105), only participants are relevant to the case frame for a predicate. Thus limitation of the set of participants to four, as proposed here, imposes a significant constraint on the form of lexical entries, at least in so far as these make reference to the set of (adjoined) CRs associated with a particular item. (This is made rather more precise in § 2.8.) On such a view, a verb like *send* shows the maximal case frame, realised in (107):

(107)   Fred sent a letter from New York to London

which contains (in order of precedence) an agentive, an absolutive, an ablative and a locative, i.e. the four CRs allowed for by the localist theory of (60)/(61).

2.6.6. Such a case frame for *send* etc., however, raises a couple of problems which are central to the discussion in the following section. Observe in the first place, that, as Stockwell *et al.* (1973, 746) observe, whereas both (107) and (108):

(108)   Fred sent a letter from New York to his brother (in London)

are viable sentences, only (109.b) of the pair:

(109)   a.*Fred sent London a letter from New York
        b. Fred sent his brother (in London) a letter from New York

is, unless '*London* is an abbreviation for *our branch in London* or some other entity with human associations'. We can distinguish between the two instances by designating *to his brother* a dative rather than a locational. (See too Green, 1974*a*, 118.) However we have otherwise found little support for such a notion, and we shall in § 2.7 encounter further arguments against the recognition of such a CR. Does this mean that we must attribute the distinction between (109.a) and (109.b) simply to animateness as such? As I have indicated, we return to this question below.

Notice, secondly, that such a distribution of CRs raises a further problem in the light of our earlier discussion. In § 2.3 we associated co-selection of [abl, erg, loc] (in terms of the rule in (29)) with a sentence like (54.a), repeated here as (110):

(110)   The local government officer received a crate of whisky
         from the businessman

such that the subject is [loc, erg] and the object [abs] and *from the businessman* [abl]. Clearly if we are to distinguish in terms of a rule like (29) between *send,* in which the ergative and locative arguments are distinct, and *receive,* where they are not, the set of options must be extended. More importantly, there is now a discrepancy in the status of erg. Thus far we have been able to associate agentivity with an erg which is not associated with a locational predicate. Thus *know,* which is [loc, erg], *occupy,* [loc, abs, erg] and *receive* [loc, erg, abl] are all non-agentive, whereas *read* [erg] or *work* [erg, abs] are agentive. But *send* is a locational (specifically a direction) verb which is nevertheless agentive, as is, say, *move,* in which the abs and the erg CRs may or may not have distinct arguments. They both, for instance, permit agentive adverbials and benefactives. Cf. as examples of the former (111):

(111)   a. Fred sent it off carefully
         b. Fred moved it carefully
         c. Fred moved carefully

Now we might try to save something like this generalisation by observing that whereas with the non-agentives the erg CR is actually combined with the locational, i.e. they constitute a multiple CR, in the agentive examples (*send, move*) the erg is either simplex or combined with abs. Unfortunately, this fails to include *occupy* as non-agentive; and we shall discover in the section that follows that there are agentive verbs the most plausible interpretation of which involves positing an argument which is simultaneously loc and erg.

2.7 On the Derivative Status of Indirect Objects, 1: Case relations

2.7.1. In this and the following section we return to datives from a rather different perspective. In the preceding section we found that this putative CR appeared to lack a distinctive distribution: in terms of the complementarity criterion its casehood could not be motivated. We shall now find that there exist syntactic and semantic generalisations the adequate formulation of which depends on there not being such a CR. These conclusions also hold for those non-case grammars which include as basic either the grammatical relation 'indirect object' or a unique configuration of which the relation can be defined. In view of the conclusion that we arrive at that 'indirect objects' can and must be defined in terms of a conjunction of independent properties, any grammar which contains such a notion as an unanalysed primitive must be reckoned inadequate in this respect.

Let us then look more closely at what Fillmore (1968*a*) calls datives, 'the case of the animate being affected by the state or action identified by the verb', in particular triples of the character of (112):

(112)   a. The secretary has sold this car to the professor
        b. The professor has bought this car from the secretary
        c. The professor owns this car

In these sentences *to the professor* in (a) and *the professor* in (c) are presumably datives. In (112), *the professor* appears to be, in Fillmore's terms, an A; cf. e.g. the imperative and the agentive adverbial in (113):

(113)   a. Buy this car
        b. The professor bought this car on impulse

But it can also, given the multiple CRs hypothesis, be a dative, which is clearly desirable on notional grounds. (The considerations which Huddleston advanced in favour of multiple CRs (cf. § 1.4) clearly apply here also.) Whatever the CR associated with *from the secretary* in (112.b), it is similarly also present in (112.a), but on this occasion in conjunction with an A:

(114)   a. Sell this car
        b. The secretary sold this car on impulse

Compare the scopes of the agent-modifying adverbial in (115):

(115)   a. She sells apples skilfully
        b. He buys apples skilfully

(Fillmore, 1972, § 30). It looks then as if we can allow for various aspects of the meaning and the syntax of (112) if they all contain an objective and a dative, but (112.a) and (112.b) contain an extra 'merchant' CR and differ in whether the dative 'customer' or the 'merchant' is also an A. (Cf. Fillmore, 1972, §§ 25-30.)

However, observe that the implicational relation that we found to

hold between appropriate directional/locational pairings like those in
(33)/(34) also holds between (112.a)/(112.b) and (112.c) and (116):

(116)   The secretary doesn't own this car

That is, to spell it out more precisely, just as, under a resultative
interpretation, (117);

(117)   Ulysses has gone from London to San Francisco

implies both of (118):

(118)   a. Ulysses is in San Francisco
         b. Ulysses is not in London

so (112.a-b) imply both (112.c) and (116).

This can be generalised if the 'datives' in (112) are simply (allative)
locatives, and the 'merchant' CR is an ablative. Observe too that we
also thereby arrive again at a lexically more natural account: the
occurrence of *to* and *from* is not fortuitous. (Cf. too, corresponding to
(112), *This car belongs to the professor.*) Such an identification also
accounts for another correlation noted by Mittwoch (1971, 258).
Non-elliptical sentences with *give* normally cannot omit the 'indirect
object': **Mary has given the books.* The major exception is in sentences
containing a directional particle like *out/away:*

(119)   Mary has given the books away

This is not exceptional if 'indirect objects' are also directional.

In § 2.3 we associated the ambiguity of sentences like (49) (*The
water rose to this point for several days*) with a structure for allatives
whereby they contained an embedded locational predication, such that
the adverbial could modify either the directional or the locational
predication. Only the instance modifying the main clause can be
preposed, and so *For several days the water rose to this point* is
unambiguous. 'Dative' *to*-phrases allow a similar scope ambiguity (see
Green, 1974*a*, § 3.4.7), as in *John lent his hoe to Hill for several days,*
with again *For several days John lent his hoe to Jill* being unambiguous;
and the same situation obtains with the prepositionless 'indirect object':
John lent Jill his hoe for several days (ambiguous); *For several days
John lent Jill his hoe* (unambiguous). This is to be expected if 'indirect

objects' are allatives.

Underlying (112) are thus the respective representations abbreviated in (12) (ignoring for the moment questions of sequence):

(120)   a.

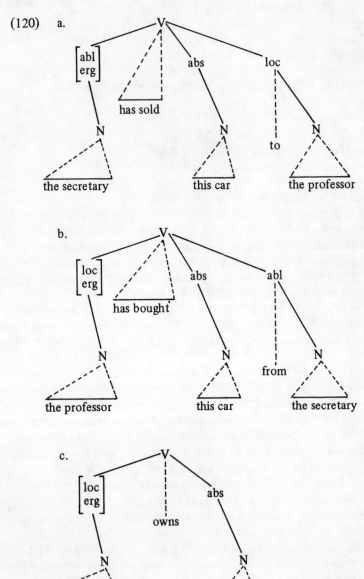

In accordance with the case-hierarchy, the phrase labelled with erg occupies subject position and that marked abs is the object. The erg associated with the loc in (120.c) allows for the *by*-passive:

(121)   This car is owned by the professor

and for the animacy restriction.

However, such a structure as (120.c) also, in conjunction with the other representations in (120), gives rise to a problem which, together with some other evidence, will require us to modify somewhat the analysis I have just outlined. Notice once again that the [loc, erg] conjunction in (120.c) is, as with *receive,* non-agentive. But in (120.b), as we have seen, we have an agentive subject. We thus cannot, as suggested in the preceding section, associate non-agentivity with conjunction of loc and erg and agentivity with non-conjunction. Nor does the agentivity distinction correlate with the locational/directional distinction: both *receive* and *buy* are directional. I shall propose below a modification to our analysis of *buy* and *sell* which allows us to maintain the original generalisation (that locational predications exclude an agentive interpretation for erg) and which can be motivated on quite other grounds.

2.7.2. However, observe first of all, that such an analysis will allow even for abstract 'transactions' like that in (122):

(122)   a. The secretary has taught demotic Greek to the professor
         b. The professor has learnt demotic Greek from the
             secretary
         c. The professor knows demotic Greek

Notice that in this instance (122.b) (interpreted as resultative) again implies (122.c), but does not imply (123):

(123)   The secretary doesn't know demotic Greek

But, as we observed in § 2.3, there are 'spatial' pairs that share this property; extension rather than displacement motionals:

(124)   a. Fog spread from London to Brighton
         b. There is no fog in London

And thus (rather than (123) constituting a problem) the existence of such a further shared distinction lends additional support for the analysis. It is now apparent that the loc invoked in §§ 1.7/.9 along with erg for the subject of *know* was indeed well-motivated.

The various groups of predicates belonging to this kind of paradigm otherwise differ in whether the 'giving' (the 'nuclear' predicate – Dixon, 1973) is associated with a reciprocal 'giving', as *buy/sell, hire from/to, lend/borrow* (reciprocated by a promise to return) or not necessarily (*give/take*). The former group are distinguished in terms of the character of the reciprocation.

2.7.3. A simple extension of the analysis will also apparently allow for the sentences in (125):

(125)   a. The secretary has sold the professor this car
        b. The secretary has taught the professor demotic Greek

and the like. They can be differentiated from the respective (a) sentences in (112) and (122) by virtue of an abs associated with the loc. In conformity with the hierarchy of cases, the erg phrase still becomes subject, but now the [loc, abs] phrase outranks the simple abs – as too in the passives:

(126)   a. The professor has been sold this car (by the secretary)
        b. The professor has been taught demotic Greek (by the secretary

Cf. (127):

(127)   a. This car has been sold to the professor (by the secretary)
        b. Demotic Greek has been taught to the professor (by the secretary)

which are the passive equivalents of (112.a) and (122.a) respectively. And a non-transformational relationship between such pairs as (112.a)/(125.a) and (122.a)/(125.b) is supported by other phenomena.

Above we differentiated *teach* from *sell* as an extension rather than a displacement motional. Green (1974*a*, § 4.B) argues that they differ in a further respect which she illustrates by (128):

(128)   a. Mary gave John an apple

       b. Mary gave an apple to John

v. (129):

   (129)   a. Mary taught John linguistics
           b. Mary taught linguistics to John

Of these she writes (1974*a*, 157): 'while sentences [(128.a)] and [(128.b)] are, as far as I can tell, synonymous with each other, [(129.a)] does not mean the same thing as [(129.b)]. Sentence [(129.a)] implies or entails that John learned linguistics, while [(129.b)] merely states that he was a student of linguistics'. Now, it does not seem to me that this distinction (between (a) and (b) in (129)) is as firmly based as Green claims. Moreover, its existence with such pairs depends on the character of the (direct) object rather than of the verb, since, on the one hand, as Green herself observes (1974*a*, 158, n.1), there are objects which neutralise the distinction she observes in the case of *teach,* as in (130):

   (130)   a. Eloise taught her nephew the Lord's Prayer
           b. Eloise taught the Lord's Prayer to her nephew

and, on the other, the (129.a)/(129.b) distinction depends on two understandings that can be accorded *linguistics,* 'knowledge of linguistics' and 'a course in linguistics'. If we overrule this, the distinction again disappears in both (131):

   (131)   a. Mary taught John a course in linguistics
           b. Mary taught a course in linguistics to John

and (132):

   (132)   a. Mary gave John a course in linguistics
           b. Mary gave a course in linguistics to John

Pointing up the 'knowledge of' interpretation for such a noun renders the *to*-variant somewhat deviant for some speakers with both *teach* and *give,* as illustrated by (133):

   (133)   a. Mary taught John an appreciation of good cooking
           b.?Mary taught an appreciation of good cooking to John

and (134):

(134)   a. Mary gave John an appreciation of good cooking
        b.?Mary gave an appreciation of good cooking to John

Green also observes (1974*a*, 158-9) that only the prepositionless variant permits an abstract subject with *teach* (as *Several mistakes taught John the secrets of Chinese cooking v. *Several mistakes taught the secrets of Chinese cooking to John*). But this is not distinctive, as (Green, 1974*a*, 84) it is also true of *give* (*Mary's behaviour gave John an idea v. *Mary's behaviour gave an idea to John*).

Whatever the precise character of the distinction between (129.a) and (129.b) and the circumstances in which it is manifested, it provides if confirmed a motivation with all these verbs for not suggesting a transformational relationship between indirect object + direct object constructions and the corresponding direct object + *to*-phrase. Notice that there is clearly not involved a rule of surface structure interpretation, in that the distinction remains constant under e.g. passivisation:

(135)   a. John was taught linguistics by Mary
        b. Linguistics was taught (to) John by Mary

or clefting

(136)   It was linguistics Mary taught (to)
        John

Thus the phenomena observed by Green support an analysis of these constructions such as was suggested above, whereby different representations are assigned to pairs which under other analyses are related by dative movement (in either direction). This conclusion is also supported by Green's (1974, 74-7) observation that the positing of a rule of dative movement requires in the case of *to*-datives that five different kinds of exceptions to the rule be recognised. (Lakoff (1970*a*, § 7.2) found evidence for only two kinds of exception, and even these have been disputed.)

The verbs to which we have assigned [abl, erg] subjects (rather than [loc, erg]) − *give, sell, teach*, etc. − belong to Green's class 2 *to*-dative verbs (1974*a*, 80-85). Classes 1 and 3, *bring, send* (80, 85) differ, according to the present analysis, in having separate ergative and ablative arguments. Thus, as Green later (1974*a*, 140) observes, 'the *give*-class verbs of *to*-class 2 . . . have only a reading in which only the place of causation . . . is referred to' by an ablative (rather than the source of the movement). She compares the pair in (137):

(137) a. Jack brought the Ming vase to Jill from Urbana
       b. Jack sold Mary a house (in Urbana) from Chicago

The *from*-phrase in the second sentence is also shown to be circumstantial by the '*do-what*' test:

(138) What did Jack do from Chicago?
       a.*He brought the Ming vase to Jill
       b. He sold Mary a house (in Urbana)

In the latter instance the participant source is cumulated with the ergative (*he*), and thus *from Chicago* can only be circumstantial. Classes 1 and 3 differ from each other, on the other hand, in whether or not the object that moves is accompanied by the agent who brings about the transfer, as revealed by the contradiction established by (139.a) but not (139.b):

(139) a.*Fred brought his niece to Melrose } instead of
       b. Fred sent his niece to Melrose   } coming himself

It is inappropriate in the present context for us to explore the detailed classification proposed by Green, though we should note that she finds that the character of the constraints on different classes of verb is such that 'the dative-movement phenomena cannot be characterised as a single transformational rule applying to a class of verbs specifiable by a single (generalised) semantic structure' (1974*a*, 148-9). The rejection of dative-movement is just; however, we shall in what follows try to establish for *to*-datives at least rather more commonality of structure than Green felt able to suggest.

Let us therefore note, for completeness, the final two classes of *to*-datives that she sets up. Class 4 involves 'instrumental' communication verbs like *radio* or *shout* which incorporate the means of communication and 'enunciatory' verbs like *tell, read, write*. Both these classes impose rather heavy constraints on their objects: the former verbs take objects which 'are typically nouns like *news, information, response,* which describe (rather than denote) the communicated information'; with the latter, 'the objects . . . are typically nouns or noun phrases which respectively denote or describe narratives *(joke, story, anecdote; the one about the farmer's daughter)*' (Green, 1974*a*, 86). And

> The fifth class . . . is composed of verbs which refer to a situation in the future relative to the tense of the verb, in which the individual denoted by the indirect object expression will have the object described by the direct object (Green, 1974*a*, 90).

These differ from the other classes in that two movements (and two times) are involved. Thus, as Green observes elsewhere (1974*a*, 135), the scope of the temporal adverbial is ambiguous in sentences like (140):

(140)   Biffo promised Eloise a new car on Thursday

such that either it denotes the time of the transmission of Biffo's promise to Eloise or the time of Eloise's reception of a new car. The first reading can be suppressed by choice of an appropriate adverbial:

(141)   Biffo promised Eloise a new car tomorrow

and the latter (once more) by preposing:

(142)   On Thursday Biffo promised Eloise a new car

Since in general, as we have seen, such adverbs can be preposed only to a clause they modify this suggests that in (141) the adverbial modifies an embedded clause which has disappeared rather than the overt clause modified by *on Thursday* in (142). However, this is to anticipate somewhat the course of our discussion.

2.7.4. Thus far we have found some support from the identification of 'indirect objects' and Fillmorean datives in general with a locative, and for providing pairs like (122.a)/(125.b) with distinct underlying representations rather than deriving one from the other. Fillmore (1971*c*) moves part of the way in the direction of the first conclusion in interpreting the 'indirect objects' and *to*-phrases with verbs like *give* as goals (rather than 'datives') but he introduces the CR experiencer for the subject of sentences like (122.c). This renders the relationship between that sentence and (122.a/b) opaque, whereas it is clearly an instance of the goal/location relationship illustrated by (117)/(118.a). Observe too that if the contrastiveness of the original dative (as adopted by Stockwell *et al.*, 1973) is not demonstrable, the subset of datives characterised in terms of the notion experiencer is even more obviously in complementary distribution with the other participant cases. There thus exists sufficient evidence against the concept of a basic relation of dative or 'indirect object' in English to enable us to discount it as a putative counter-example to the localist theory. And the illustrative function of this section is therefore fulfilled. However, the localist analysis we have substituted itself raises a number of problems, some of them already noted. While these remain there exists a strong possibility that an alternative, non-localist interpretation may prove preferable. I now therefore want to turn to these problems. We shall find that a resolution of these will uncover further support for the localist analysis rather than the contrary. What has to be adjusted is our interpretation of the character of the case frames for such verbs as *buy* and *sell*.

Recall again first of all that when we decided in ch.1 to exploit the notion of multiple CRs per NP we were able to make a generalisation concerning the distribution of erg of the following sort: in a proposition lacking a locational CR, erg is a full agentive, and permits imperativisation etc, but in a proposition containing a locational, this is not the case. Thus, (143), say:

(143) a. John worked hard
       b. John read the book

containing an erg (*John*) and no locational, contrast in this respect with (144):

(144) a. That obelisk occupied the plinth
       b. The plinth is occupied by that obelisk

or (112.c) and (122.c), or the directional (145):

(145) a. The professor received the present on Friday
       b. The present was received by the professor on Friday

but (112.a), (112.b), etc. are locational (specifically directional) sentences containing an erg, indeed an erg in conjunction with a locational CR; and there the ergative phrase functions as a full agent (cf. (113)–(115)). Thus the accommodation of sentences like (112.a/b), with *buy/sell*, and (108), with *send*, is not simply a question of adding to the rules in (56/57). Within the kind of framework allowed for by these rules, *receive* and *buy* are assigned the same set of case features. Now it may simply be that our interpretation of the notion of multiple CR needs refinement; but there are other indications that the problem is not simply that.

Sentences with *send* raised another problem, as revealed by the pair in (109), wherein only an animate allative appears in 'indirect object' position. If 'indirect objects' are, as suggested above in reference to (125), simply (allative) locatives which are also absolutive, what is the motivation for this restriction? In arguing in § 1.7 that *know* took an active subject that was [loc, erg] , I pointed out that we thereby associated the animacy restriction uniquely with erg: erg was the only CR which requires of its arguments a relatively higher position on the 'humanness hierarchy' than would otherwise be the case. Must we now also associate such a requirement with a [abs, loc] argument in sentences which are also [erg] ? But there are other [abs, loc] verbs apparently, which lack this requirement; namely the *load/spray* class discussed in §§ 1.8-.9. We associated with the holistic variants containing these verbs an agentive subject and an absolutive locative object. But their objects are not restricted to animates. Rather, as we observed in §§ 1.8-.9, they impose a quite different constraint on interpretation, a property which, following Stephen Anderson (1971), we labelled holistic. The indirect objects of *give,* on the other hand, do not differ from the corresponding *to*-phrases as holistic/partitive (as Anderson demonstrated). There is the further, by no means trivial problem that whereas the absolutive that is displaced from immediate post verbal position by the [loc, abs] argument of a verb like *load* is marked by *with,* this is not true of the abs which follows a [loc, abs] in sentences with *sell* etc. Thus any generalisation that might be made about *with* as the marker of an abs displaced from object position by another absolutive phrase (cf. e.g. § 2.4) is compromised by the interpretation we have been proposing for sentences containing indirect objects.

There are thus, it would appear from our analysis, two kinds of sentence with a [loc, erg] active subject, one in which we have a true agent (*buy*) and another in which the subject is not agentive (*receive*). Our analysis does not enable us to differentiate between these in any principled way. Similarly, there are two kinds of agentive sentence with a [loc, abs] object, one of which imposes an animacy restriction on the object (*send*), the other of which is associated with a holistic interpretation (*load*), and which also differs in marking the other (simple) absolutive phrase with *with* rather than (typically) zero. Again, this is not predicted by the analysis.

2.7.5. A further, seemingly quite distinct problem is posed by the fact that in some varieties of English, but not the one with which I am most familiar, passives like those in (146) are apparently well-formed:

(146)   a. (*) This car has been sold the professor (by the secretary)
        b. (*) Demotic Greek has been taught the professor (by the secretary)

Even though the 'corresponding' actives:

(147)   a.*The secretary has sold the book the professor
        b.*The secretary has taught demotic Greek the professor

('corresponding', on the assumption that the passive 'affects' only the object NP closest to the V) seem to be universally rejected.[34] (I am not taking into account pronominal instances which introduce other considerations.) I do not see how we can in any plausible way constrain, say, the case hierarchy in such a way as to permit, for the appropriate dialect, just (146) and not (147). There are two problems then: (a) the dialectal limitations of the (146) passives; (b) the general rejection of the corresponding actives in (147).

2.7.6. Before proceeding with our own analysis, it is in order to point out that such sentences as (146) also pose a problem, one for which I can see no non-ad hoc solution, for grammars which unlike ours include indirect objects (either directly or by definition). Both Stephen Anderson (1971) and Jackendoff & Culicover (1971) consider dative movement to be a rule or rules which relates sentences like those in (148):

(148)   a. Bill gave a book to Mary
        b. Bill gave Mary a book

by in the derivation of (148.b) permuting *a book* and *to Mary* and deleting *to*. Certainly if there is such a relationship, this direction for it, rather than extracting *Mary* from before *a book* and inserting (or retaining) *to,* is preferable (Anderson, 1971, 392-3; Jackendoff & Culicover, 1971, 402). However, this is unimportant for the present discussion. Jackendoff & Culicover note a problem in ordering this reordering of the *to*-phrase (henceforth DATIVE MOVEMENT) with respect to passivisation. Thus, if dative movement follows passive, then we can generate (148.a) (neither has applied), (148.b) (dative movement only) and (149):

(149)   A book has been given to Mary by John.

(passive only). However, in order to allow for (150):

(150)   (*) A book was given Mary by John

we must allow 'the indirect object . . . to permute, as it were, around nothing' (1971, 398), after the direct object has been moved away under passivisation. Further, (151):

(151)   Mary was given a book by John

cannot be generated at all, given their assumption that passive moves only the NP nearest to the verb (in this instance *a book*). The appropriateness of this assumption is illustrated by sentences like (152):

(152)   a. This table has been eaten at by many famous people
        b.*This table has been eaten food at by many famous people.
        c. Food has been eaten at this table by many famous people

As Jackendoff & Culicover observe, 'only when there is no direct object intervening between the prepositional phrase and the verb can the object of the preposition undergo the passive'. We would then apparently have to exclude such as *Jo was taken care of by the boss* as 'idiomatic' or perhaps as showing 'object-incorporation' (cf. § 3.6).

However the reverse order of application does not provide a solution either. Under the order dative movement then passive, again (148.a) (neither apply), (148.b) (dative movement only) and (149) (passive only) can be generated. So too can (151) (dative movement followed by passive). But (150) remains a problem, since it apparently shows dative movement followed by passivisation of the original direct object, which is no longer next to the verb. Thus neither ordering assumption will provide for the full range of forms.

The solution proposed by Jackendoff & Culicover (1971, 403-4) involves the adoption of the latter ordering and the positing of an ad hoc rule of *to*-deletion: 'we can simply add an optional rule of *to*-delete, ordered *after* Passive, and governed only by verbs which are subcategorised for ——NP-*to*-NP'. Concerning this proposal they observe: 'The reader may have become a bit uneasy to see that the two preposition deletion rules have identical environments, so that there are now two different ways to delete *to* when it is next to the verb'. In this

they are undoubtedly correct, and their attempt to obscure the lack of
support for such a suggestion by references to 'the generality of the
resulting solution' and alleged 'similar situations . . . in phonology'
does not do anything to dissipate uneasiness. I should add that the
reader may also be 'uneasy' about the arbitrary use of ordering as a
'blocking device' for unwanted derivations.

2.7.7. Sentence (150) and the like also pose a challenge to one of the
basic tenets of relational grammar, as I understand it.[35] Within such a
theory the grammatical relations, subject, object, indirect object are
primitives, and they are hierarchically ordered in the sequence given:
I = subject, II = direct object, III = indirect object. Noun phrases which
bear one of these relations to a predicate are TERMS. NPs/PPs bearing
other relations to the predicate are non-terms, and they are ranked
below terms. Only terms take part in certain syntactic processes, like
requiring agreement by the predicate. Certain cyclic rules called RELATION
RULES also affect term-hood. For instance passive involves the
advancement of an object to become a subject (II → I). Relation rules
are subject to the RELATIONAL ANNIHILATION LAW, which
requires that when a NP is replaced by another as the term of a
grammatical relation, the NP that originally bore the grammatical
relation ceases to bear any grammatical relation; it becomes a
CHOMEUR, and as such ceases to be eligible for subsequent
term-referring rules. The *by*-phrase in a passive represents such a chômeur,
as it has been replaced as subject by the direct object.

In the case of dative movement, an indirect object is advanced to
become a direct object, as in (148.b) (III → II) *v.* (148.a). Passive can
also apply in either instance. If dative movement has not applied then
the original direct object is advanced to subject, as in (149). With
prior application of dative movement, it is the original indirect object,
now the direct object, that becomes subject, as in (151).

But consider again (150). Here dative movement has apparently
occurred (in that the original indirect object is *to*-less, as in (148.b)),
but it is the original direct object that has been subjectivised by passive.
The problem is not just that the original direct object has been
preferred for subjectivisation over a NP that has been advanced over it
by dative movement; by the relational annihilation law the NP that was
originally direct object should not be eligible at all for a relation rule
like passive in that it has been displaced from term-hood by the
application of dative movement, it is a chômeur.

Two conclusions are possible: (1) (150) constitutes a counter-example to the relational annihilation law; or (2) the status of indirect objects is other than has in general been supposed by the adherents of relational grammar. The burden of the present discussion would support the latter conclusion. This has interesting consequences for our view of the relationship between case grammar and relational grammar, and we shall return to this question below. At this point, however, let us note that the conclusions of this paragraph are subject to a qualification. And it is in this qualification that a defence might be sought for a standard relational account, i.e. one in which subject, direct object and indirect remain as primitive and the relational annihilation law can be maintained.

2.7.8. Suppose we can show that *Mary* in (150) does not 'behave like' an object; specifically, that the lack of a *to* is not an index of objecthood. This would give us some support for supposing that this NP had not undergone dative movement but had lost its *to* by a later rule such as Jackendoff & Culicover's *to*-deletion. Are there then phenomena which would render such a strategy non-ad hoc? Consider, say, the distribution with such verbs of a 'particle' like *back,* which seems to occur immediately after the verb, as in (153):

   (153)   John gave back the book to Mary

or the object, as in (154):

   (154)   John gave the book back to Mary

but not after the *to*-phrase:

   (155)   *John gave the book to Mary back

The dative passives of (153-4) are as in (156):

   (156)   a. Mary was given back the book (by John)
           b. Mary was given the book back (by John)

In this respect *Mary* in (157):

   (157)   *The book was given Mary back (by John)

behaves like the *to*-phrase in (155) or (158):

(158) *The book was given to Mary back (by John)

rather than the objects in (153), (154) and (156) in not permitting a following *back*. This is allowed for if the *Mary* in (157) is a *to*-phrase until after the application of the other relevant rules and then undergoes *to*-deletion.

However, a widening of our data reveals that this conclusion is perhaps premature. One issue arises from further consideration of the fact that all occurrences of the particle at the extreme right of an indirect object construction are ruled out by Emonds (1972, 557), though he admits to some exceptions, of which, however, he says 'I am ignoring these differences which seem unsystematic and quite limited in number.' But in the English with which I am familiar the particle is quite regularly locatable after the direct object following an indirect, i.e. in examples like (159):

(159) John gave Mary the book back

except with Green's class 4 *to*-datives and with *for*-datives. However, other considerations are more problematical for the *to*-deletion proposal. Observe, for instance, that whereas the *to*-phrase can be immediately preceded by *back,* as in (154) or (160):

(160) The book was given back to Mary (by John)

this position is only marginally possible when the *to* is absent:

(161) ?*The book was given back Mary (by John)

(161) is similar to (162), which shows dative movement and no passive, in this respect:

(162) ?*John gave back Mary the book

That is, whereas (157) seems to group sentences like (150) with *to*-phrase sentences like (158), the parallelism of (161) and (162) groups them with sentences that have clearly undergone dative movement. This paradox must be resolved by any attempt to provide a specification for the distribution of *back*. It will also have to allow for (163):

(163) John gave Mary back the book

in which *back* immediately follows neither the verb nor the (direct) object, but the post-dative movement indirect object, which thus, unlike (150), does not behave like a *to*-phrase. This invites a relational account. It is already apparent, however, that such phenomena, involving particles like *back,* do not unequivocally support an analysis for (150) which involves *to*-dropping, and sentences like it therefore remain a problem for the 'traditional' analysis of Jackendoff & Culicover (1971), and, more crucially, for certain basic notions in the theory of relational grammar.

2.7.9. If the *back*-ing evidence is inconclusive in showing that the postverbal NP in (150) is distinct from a prepositionless indirect object like that in (148.b), there is on the other hand evidence that prepositionless indirect objects are distinct from direct objects; i.e. that a formulation of dative movement in terms of which the (preposition-full) indirect object takes over the direct object relation is incorrect. One piece of evidence derives from COMPLEX NP SHIFT. A complex object like that in (164):

(164)   I gave a book about spiders to the man in the park

may be moved to the right over the following phrase (if we assume for convenience of exposition a movement formulation):

(165)   I gave to the man in the park a book about spiders

However, the prepositionless indirect object in (166.a) cannot be moved over the following phrase:

(166)   a. I gave the man in the park a book about spiders
         b.* I gave a book about spiders the man in the park

(Wexler & Culicover, 1974). (166.b) can be excluded by having complex NP shift apply before dative movement and thus bleed it. But if such appeals to extrinsic order are excluded, and indeed if complex NP shift is part of the shallow structure conditions on serialisation (§ 1.11), then the most obvious conclusion is that the immediately postverbal NP in (166.a) is not relationally identical to that in (164). Specifically, the shift affects simple absolutives rather than the [loc, abs] NP that the analysis we developed above claims that the indirect object in (166.a) is. Better, to allow for shift with *spray paint* forms: only the second of two objects (§ 3.8) shifts.

Of course, it may be that (166.b) can be excluded with reference to some independent constraint. However, some of the more obvious candidates turn out not to be appropriate. For instance, one gross difference between the movements in (165) and (166.b) is that the phrase moved over in (165) is a prepositional phrase whereas in (166.b) it is only a NP. Is complex NP shift then perhaps simply ruled out over NPs (cf. Hankamer, 1973, 53-4)? But such a hypothesis is shown to be insufficient by examples like (167.b):

(167) a. They made the one who had least influence the scapegoat
       b. They made the scapegoat the one who had least influence

(Of course (167.b) has a further interpretation in which it does not represent a shifted variant of (167.a) but rather a simple causative equative in its own right. Moreover, such sentences seem to me to be fully acceptable only if the shifted material constitutes 'new information'.) Again in this instance a simple absolutive is moved, but here over a NP rather than a prepositional phrase. Thus, (166.b) cannot be excluded on this basis.

(166.b) also differs from (165) in involving movement over a chômeur (the displaced original direct object). Perhaps we should look for an explanation in this. However it is clear that in other instances this circumstance does not inhibit movement:

(168) a. I was given two books by my uncle
       b. I was given by my uncle two books describing the effects of excessive intake of alcohol

So (166.b) is not deviant because the shift is over a chômeur. Notice too that the displaced object, on the other hand, is still available for complex NP shift after dative movement has applied. Consider (169.b):

(169) a. I gave John the key that morning
       b. I gave John that morning the key that opens our safe

On the present account, this is because such 'direct objects' remain simple absolutives throughout the relevant derivations. Whereas the indirect object in (166.a) is at no point a 'direct object' and thus fails to meet the conditions for complex NP shift. Such a pattern of acceptability, however, seems to be inexplicable within a framework in which 'indirect objects' 'become' 'direct objects' as a result of dative movement. We return below to further evidence of this character.

2.8 On the Derivative Status of Indirect Objects, 2: Decomposition

2.8.1. We must now try to provide a derivation for indirect objects which will accommodate the various phenomena we have observed, in particular:

(170)   a. The parallelism in semantic relations with
              directional sentences (cf. (112) with (117)/(118)
              and (122)/(123) with (124); and consider (138));
          b. agentive properties ((113)-(115));
          c. lexical naturalness;
          d. the difference in meaning potential between the
              prepositionless and prepositionful indirect object
              (cf. (129)), together with the problem of the 'animacy'
              restriction on prepositionless indirect objects;
          e. the problem of determining when erg has an agentive
              interpretation ((143), (144), (145) *v.* (112));
          f. the distinction in interpretation and form between
              indirect object and *spray paint* verbs;
          g. passives like (150), their dialectal limitation, and the
              deviance of (157).

The account we developed above involving multiple CRs, specifically combinations of erg with loc or abl, and abs with loc, provides something like an adequate account only of the phenomena underlying the first three of these observations. We must now try to establish whether some simple extension of such a localist account will accommodate this full range of data, most of which are, let us reaffirm, incompatible with an analysis whereby indirect object constructions are basic.

All of these phenomena are accommodated by the positing of a complex source for *buy/sell* etc; specifically, as suggested in Anderson, 1971*b*, a structure embedding a directional into an agentive predication, as in, say, (171), underlying the relevant aspects of (112.a/b):

(171)

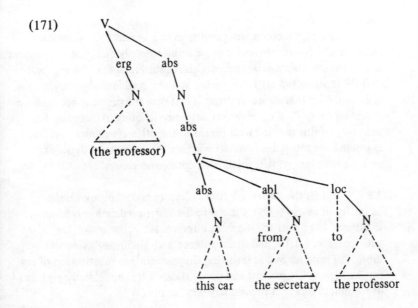

which assumes, as suggested in § 1.11, that, early in the cycle at least, modifiers to the predicate are serialised to its right in English, and wherein the (lower) abl, loc and abs Ns are lexically as in (120.a/b), and (112.a) and (112.b) are differentiated as to whether the abl or the loc phrase is respectively identical with the erg in the upper predication. (Whether or not this identity relation involves lexical identity, as assumed here for convenience of exposition, is not at issue at this juncture.) The upper abs is lexically empty (or minimally specified semantically). The abs governing the lower V is the source for overt complementisers.

In such a representation, the ergative no longer appears in a locational predication, and therefore receives unambiguously an agentive interpretation, in accordance with our original generalisation. I.e., the structure underlying *buy* now differs from that for *receive* in that whereas with *receive* the active subject originates as a [erg, loc] argument ((120.b) is an appropriate representation), with *buy* there are distinct (though identical) erg and loc arguments such that they originate in distinct predications. If such an interpretation is extended to locational/ directional sentences which are agentive in general, then the formula that an erg phrase is agentive only in a predication which lacks a locational argument can be universally maintained; i.e. (170.e) is resolved.

Of course this account still permits us to formulate the semantic relations which such sentences share with obviously directional sentences; indeed the formulation is more straightforward now that the erg (and abs) CR is separated off from the loc and abl. And lexical naturalness is maintained. In this respect nothing is lost over the previous account, i.e. providing for (170.a-.c). However before proceeding to examine the adequacy of this revision with regard to the other phenomena we have examined, we must also consider whether the subsequent derivation such representations will entail is acceptable on general grounds.

2.8.2. Consider the derivation for (112.a). In accordance with the hierarchy of cases (§ 1.9), the abs in the lower predication is selected as subject. Let us for the moment interpret subject-selection (as . anticipated in § 1.10, and in accordance with Hjelmslev's view of subjective nominatives as involving 'éloignement') as substitution of erg for the highest CR present in a predication (if it is not already erg). Let us formulate this, in a preliminary way, as (172):

(172)   SUBJECT-FORMATION: abs → erg,

where $\begin{bmatrix} \text{case} \\ \text{abs} \end{bmatrix} > \text{abs}$

(172) involves substitution rather than addition of erg, and thus makes the claim that neutralisation occurs at this point. And if serialisation has already occurred, as again suggested in § 1.11, i.e. with in English all modifiers of a V following it, then subject-positioning (i.e. preverbally) will be applicable with respect to the output of (172), though it is probably post-cyclic (McCawley, 1970; § 1.10) or rather part of the shallow structure conditions. We return to the relationship between subject-formation, subject-positioning and the CR hierarchy in § 3.6; let us formulate the process of positioning as in (173):

(173)   SUBJECT-POSITIONING: erg $\rightleftharpoons$ V $\supset$ erg $\ll$ V

($\rightleftharpoons$ = 'is dependent on'; $\ll$ = 'precedes'). In what immediately follows I shall for expository convenience silently apply subject-positioning cyclically. This subject is then (moving to the upper sentence) available for raising into the abs position in the agentive predication while the lower V is attached directly (via abs) to the upper, as in (174):

(174)

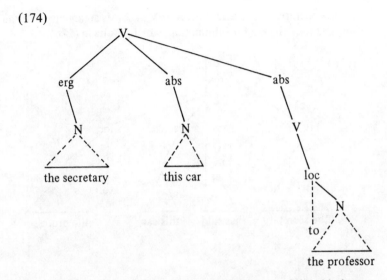

(174) also assumes for *sell* (but not *send* etc) deletion of the abl phrase under identity with the erg (equi), and subject-selection and positioning in the upper S. The raising rule invoked is simply the equivalent in terms of a dependency case system of the rule examined by Postal (1974), and thus also applied in the derivation of sentences such as (1.100) (*I expected John to like Fred*) discussed above. A rough formulation for the rule (in sequence-free terms — i.e. where only dependency relations are invoked) is given in (175):

(175)   RAISING:

$$V_1 \overset{\Rightarrow}{\rightarrow} abs \overset{\Rightarrow}{\rightarrow} N_0 \overset{\Rightarrow}{\rightarrow} abs \overset{\Rightarrow}{\rightarrow} V_2 \overset{\Rightarrow}{\rightarrow} erg \overset{\Rightarrow}{\rightarrow} N_1 \rightarrow$$

a) $V_1 \overset{\Rightarrow}{\rightarrow} abs \overset{\Rightarrow}{\rightarrow} V_2$ b) $V_1 \overset{\Rightarrow}{\rightarrow} abs \overset{\Rightarrow}{\rightarrow} N_1$

(where $\overset{\Rightarrow}{\rightarrow}$ = governs; N_0 is the lexically empty N). If sequence is determined early in the cycle then that of (174) is predictable from those of its component parts; if it follows raising, then a special subpart must provide for the abs-V dependent (unless such an abs when subordinated to V is switched to loc, as suggested in § 1.10). Of course, (175) can be analysed into two parts, raising of the lower V, henceforth V-RAISING, and raising of the lower subject NP as such, henceforth SUBJECT-RAISING. It will sometimes be necessary in what follows to refer to these individually; moreover, both of them may not apply in a particular derivation (see below).

By the operation of raising, the lower V becomes an argument of the upper, and thus eligible for subjunction, which results in (176):

(176)

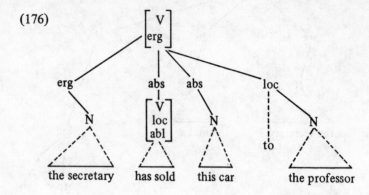

(By convention, the arguments of the subjoined element are assigned to the element to which it is subjoined.) Thus *sell, buy, hire* etc. are substituted for not just one set of case features but two. So that apart from avoiding the problem of the unpredictable agentivity of ergatives, such an account enables us to avoid adding any further addition to the set of subcategorisation and dependency rules for cases in order to allow for these verbs. It also has some important consequences for the structure of the grammar.

2.8.3. The derivation resulting in (176) reveals, in the first place, that lexicalisation (of such verbs at least) cannot be pre-cyclic in that the configuration for which *sell* etc. can be inserted only arises as a consequence of the cyclic rule of raising, which by making the lower V an argument of the upper makes it possible for subjunction and thus lexical insertion to take place. (This on the assumption that only dependents can be subjoined.) Thus the structure meeting the conditions for lexicalisation (the element to be subjoined is a dependent of the element it is to be subjoined to) is achieved via the application simply of the raising rule whose syntactic status Postal has recently argued for (1974) rather than by invoking the even more controversial predicate raising/lifting (cf. e.g. McCawley, 1968*b;* Newmeyer, 1974; de Rijk, 1974). This is a consequence of adopting a condition on subjunction that does not require that lexicalisable elements form a single constituent but is framed in terms of dependency[36].

That at least subjunction (if not actual lexical insertion) is also not post-cyclic is suggested by a number of other considerations. For instance subjunction trees can be built up by subjoining on successive cycles, as in the derivation of *bring* sentences from such a source as (177):

(177)

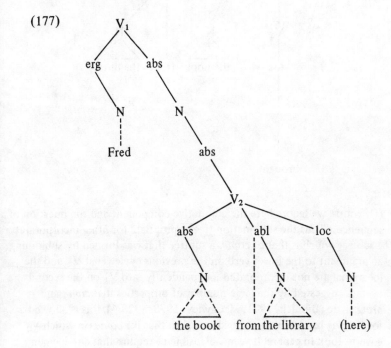

On the cycle which applies to V_2 the locational (again inadequately abbreviated as *here*) is subjoined to V_2, as in the derivation of *come*; on the second cycle, after the lower subject has been raised into absolutive position and V_2 attached as an argument to V_1, the former is available for subjunction to the latter, as in (178):

(178)

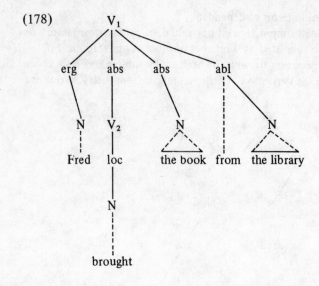

(Of course we ignore here the comitative component and the question of sequence.) Thus the subjunction tree appropriate for *bring* incorporates a subtree which is that of *come,* a subtree that was formed by subjoining an argument to the lower verb on the previous cycle. That V_2 and the locational are not incorporated independently into V_1 on the second cycle is suggested by the large number of properties that *come* and *bring* share (Binnick, 1971; McCawley, 1973*c*, 323-4); this is allowed for if *bring* has a substructure identical to that for *come* (in which V_2 governs loc). In general it seems plausible to require that any element can subjoin only one argument: let us call this the SINGLE-ARGUMENT SUBJUNCTION condition. Clearly it is tenable only if subjunction is cyclic.

Notice too that under the '*do what*' test the locative and ablative arguments of such verbs behave as participants (cf. (128)):

(179)   a.*What did the professor do from the secretary?
            He bought this car.
        b.*What did the secretary do to the professor?
            She sold this car.

We can now characterise participants as arguments of a predicate at the point at which subjunction (and insertion) takes place. Other arguments are added on subsequent cycles, but these are of course circumstantial.

Consider, for instance, a sentence like (180):

(180)   The professor bought the book in Sicily

Suppose that at the point at which the subjunction that underlies *buy* occurs we have the structure in (181):

(181)

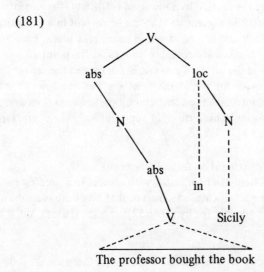

The surface structure can be derived by reapplication of raising in the highest sentence followed by subjunction of the second V to the topmost:

(182)

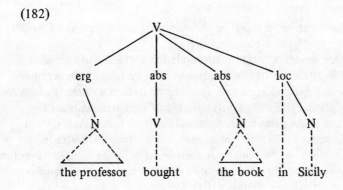

But since *buy* has already been inserted, the locational argument is a circumstantial; the final cycle does not add to the set of participants. Such a derivation also reveals that subjunction applies both pre- and post-lexically.

It now emerges that the formulation concerning the maximum number of participants that we arrived at in § 2.6 — that they comprise the set allowed for by the localist hypothesis of (60)/(61) — represents a constraint on the array of arguments that can be present in a predication when subjunction of a V and lexical insertion are to take place. Even though *buy, sell, hire* etc. involve complex sources, at the point at which they are inserted the array of cases does not exceed the set of (60), or better, to provide for two instances of abs, the set allowed for by rules (56). We can interpret the constraint on participants then as a hypothesis concerning lexical insertion, of approximately the character of (183):

> (183) *Localist constraint on lexical insertion*
> A lexical item can be inserted with respect to a predicate only if the set of cases adjoined to that predicate is a subset of the set allowed for by (56)/(57): erg, abs (twice), loc, abl.

This hypothesis too can be formulated only if lexical insertion is cyclic, in that the postcyclic structure obviously may exceed the limit specified in (183). Consider, for instance, (182) or (184):

> (184)   Fred travelled to London on Tuesday

with two locatives, the allative *to London* and the temporal *on Tuesday*. However, the latter is circumstantial.

Notice incidentally that the formulation in (183) also depends upon lexical insertion taking place with respect to subjunction trees rather than with respect to arguments (participant or circumstantial) which are then (optionally or obligatorily) deleted. If such arguments are not subjoined at the point at which lexical insertion takes place, then in many instances (183) will not be met. For instance if the verb *motor* incorporates lexically some such component as *by car*, then however this argument is analysed, insertion of *motor*, if it is also a directional verb, will almost certainly infringe (183). Say *by car* is a *through*-phase, an abstract path of some sort; then *motor* will (in the absence of subjunction) take both a path (i.e. a [loc, abl] argument) and a separate goal and source at the point at which it is inserted.

2.8.4. Return now to *buy, sell, hire* etc. and the representation in (176). The subjunction tree there is appropriate for all three and indeed for *send*. The other three differ from *send* among other things in that either the lower ablative (*buy, hire*) or the lower locative (*sell, hire*) has been deleted under identity with the ergative in the upper predication. They are thus characterisable lexically by the subjunction tree in (176) (plus whatever subtree(s) differentiate *buy* and *sell* from *borrow* and *lend* etc) together with the information that they are necessarily ablativeless or locativeless. This is distinctive provided that the deletion that results in, say, *Fred sold a book,* whereby *sell* also lacks a locative (though as indefinite, rather than removed under identity) as well as an ablative, occurs after lexical insertion has taken place. It may be that the deleted locative with *buy* and the ablative with *sell* leave behind a copy subjoined to the predicate, in which case of course *buy* and *sell* etc. will differ in the subjunction trees to which they are attached. However, this would apparently infringe the constraint proposed by Seuren (1975) whereby (in the present framework) elements which refer may not undergo subjunction. Perhaps then we should interpret equi as copying the lower argument on to the upper identical one before deletion. So that the subject in a *sell* sentence will have a derived [erg, abl] specification, whereas that with *buy* will be [erg, loc] : that is for *sell,* a derived representation like (120.a); for *buy,* like (120.b). Insertion of *buy/sell* must then be sensitive to the character of the subject. However, the precise characterisation of such lexical information is unimportant for the present discussion: but see further § 3.4. I shall nevertheless assume henceforth that equi involves raising of a case phrase into a co-referential case phrase in the main clause.

2.8.5. Such a (two-predication) derivation for causative directionals and specifically indirect object constructions also accounts for some anomalies concerning coordination observed by Gleitman (1965, 264-5). Chomsky (1957, 36-7) suggested that one criterion in setting up constituents should be capacity for coordination. So that the viability of, say, *John payed the bill and ordered a taxi* as a coordination supports the positing of some constituent which includes just *payed the bill* (and *ordered the taxi*). And indeed in general independently established constituency and conjoinability seem to correlate rather well. However, as Gleitman observes, '. . . certain conjunctions of non-constituent sequences of constituents are uniformly accepted by speakers' (1965, 264), whereas

(1965, 265) 'Other conjunctions that cross constituent boundaries are judged awkward but acceptable. Still others are rejected.' As examples of awkward or unacceptable sentences of this kind she offers examples like: *?The man saw and the woman heard the shot fired* and **I want to know why John and when Mary are coming.* However, what is of interest in the present context is that one of her examples of acceptable conjunctions of non-constituents involves what is by the present analysis a causative directional, viz. *He took John home and Mary to the station.* Now clearly at a certain point in the derivation *John home* together with the directional verb that later gets incorporated into the causative does in terms of the account presented here make a constituent. And so too does *the boy a nickel* (in terms of the derivation pursued below) in *I gave the boy a nickel and the girl a dime,* another of Gleitman's examples of well-formed conjunctions of 'non-constituents'. So the derivation we are proposing removes some of the major counter-examples to Chomsky's generalisation. Clearly these remain as such under an analysis whereby 'indirect objects' originate in a simplex structure.

2.8.6. Let us now turn specifically to the question of the derivation of prepositionless indirect objects, bearing in mind the various observations concerning them we have made: their positioning before the direct object in active sentences (often accounted for by dative movement); their availability for passivisation; the animateness restriction (cf. (107), (108) *v.* (109)); the potential difference in interpretation from *to*-indirect objects (170.d); the necessity for distinguishing them from the *spray paint* verbs (170.f).

Observe, in the first place that the animateness restriction exemplified in (107)/(108)/(109), reproduced as (185):

(185)   a. Fred sent a letter from New York to London
         b. Fred sent a letter from New York to his brother (in London)
         c.*Fred sent London a letter from New York
         d. Fred sent his brother (in London) a letter from New York

is exactly paralleled in (186):

(186)   a. A letter travelled from New York to London
         b. A letter travelled from New York to his brother (in London)
         c.*London received a letter from New York

     d. His brother (in London) received a letter from New York

Moreover, the corresponding sentences in (186) are implied by those in
(185). (For some speakers the (a) and (b) instances in (185) (at least)
do not imply that the letter necessarily reached its destination; for me
this is only true of *send off* or *mail/post* rather than *send*. At any rate,
with this proviso, there still exists an obvious relationship.) We
distinguished *receive* from ordinary directionals as taking a [loc, erg]
argument which is subject in active sentences and occurs in a *by*-phrase
in passives:

(187)   A letter was received by his brother (in London)

(cf. **A letter was received by London*). We can allow for the semantic
relationships between (185) and (186), the sequence of prepositionless
indirect objects, their lack of preposition and availability for
passivisation, and the animateness restriction (cf. (170.d)) if the structures
underlying verbs like *send* and *sell* involve a lower directional which
may be erg (like the predications associated with *receive*), such that the
locational phrase (rather than the absolutive) in the lower predication
corresponding to that in (171) is subject and then undergoes raising,
resulting after subject-positioning in V_1 in (188):

(188)

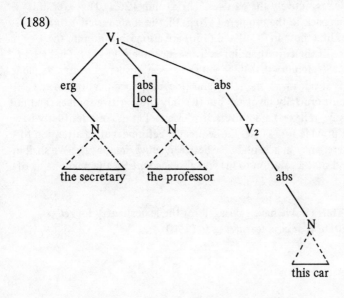

(which underlies (125)).

I have interpreted subject-raising as involving the carrying along of any case relation other than erg (which is not distinctive for subjects) into the upper predication (cf. the interpretation of equi suggested above): so *the professor* is [loc, abs] rather than simply abs. This will ensure that the resulting configuration (after subjunction of the lower V) will conform to the post-cyclic serialisation constraints: [abs, loc] before [abs]. In some languages this [loc, abs] (originally [loc, erg]) argument is provided with a special marker, like the Basque 'dative', distinct from markers of both absolutive and goal:

> (189)   Paulor*i* liburu bat eman diot
>   ('Paul-dative book a given have-I-him-it'
>   = 'I have given/gave Paul a book')

(Of course this marker is used in other predication-types, but I think the [loc, abs] or [loc, erg] can be motivated in most if not all of these instances, which involve, for instance, arguments corresponding to the object of *please* in English and possessives raised into the main clause.)

On the assumption (examined above) that passivisation involves (whatever else) the making into a subject of the argument to the immediate right of the verb, (176) and (188) will also (at least in part)' underlie respectively the passives (127.a) and (126.a). However, this brings us back to the problem (170.g) that in some varieties of English passives like those in (146) and (150) are also viable, despite the deviance of the corresponding actives (such as e.g. (147)). That is, (a) (146)/(150) require that their active 'sources' display a relative sequence which is at odds with the [abs] and [loc, abs] specifications of the arguments crucially involved; but (b) only those active sources (and not the passive reflexes) are universally deviant. Let us consider firstly how we can provide for (a), i.e. the sequence, before devoting attention to the discrepancy in acceptability between active and passive. We shall in fact find that a solution to (a) will also account for the phenomena of (b).

2.8.7. Thus far, we have envisaged for the lexical entry for *sell*, a configuration of case features as in (190):

(190)

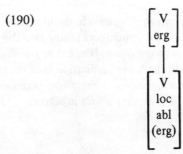

The optional erg allows for (125) as opposed to (112). By the rules of (57) such an erg is attached to loc which then assumes precedence over a simple abs in the hierarchy of CRs. The difference in meaning potential between the *to*-ful and *to*-less variants can be associated with this difference in source and derivation. Also, 'exceptions' to dative movement like *allow,* which has only a *to*-less variant, and *delegate,* only *to*-ful, can now be accommodated without recourse to exception features. Rather, *delegate* simply lacks the lower erg in (190); with *allow* it is obligatory.

We can also now allow for the appropriate sequence in the sources for (146)/(150) if the lower (directional) predication corresponding to that in (171) is abs as well as erg; i.e. is specified as [loc, abl, erg, abs]. By the rules in (57), such a specification introduces a directional predication (involving a locative and ablative and an absolutive) in which an erg is combined in a complex with the abs and the extra abs is attached to the locative argument, as represented by the (post-subject-positioning) structure in (191):

(191)

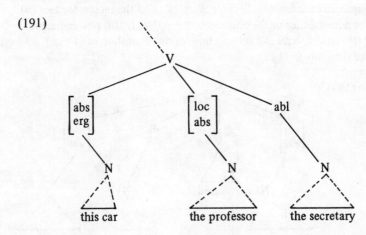

in which the [abs, erg] argument, having precedence in the hierarchy, has undergone subject-formation, and then undergoes raising into the upper predication and eventually, as (non-subject) NP next to the V, passivisation, to give (146.a). That is, the lower predication is of the character of that associated with *reach,* which is a directional verb that also takes an [abs, erg] subject and a [loc, abs] object in active sentences.

Thus *sell* must be classified as in (192):

(192)

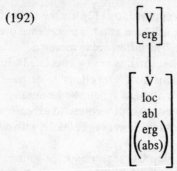

for those dialects in which (146)/(150) are viable, but as (190) where they are excluded. Why this particular variant should be the marginal one follows from such a specification as (192), which is more complex than (190) and in which the presence of abs in the lower complex (which is what allows for the (146)/(150) variants) is dependent upon the presence of erg.

In this way we provide for fact (a) about such passives, namely the sequence of arguments in their 'sources'. And the reason for fact (b), the non-viability of the corresponding actives is also now apparent. After raising, equi and subjunction, in the derivation of (146.a), we have the structure in (193):

(193)

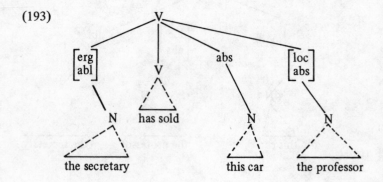

To form (146.a) the immediately post-verbal argument is made into a subject under passivisation. However, if passivisation fails to occur, we are left at the output to the cyclic rules with a sequence, [abs] followed by [loc, abs], which contravenes the serialisation constraints; only the sequence [loc, abs] + [abs] is permitted. Thus (147.a) is impossible as an active corresponding to (146.a). The non-viability of (147) is due to an infringement of the independently motivated constraints on sequence.

2.8.8. The positing of a (second) *to*-dropping rule to allow for (146)/(150) is accordingly unnecessary. The account we have arrived at involving a complex source for indirect object sentences will allow for these as for the other properties associated with indirect objects in terms of independently motivated rules and constraints. Jackendoff & Culicover (1971) offered no evidence to justify the positing of a rule of *to*-dropping. The phenomena involving particles like *back* we found to be inconclusive: on the one hand, the non-viability of (157) associates the putative *to*-dropping NP with the *to*-phrase in (158), and thus supports the notion of *to*-dropping; on the other hand, the fact that (161) and (162) are equally dubious suggests that *Mary* in (161) is a genuine indirect object like (162) rather than a *to*-phrase, which allows a preceding *back,* as in (160). The behaviour of the particle thus does not overall provide evidence for *to*-dropping. However this behaviour is compatible with the source of indirect objects advocated here. Let us now establish that this is so.

For ease of discussion I draw together the various examples involving the particle in (194):

(194)   a. John gave back the book to Mary
           b. John gave the book back to Mary
           c.*John gave the book to Mary back
           d.?*John gave back Mary the book
           e. John gave Mary back the book
           f. John gave Mary the book back
           g. The book was given back to Mary
           h.*The book was given to Mary back
           i. Mary was given back the book
           j. Mary was given the book back
           k.?*The book was given back Mary
           l. *The book was given Mary back

(k) and (l) involve the putative *to*-dropping NP. (l) behaves like the *to*-phrases in (h) and (c) rather than the indirect object in (e), whereas (k) resembles the indirect object in (d) rather than the *to*-phrases in (g) and (b).

Emonds (1972, §§ I-VI) presents various arguments which support the view that a particle like *back* originates as an adverbial which may optionally be preposed over the object. The application *v.* non-application of what I shall refer to as BACK-ING is illustrated by (194.a) *v.* (194.b) and (194.e) *v.* (194.f). Let us adopt such a view of the relationship between these sentences, though it does not matter in the present context whether or not they are related by a movement transformation of this kind. (Jackendoff (1974) offers a structure-preserving formulation, but it fails to allow for variants (194.f) and (194.j), which, as I have indicated, are acceptable to me.) Thus *back* originates to the right of the object and optionally moves over it, as indicated schematically in (195):

(195)   optional *back*ing: *back*   abs

Back, however, cannot occur after *to*-phrases. If we assume that *back* (whatever its source) originates always to the far right of the (directional) predication concerned, then it is obligatorily preposed to a directional phrase — though again the formulation of this as a movement is not crucial. We thus get (194.b) rather than (194.c), by (196):

(196)   obligatory *back*ing: *back*   loc

However, on such a view, (194.a) apparently shows two applications of *back*-ing, one obligatory (as in 194.b)), one optional (over abs). But if such sentences are complex, the first application is on the cycle associated with the lower sentence, the second with the following cycle. In this way we can allow for (the deviance or non-deviance of) (194. a,b,c,e,f,g,i,j).

(194. d,k), on the other hand, are excluded by a constraint throwing out the sequence *back* + [loc, abs] . That this is general is shown by the deviance of (197):

(197)   *The cows crossed back the river

v. the well-formedness of (198):

(198)   The cows crossed back over the river

if (197) differs from (198) in having *the river* argument labelled as abs
(as well as [loc, abl] , i.e. path) thus enabling it to assume object
position in the active and subject in the passive:

(199)   a. The cows crossed the river
         b. The river was crossed (by the cows)

At any rate, as we have seen, the parallel deviance of (194.d) and (194.k)
argues against a derivation involving *to*-dropping. It is, however, to be
expected in terms of the analysis presented here. Notice too that since
the *the river* arguments in both of (197) and (198) are directional,
(196) applies (obligatorily); so that both sentences in (200) are deviant:

(200)   a.*The cows crossed the river back
         b.*The cows crossed over the river back

On the same grounds, then, not only, as we have observed, are (194. c,h)
ruled out, but also (194.l). That is, the deviance of this last is dependent
not on its being a *to*-phrase (as posited by the *to*-dropping analysis) but
merely on its being directional (like (200.a)).

However, what now of (194.e)? Should not obligatory *back*-ing also
occur over the directional *Mary* and (194.e) thus also be deviant? There
is such a derivation, it eventuates in (194.d). The derivation involves
back-ing over the absolutive *the book* on the first cycle and over the
[loc, abs] *Mary* on the second, so that *back* ends up in the banned
pre-[loc, abs] position. But recall that *back*-ing over abs is optional.
There is therefore another derivation for a sentence of the form of
(194. d.e.f) whereby *back*-ing does not occur on the first cycle. If it
also is not applied on the second, then (194.f) is the result. However,
if *back*-ing applies only on the second cycle, the result is (194.e), whose
well-formedness is then to be expected, given the optionality of
back-ing over (simple) absolutives. Accordingly, the set of phenomena
tabulated in (194), while partly predicted by the *to*-dropping analysis
but partly incompatible with it, is perfectly compatible with the
complex source we have posited.

2.8.9. We are also now able to distinguish in a principled way between
the structures underlying 'indirect object' constructions and those to be
associated with *spray paint* verbs (170.f). In ch.1 it was argued that

swarm was a locational verb that could take an extra abs feature; and the presence or absence of this abs distinguished between the pair in (201):

> (201)   a. Bees are swarming in the garden
>   b. The garden is swarming with bees

such that (b) has a [loc, abs] subject and a 'holistic' interpretation thereof. The *with* in (b) is interpretable as the marker of an absolutive phrase that has been denied subject position by another, complex absolutive phrase. Now, the sentences in (202):

> (202)   a. Fred sprayed paint on the wall
>   b. Fred sprayed the wall with paint

are like 'indirect object' sentences in showing both an agentive ergative and a locational phrase. On these grounds a complex source is once more to be preferred. In the lower predication, in the (a) instance the simple absolutive *paint* will be in subject position and thus undergoes raising, but in the (b) structure this absolutive is again (cf. (201.b)) 'displaced' by a [loc, abs] phrase, with which also a 'holistic' reading is associated. This contrasts with 'indirect objects' such as (125), where the locative is subject in the lower predication not by virtue of also being absolutive but as an erg. The 'indirect object' thus imposes an animacy rather than a 'holistic' interpretation on the locative, and does not require that the simple abs be marked by *with*, which lack of marker is normal in sentences with ergative subjects. So that if the (relevant part of the) subjunction tree appropriate to *sell* is as in (192), for *swarm* and *spray* we have respectively (203.a) and (203.b):

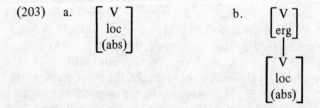

> (203)   a. $\begin{bmatrix} V \\ loc \\ (abs) \end{bmatrix}$ b. $\begin{bmatrix} V \\ erg \end{bmatrix}$
>
> $\begin{bmatrix} V \\ loc \\ (abs) \end{bmatrix}$

2.8.10. Anderson (1971*b*, § 9.5; 1971*c*) proposes extending such an 'indirect object' analysis to superficially transitive verbs like *help, advise, kiss, obey,* such that the structure underlying (204.b) is more overtly represented in (204.a):

(204)   a. Fred gives his nephew advice
         b. Fred advises his nephew

(cf. too Porzig, 1934). In the derivation of *advise* the direct object has
been subjoined to the verb. The 'indirect object' left behind nevertheless
retains in many languages the distinctive (dative) marker even though the
sentence is superficially otherwise a simple transitive, as exemplified by
Old English, German or Basque.[37] As an example cf. (205):

(205)   obeditzen du $\left\{ \begin{array}{l} \text{aitari} \\ \text{aita} \end{array} \right.$

         ('Obey he-him father(-to)' = 'He obeys his father')

which reveals that the dative *i* is optional in Basque with a verb like *obey*,
even though the (auxiliary) verb *du* is a simple transitive in form rather
than dative, like *diot* in (189).

At first sight this derivation might seem to constitute yet another
counter-example to the contiguity requirement on subjunction. However
this is not necessarily so, in that subjunction of the absolutive phrase
(*advice*) can take place on the first cycle; i.e. it can be subjoined initially
to the lower verb (on which it is dependent). The whole complex is
then subjoined to the upper verb on the second cycle. Such a derivation
is indeed required by the single-argument subjunction condition. Of
course, as already observed, this second subjunction does indeed violate
the contiguity requirement. Perhaps, then, the contiguity requirement can
be imposed in general on subjunction not involving predicate-to-predicate
(which differ from the others in that a configuration involving a predicate
adjoined (via a CR) to another is always derived). As we have seen, for
this to be true in the present instance (*advise* etc.) subjunction must
apply cyclically. If such a derivation is just, and if the weakened
contiguity requirement is maintainable, we have indeed here a further
argument for the cyclicity of subjunction. Note too that if such a
derivation for *advise* etc. does not falsify the contiguity requirement, it
does if just disconfirm the requirement that only a constituent can be
lexicalised (McCawley, 1968*b*, 1971*a;* de Rijk, 1974). There is no
point prior to subjunction at which the *advice* NP forms by itself a
constituent with its predicate.

Let us accordingly sum up the observations we have thus far made
concerning the preservation of structure and sequence, informally, as
follows:

(206)   *Output conditions for cyclic rules:*
    a. Only V-raising creates dependencies, specifically the
       unique configuration $V_i \rightrightarrows abs \rightrightarrows V_j$;
    b. If subject-positioning is post-cyclic, V-raising is nevertheless
       sequence-preserving.

It remains to be seen, however, whether the sequence-preserving
constraint can be maintained in general — cf. the discussion of
extraposition in § 1.11: only if extraposition involves cyclic V-raising
and post-cyclic movement to the right can either part of (206) be
maintained in that form. At any rate, the weaker sequence-preserving
constraint applies more generally than the structure-preserving constraint,
with respect to which the configuration alluded to in (206.a) is
exceptional. We can then formulate the conditions on subjunction
outlined in (207):

(207)   *Conditions on subjunction:*
    a. subjunction is applied cyclically;
    b. only dependents are subjoined;
    c. only subjunction of the dependents in
       $V_i \rightrightarrows abs \rightrightarrows V_j$ violates condition d;
    d. only a contiguous element can be subjoined to its
       governor.

Of course, again, these are offered in the knowledge of our (or at least
my) ignorance concerning much of the relevant aspects of the grammar.
However, I hypothesise that (207), at any rate, will be maintainable,
and indeed perhaps will eventually incorporate even tighter constraints.

2.8.11. There are various other phenomena which depend (a) on a
complex source for indirect objects and (b) on the prepositionless and
prepositionful variants not being related by a rule of dative movement.
And I would like to conclude this discussion of indirect objects with a
brief consideration of some of these areas. We shall in the first instance
be concerned with the phenomenon (or group of phenomena) known
as quantifier-postposing and/or -movement or Q-float.[38] In terms of
most accounts it is suggested that (208.b) is related to (208.a) by some
rule the effect of which is to move a universal quantifier out of and to
the right of its NP:

(208)   a. Each of the men caught two fish

      b. The men each caught two fish

It seems to me that this is a rather unilluminating way to look at the
relationship between such pairs (cf. Anderson, 1975*b*), but it will suffice
in the present context. What is of interest to us at this point is that the
quantifier cannot be moved out of an object NP;

    (209)   a. Someone caught all of the fish
               b.*Someone caught the fish all

unless it is a pronominal (for discussion, see Postal, 1974, § 4.5);
movement is limited strictly to (derived) subjects, as shown by (210):

    (210)   a. All of the fish were caught
               b. The fish were all caught

and (211):

    (211)   a. Two fish were caught by each of the men
               b.*Two fish were caught by the men each

(I am of course ignoring here differences in scope which in certain
dialects are associated with these 'corresponding' actives and passives.)
    There is also no movement out of prepositional phrases other than
that in (211), as revealed by (212):

    (212)   a. Mary gave a kiss to each of the men
               b.*Mary gave a kiss to the men each

However, *each* at least can in certain circumstances be moved out of a
prepositionless indirect object (and for some speakers movement of *all*
is marginally possible):

    (213)   a. Mary gave each/all of the men a kiss
               b. Mary gave the men each/?all a kiss

Movement of *each* is even marginally possible out of a direct object in
a sentence with a prepositionful indirect object:

    (214)   a. Mary gave each of the pigs to a different farmer
               b.?Mary gave the pigs each to a different farmer

Of course, it is possible to allow for this by formulating a distinct rule of quantifier movement which applies after dative movement and relates the (a) instances in (213)/(214) to the (b). But this leaves unexplained why there is movement in just these circumstances: namely, if the NP is a derived subject or a *to*-less indirect object or a direct object in a *to*-ful sentence. One plausible candidate for a generalisation would relate viable shifts to the fact that in such the quantifier comes to occupy a position before a NP (or PP, or with subjects VP, say). But this is shown to be insufficient by the deviance of sentences like *A messenger went from the towns each to several adjacent villages. Under the analysis developed in this section, however, all of the NPs which permit movement are the subjects of the predication in which they originate. We can thus allow for the (b) variants in (213)/(214) by the same means as provide for (208.b) and (210.b), if the movement occurs on the cycle that applies to the lower predication underlying the former. However, the subjects of the lower predications in the structures underlying (213.b)/(214.b) subsequently lose their subjecthood, which apparently affects the viability of quantifier movement variants in the manner tabulated in (215):

(215)   *sources for*   Movement of
         moving quantifiers

		each	all
	subject	√	√
from	subject → indirect object	√	?
	subject → direct object	?	
	others		

That is, movement is most general from a subject which remains as such; from anything else than a subject it is impossible; from a subject which becomes a direct object, from which movement is otherwise impossible, movement of *each* is marginally possible. A prepositionless indirect object, which is a subject which has come to occupy a unique position between the verb and the direct object, is intermediate, in readily permitting movement of *each,* and marginally of *all.*

The ability to 'launch' quantifiers is a property associated within relational grammar with *terms*. However, this is clearly not a necessary condition for termhood, since, in particular, quantifier movement is only marginally possible with direct objects and then only in certain circumstances. It is also impossible with *to*-indirect objects. Moreover, the interest of the association between termhood and quantifier-launching is somewhat lessened by the fact that in the hierarchy defined in (215) prepositionless indirect objects come above direct objects and prepositionful below. Why should this be? This is not arbitrary if prepositionless direct objects are not the result of dative movement but are subjects in an embedded predication. Against the existence of dative movement is thrown into doubt, and with it the notion that 'indirect object' is a primitive term.

2.8.12. Further doubt is cast on the existence of a process whereby 'indirect objects' are converted into 'direct' by other phenomena concerning quantifiers, in this instance involving scope of quantification. This is an issue of some complexity which I shall not pursue here. However of immediate relevance are some observations of Ioup's (1975) concerning the hierarchy of grammatical relations with respect to scope. She notes, for instance, that both indirect objects (prepositionless or -ful) and the objects of prepositions take precedence over direct objects, such that a quantifier occurring in the former positions will tend to have 'higher scope over the same quantifier occurring in the direct object' (p.43). Thus, the preferred scope relation in (216) is constant:

(216)   a. I told every child a story
        b. I told a story to every child

such that on the preferred reading *every* includes *a*, whereas in (217) the preference is reversed:

(217)   a. I told a child every story
        b. I told every story to a child

That is, in both pairs the quantifier in 'indirect object position' includes the 'direct object' quantifier in its scope, whether the 'indirect object' has putatively undergone dative movement or not. That is, again the prepositionless 'indirect object' does not behave like a 'direct object'. Such phenomena offer further counter-evidence to a rule of dative movement. This conclusion holds whether it is proposed that quantifier scope is interpreted at surface structure (or even at the end of each cycle) or it is assumed that quantifiers are provided with a source outwith the predication they appear in superficially. In either case the quantifier and its scope are associated with the appropriate NP after the putative application of dative movement. If there is such a rule which converts indirect into direct objects, then one would expect that the first NP in (216/217.a) should be included in the scope of the second. That we cannot account for this by invoking the status of the second NP as a 'chômeur' (and therefore outside the hierarchy) is shown by such examples as (218):

(218)   a. I was told a story by every child
         b. I was told every story by a child

in which on the preferred reading the 'chômeur' *by every/a child* includes the direct object in its scope.

2.8.13. Further evidence against the kind of account of indirect objects offered by advocates of relational grammar is provided, for example, by Postal's (1974, §§ 4.11, 8.2) attempt to formulate the constraint which underlies the deviance of (219):

(219)   a.*Tom believes, if I am not mistaken, Melvin to be a
            Martian
         b.*I like very much Bob
         c.*I visit very frequently my aunt

He expressed this as the INTERPOLATION BAN, which rejects surface structures of the character of (220):

(220)

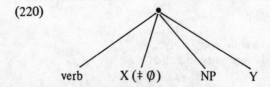

provided that the NP therein is the (direct) object of the verb. (Thus, for example, in contrast with (219), a sentence like *I would guess first Harry*, as an answer to, say, *Who do you think won?*, is well formed, since *Harry* is not the object of *guess*.) However, Postal goes on (p.145, n.49) to credit to Perlmutter the observation that (220) might appear to rule out such sentences as (221):

(221)   Jim gave the girls necklaces

since an element (*the girls*) is interpolated between *gave* and *necklaces*. Postal's response, consistent with the account of dative movement in terms of relational grammar outlined above, is to deny that *necklaces* is indeed an object in such sentences. By dative movement the original indirect (*to*-phrase) is converted into a direct object and the former direct object ceases to bear any relation to the verb, it is a 'chômeur'. However, this suggestion has rather unfortunate consequences. It will, admittedly, account for the deviance of (222):

(222)   *Jim gave very frequently the girls necklaces

again with respect to (220). But the deviance of (223):

(223)   *Jim gave the girls very frequently necklaces

as compared with, say, (224):

(224)   a. Jim gave necklaces very frequently to the girls
         b. Jim gave necklaces to the girls very frequently

is quite unaccounted for. We cannot relate it to the interpolation ban, because *necklaces* in (223) is a 'chômeur', not an object; moreover it is already preceded by an object on whose objecthood the deviance of (222) depends. The generalisation seems to be that only an object can intervene between an object and its verb. Such a generalisation is incompatible with the account of indirect object sentences espoused by Postal. An appropriate definition of object is offered in § 3.6. Observe for the moment that both 'direct' and 'indirect objects' are absolutives.

Such phenomena require, then, that 'direct' and (prepositionless) 'indirect objects' have something in common (at the same point in a derivation), which is denied by relational grammar. The scope phenomena, and the failure of prepositionless indirect objects to undergo complex NP shift (noted in § 2.7), require that they nevertheless be distinct, and specifically that 'indirect' objects do not become 'direct objects' by dative movement (as required by relational grammar). Apart from this, the Q-float evidence surveyed briefly above (in § 2.8.11) suggests that at some point in their derivation prepositionless indirect objects are subjects.

2.8.14. Postal, on yet another hand, also provides some further evidence
for the subjecthood of indirect objects. Let us note one particular
instance which relates to another issue of relevance. He observes (1974,
§ 5.1), following Chomsky (1973), that (for many speakers) extraction
of a certain class of NPs from a subject NP that contains them is ruled out.
Thus whereas, to illustrate with WH-REL-MOVEMENT, (225), showing
extraction from an object:

(225)   The girl who(m) you bought pictures of

is perfectly well-formed, both of (226):

(226)   a.*The girl who pictures of lay on the table
         b.*The girl who Bill thinks pictures of were on the table

with extraction from subject-position, are deviant. However, as Postal
(utilising some examples suggested by McCawley) observes (p.192, n.4),
extraction from indirect object position in (227):

(227)   *The scholar who I gave a disciple of a lot of money is in jail

is also impossible. Now, this admits of explanation in terms of the same
ban on extraction as underlies the deviance of (226) if 'indirect objects'
derive from subjects, as in the account developed above. Interestingly,
there is a dialect (instantiated by Roger Lass at least) in which extraction
is possible from those NPs which lose their subjecthood (i.e. (228)
and (227)).

But notice now that (for the non-Lassian dialect) the ban requires a
global formulation, since at the point in the derivation of (227) at
which extraction takes place the NP concerned has ceased to be a
subject. Lightfoot's (to appear) only objection of substance to the
raising rule depends upon the fact that under a raising analysis, the
deviance of NPs like (228):

(228)   *The girl who you believed pictures of to be on sale in
         Tunisia

can only be related to the extraction-of-subjects ban if this is given a
global formulation, since once again, if raising has applied, at the point

at which extraction applies the relevant NPs have ceased to be subjects. However, we have just encountered a case (227) in which just such a formulation is required, since no one would presumably want to argue that 'indirect objects' are subjects at the time of extraction. Moreover, the degree of globality required, either under a movement or deletion (Gundel, 1975) formulation of 'extraction', is no more than is invoked by the 'trace theory' of movement rules.

Of main interest, however, at this point in our discussion, is once again evidence for the cyclic subjecthood of 'indirect objects'. Only an account such as we have developed allows for this and the partial similarity to 'direct objects', as well as the semantic and lexical properties we have noted.

3 ON THE NATURE OF GRAMMATICAL RELATIONS

3.1 Introduction

In this chapter we shall try to establish rather more precisely the role in the grammar of the CRs proposed in the previous one. We have seen that the CRs determine subject and object selection. To what extent must other syntactic generalisations invoke them? In particular, if subject-formation has a neutralising role, at what point does this neutralisation take effect, and thus at what point do the CRs that become subjects cease to be referable to as such in the formulation of syntactic regularities? The plausibility of case grammar as a genuine alternative to other hypotheses depends to some degree on the extent to which subject-formation can be assigned a rather 'late' position in the set of syntactic rules.

In the initial discussions of ch.1 we distinguished case grammars from 'standard' transformational grammars in two crucial respects: (a) the inclusion as primitive of relational information, e.g. the case nodes, in underlying and derived representations; (b) the relegation of the relations 'subject' and 'object' to a derived status, relations which arise as a neutralisation of CRs or which can be defined in terms of the distribution of CRs. Now, clearly it is possible to envisage an intermediate position, i.e. one which denies (b) but subscribes to (a) or vice versa. While I am not aware that the latter intermediate position (yes to (b), no to (a)) has been explicitly adopted in the literature (though one can imagine variants of generative semantics to which such a characterisation might be appropriate), it seems to me that we can associate the former (yes to (a), no to (b)) with proposals in 'relational grammar'. The following sections attempt in the main to re-examine the critical distinction between case grammars and relational grammars, viz. the status of subject and object, and to explore some of the consequences of adopting either framework. The discussion is somewhat hampered by the fact that at this point in time and space not much in the way of exposition of relational grammar is available to me.[39] But I think that we can nevertheless arrive at a preliminary decision on what I have suggested is the crucial issue.

In terms of the preceding discussion, what is at stake in selecting between case and relational grammar is the status of subject-formation

(2.172) If all syntactic generalisations in so far as they refer to relations presuppose the operation of subject-formation, i.e., more generally, they refer to subjects, objects etc. rather than ergatives, absolutives etc., then the CRs are at most semantic elements. What remains of interest, if they are such, is how these semantic elements are related to representations framed in terms of subjects and objects. In principle it seems possible in the simplest instances to define ergative and absolutive in terms of subject and object (and vice versa); and we return to this below. Let us simply establish at this point that it is appropriate to define a relational grammar, from the viewpoint of case grammar, as one in which subject-formation is prior to all (other) syntactic transformations.

We can define various versions of a case grammar in terms of the extent to which this requirement concerning the status of subject-formation is not met. For instance, subject-formation could be in the cycle, at the end of the cycle, or post-cyclic. (A case grammar with pre-cyclic subject-formation is as far as I can see equivalent to a relational grammar unless prior pre-cyclic processes can be motivated.) A case grammar with mid-cyclic subject-formation is only weakly distinguished from a relational grammar, if there is any depth of ordering within the cycle. Post-cyclic subject-formation, on the other hand, incorporates a very strong counter-claim to the hypothesis embodied in relational grammar, in terms of which the rules referring to grammatical relations are cyclic. I suggest, however, that 'standard' case grammars are most appropriately characterised as occupying a position intermediate between these two other possibilities, such that subject-formation is cycle-terminating (whatever the ordering relations within the cycle). The evidence I know of seems to support this case grammar proposal over both relational grammar and the weaker and stronger variants of case grammar I have outlined here.

The variant of case grammar with post-cyclic subject-formation is clearly too strong, in that the formulation of such cyclic rules as equi and raising involves reference to, in particular, the subject of an embedded sentence. Relational grammar, on the other hand, selects subjects too early, in that, as we saw in § 1.10, raising, and possibly 'ascensions' in general, involves crucially (as far as the 'host' clause is concerned) absolutive phrases (not subjects or objects): raising is always out of a sentence embedded in an absolutive phrase; and the phrase that is raised replaces that absolutive (recall the formulation in (2.175)). The controller for equi, where one is obligatory, on the other hand, is never an absolutive. We review in what follows further evidence of the relevance of CRs to the selection of controller, and some other syntactic generalisations that depend on reference to CRs. What emerges from a consideration of these is some measure of support for the proposal that subject-formation is cycle-terminating, so that at any point in the cycle the relations referred to in the topmost clause under consideration are the (non-derived) CRs whereas the relations invoked in embedded sentences are post-subject-formation (whatever its character), i.e. derived.

Of course it is possible in treating ascensions to define a notion 'absolutive' in terms of subjects and objects and transitivity. Pullum (1975*b*), for instance, formulates the generalisation that we have been concerned with above as the 'Absolutive Host Law', such that 'The host for an ascension must be the initial (underlying) absolutive term of the trigger verb', where 'non-derived absolutive terms' are 'SUBJECTs of intransitive verbs and OBJECTs of transitive verbs'. But such a characterisation of absolutives is entirely ad hoc and does not follow in any way from other properties of the relational grammar framework. The generalisation is, however, a natural consequence of a case grammar framework in which absolutive and ergative are independently motivated terms and subject-formation is cycle-terminating.

A number of apparent counter-examples to the proposal that subject-formation is of this character seem to depend on analyses which are inadequate on other grounds. In particular, rules which appear to refer to the subject of the main clause on a particular cycle actually apply, for independent reasons, on a subsequent one. We discussed, though not from this point of view, one such 'rule' in the previous section: quantifier float, or quantifier movement. In terms of Q-float certain quantifiers can be 'moved out of' certain NPs; and we established that these NPs were subject NPs (including the subjects that become prepositionless indirect objects). However, the most plausible derivation for sentences including such quantifiers involves the incorporation of material from outside the clause governed by the superficial main verb (Anderson, 1973*d*). And the adequate formulation of quantifier movement depends on just such a source (see Anderson, 1975*b*). Thus quantifier movement is effected (whatever the process involved) on a cycle subsequent to that which establishes the subject of the main verb in surface structure. This accords with the case grammar framework. On the other hand, as we noted in § 2.8, the Q-float phenomena provide considerable problems for a relational grammar which includes indirect object as a primitive relation.

Similarly, simplex NP-movement rules like dative movement which refer to grammatical relations require on the basis of the findings of §§ 2.7-8 radical reanalysis, such that, in this instance, indirect objects arise by raising of an embedded (locative) subject rather than by an idiosyncratic simplex movement rule. I conjecture that all apparent simplex NP-movements in the cycle are to be interpreted as raisings from embedded sentences. Some further examples requiring such reanalysis are discussed below, notably passive and psych-movement. In this respect, the cyclic transformations are 'structure preserving' (Emonds, 1969, 1970) as well as 'sequence preserving' (ch.1), within the bounds proposed in (2.206). Such an interpretation is of course again in accord with a case grammar with cycle-terminating subject-formation. However, are there other syntactic generalisations affecting 'clause-mate' NPs (NPs sharing all clause memberships – Postal, 1971, ch.2)which might provide evidence in this issue? There is (for English at least) one very promising candidate.

3.2 Case relations and grammatical relations 1: Reflexivisation

3.2.1. 'Ordinary reflexivisation' (Postal, 1974, § 3.2) is a simplex ('clause mate') process *par excellence* (as formulated by e.g. Lees & Klima (1963) and Postal (1971, ch.3, A)); indeed, it is restricted to 'peers' (Postal, 1971, ch.17), clause mate NPs of zero degree of nominal embedding. The result of its application is illustrated by (1):

(1) a. Bill killed himself
     b. Bill's dad killed himself

in which the second of two coreferential NPs in a simple sentence is marked by a reflexive pronoun, given that they are peers: so that, *himself* in (1.b) is coreferential with *Bill's dad* and not with *Bill*, in that the latter is embedded in a larger NP and thus fails to meet the peer condition. In (2), too, *himself* has as antecedent only *Bill* and *him* only *Fred* or some other person (not Bill):

(2)   Fred is desirous that Bill (should) kill $\begin{cases} \text{himself} \\ \text{him} \end{cases}$

since *Fred* is never within the same clause as the reflexivised NP. And this is also the case with (3):

(3)   Fred wants Bill to kill $\begin{cases} \text{himself} \\ \text{him} \end{cases}$

even though *Bill* has subsequently been moved out of the clause that contains the reflexive. Whereas, in (4):

(4)   Fred wants himself (to be) killed

it is only after the subject NP of the lower clause is raised into the
upper one that it becomes eligible for reflexivisation with *Fred* as
antecedent. The formulation of this simplex rule need not invoke
subject, object etc. Nor are the various restrictions on reflexivisation
that have been observed dependent on these relations. On the other
hand, as I shall try to show, many of them, at least, seem to relate to
the distribution of CRs.

3.2.2. Postal (1971), for instance, observed various 'unexpected'
restrictions on reflexivisation (among other things), which he attempted
to relate to a general principle. Some of these restrictions are illustrated
by the (c) sentences in (5):

(5)   1. a. I talked to Thmug about himself
         b.*I talked about himself to Thmug
         c.*I talked about Thmug to himself
      2. a. Charley stabbed himself
         b.*Himself was stabbed by Charley
         c.*Charley was stabbed by himself
      3. a. I believe myself to be clever
         b.*Myself seems to me to be clever
         c.*I seem to myself to be clever

(Postal, 1971, 36, 15, chs. 4 and 22). Postal suggests that the (b)
examples can be excluded by virtue of ordering reflexivisation after
ABOUT-MOVEMENT (which optionally moves the *about*-phrase in front
of the *to*-phrase in sentences realised as (5.1) and after passive ((5.2))
and after psych-movement ((5.3)). However, he notes, this fails to
explain the (lesser degree of) deviance of the (c) sentences.

Reflexives in the clause which acts as host to a NP that has undergone
TOUGH-MOVEMENT (Postal, 1971, ch.3) are also excluded:

(6)   a. It was difficult for me to shave myself
      b.*I was difficult for me to shave
      c.*Myself was difficult for me to shave
      d.* $\left. {I \atop Myself} \right\}$ was difficult for myself to shave

Tough-movement takes a non-subject NP in a predication that has undergone V-raising (2.175.a) and substitutes it for the absolutive/ subject NP in the upper predication, as illustrated by (7):

(7) a. For Harry to fix the car was easy
    b. It was easy for Harry to fix the car
    c. The car was easy for Harry to fix

Tough-movement is thus compatible with cycle-terminating subject-formation and the restriction of raising to absolutive hosts. However, what is of interest in the present context is that, again, only the (b) example in (6) can be excluded by virtue of order, in this instance cyclic: in order for (6.b) to be well-formed, reflexivisation on the cycle applying to the embedded sentence would have to have not applied at the point when, on the next cycle, the object NP is raised in the upper sentence. However, (c), which would appear to constitute the result of raising the reflexive object, is also deviant. Moreover, (6.d), which would result from reflexivisation, after *tough*-movement has applied, of a *for*-phrase which is a constituent of the upper sentence, is also not well-formed. Location of the *for*-phrase in the upper sentence is argued by Postal to be the case for one reading of sentences like (7.b/c), so that the structure underlying (7.a) is one possible source and that underlying (8) another:

(8) ?*To fix the car was easy for Harry

(cf. *Fixing the car was easy for Harry*). Jackendoff (1972, 155) adduces sentences in which both *for*-phrases appear superficially:

(9) It would be easier for me for John to do the job than for me to do it myself

(though he mysteriously stars a sentence of the form of (7.a)). And he argues (1972, 156) that '*Tough*-movement can take place only if the complement subject has been deleted, since every time there is an acceptable *for*-phrase in such sentences, it turns out to be the main clause *for*-phrase'. If this is so, then (6.c) must indeed be added to our set of unexplained gaps in reflexivisation. It also means that *tough*-movement, as an instance of a raising, to some extent obeys the case hierarchy: it is only if the subject is absent that a non-subject NP can be raised by *tough*-movement. (See further § 3.4).

Postal (1971, ch.14) relates these and other anomalies involving coreferential NPs to a principle which he formulates as (10):

(10) Given: a. An arbitrary movement transformation *T* with a structure index *K*, whose *ith* item is NP, and whose operation reorders the *ith* term of proper analyses.
        b. The set of all phrase markers *S* meeting the condition *K* (that is having proper analyses with respect to *K*).
        c. An arbitrary phrase marker *P* which is a member of *S* and whose proper analysis with respect to *T* has NP$_K$ as its *ith* term.

Then: Despite the fact that *P* is a member of *S*, *T* may not apply to *P* if the application path of *T* with respect to *P* is such that this path contains an NP$_j$ coreferential with NP$_k$ and either:

        a. *T* is a *variable movement rule*.
        b. *T* is a *constant movement rule* and NP$_k$ and NP$_j$ are clause mates.

This assumes the definitions in (11):

(11) a. The *application path* of a transformation *T* with respect to a phrase marker *P*: the sequence of constituents in *P* over which a constituent is moved by *T* when it applies to *P* (Postal, 1971, 12

        b. *Variable movement rule* (transformation): one whose structure index contains at least one *essential variable* (rather than end or abbreviatory (clause internal) variables – Postal, 1971, ch.13).
        c. *Constant movement rule* (transformation): one whose structure index does not contain essential variables (*ibid.*).

The rules we have considered with respect to (5)/(6) are all (according to Postal) constant movement rules which when a NP is moved over a reflexive NP by them, or vice versa, as in (5.c) and (6.b-d), cause a violation of principle (10), the 'Crossover Principle'. Jackendoff (1972, ch.4) indicates various inadequacies of such a principle, particularly with regard to the interaction of coreference with variable movement rules. But he also notes some problems with sentences involving the rules we have been looking at here. Though none of these latter are completely destructive for the principle (and Postal, as we shall see, anticipates these objections with some degree of success), it is appropriate in the light of Jackendoff's discussion that we should consider whether some other kind of generalisation might be relevant to the reflexivisation phenomena we are concerned with. I have already indicated (§1.4) that the thematic hierarchy condition proposed by Jackendoff as an alternative to (10) is inadequate to express the relevant generalisation concerning reflexivisation (and see again Gee, 1974*a*). And further examples noted by Green (1974*a*) fail to be accounted for by either crossover or thematic considerations.

3.2.3. Let us record firstly those types noted by Jackendoff as problematical for the crossover formulation. The first of these involves *about*-movement. Jackendoff (1972, 152-3) observes that whereas (5.c) is anomalous, as predicted by the crossover formulation of (10), the corresponding sentence (12.b) is perfectly well-formed:

(12)   a. I talked to myself about myself
        b. I talked about myself to myself

Postal (1971, ch.16, § c) had noted this anomaly and attempted to accommodate it in terms of an analysis whereby sentences containing *about*-phrases have a complex source of the character of, roughly, (13) (for (12)):

(13) $_{S_3}$ [$_{S_1}$ [I talked to me $_{S_1}$] $_{S_2}$ [X was about me $_{S_2}$] $_{S_3}$]

In this case, if reflexivisation is cyclic (Postal, 1971, ch. 16, § F; 1974, § 8.2), it applies on the cycle of S_1 to the *to*-phrase in the structure underlying (12) (but not in that underlying (5.c) in which the sentence corresponding to S_1 in (13) does not meet the conditions for reflexivisation). Now, Postal had already suggested on other grounds (ch. 16, §B) that crossover constraints are obeyed only by NPs that have not undergone some pronominalisation process (like reflexivisation), i.e. NPs that are 'pronominal virgins'. (He incorporates this restriction into the formulations of the crossover principle which subsequently in his discussion replace that given in (10); other modifications are not relevant to our present concerns.) In the present instance, crossover fails to block (12.b) because the *to*-NP that is crossed over by the *about*-phrase is not a pronominal virgin.

This attempt to preserve the integrity of the crossover principle, is, however, rather weak. In the first place, as Postal himself (1971, 153) concedes, 'the proposal that the *about*-phrase starts out in a separate clause, which is fundamental to the whose explanation, has not been independently justified or supported'. Secondly, the pronominal virgin condition is motivated on the basis of phenomena involving *Y*-MOVEMENT, illustrated by (14):

(14) 1. a. Harry, I like
          b. Harry, I bought a book for
          c. Harry, Tony said I insulted
     2. a. Myself, I like
          b. Myself, I bought a book for
          c. *Him_i, $Tony_i$ said I insulted

(14.1) illustrate the application of *Y*-movement (whereby *Harry* is preposed) in the absence of considerations of coreference. (14.2.c) shows the expected violation of the crossover principle. However, the reflexive sentences in (14.2) are (unexpectedly in terms of the formulation (10)) well-formed. Postal attributes this to the order in which the rules apply (reflexivisation, *Y*-movement, pronominalisation), so that at the point at which *Y*-movement applies the object in (14.2.a) is not a pronominal virgin (reflexivisation has occurred) whereas the object in the lower sentence in (2.c) is virginal (pronominalisation is yet to occur). And he goes on to demonstrate that such an ordering has independent motivation. So *Y*-movement as well as the proposed derivation for the *about*-sentences respects the pronominal virgin condition. There is, however, as Postal again concedes (1971, ch.16, § D), a crucial problem in attributing the well-formedness of (12.b) to loss of virginity.

About-movement is, in terms of (11), a constant movement rule, *Y*-movement is a variable movement rule. The latter is post-cyclic, the former ('probably') cyclic (Postal, 1971, 148, n.9). *Tough*-movement is, like *about*-movement, a constant-movement, cyclic rule (though the former ascription is doubtful). However, it fails to obey the pronominal virgin condition, as is shown by (6.c), where a reflexive formed on the cycle applying to the lower clause (as in (6.a)) results in an anomaly when crossed over its antecedent. That is, the post-cyclic rule of *Y*-movement meets the pronominal virgin condition, but the only other cyclic rule (apart from in the derivation Postal proposes for *about*-movement sentences) that involves the relevant factors fails to do so. This suggests that something closer to an explanation for the contrasting statuses of (5.1.c) (6.c) and (12.b) is that offered by George Lakoff and rejected in a footnote by Postal (1971, 152, n.10). Lakoff suggests that the anomalous character of (5.1.c) derives from the fact that 'not only have coreferents crossed, but a pronominal form has crossed its antecedent'. In (12.b), on the other hand, the antecedent of both *myself's* is *I*. Postal objects that in sentences like (14.2. a/b) a reflexive crosses its antecedent without resulting in deviance. However the condition of no antecedent crossing can be maintained if its application is restricted to cyclic rules. Admittedly, it will fail to apply in the case for which it was introduced ((5.1.c) *v.* (12.b)), if Postal's ordering is correct, such that reflexivisation does not precede *about*-movement. However, we shall see below that (5.1.c) can be excluded on other grounds, grounds that allow (12.b) as well-formed; and that a condition that cyclic rules cannot cross reflexives over their antecedents seems to be viable. At any rate, at this point it appears to be just to conclude that the explanation offered by Postal (1971, ch.16, § C) for the viability of (12.b) (as compared with (5.1.c)) is not particularly compelling.

3.2.4. Jackendoff (1972, § 4.10.6) discusses a further restriction associated with reflexives which remains unexplained by the crossover principle. This is illustrated by pairs like (15):

(15)   a.*I sold the slave to himself
      b.*I sold the slave himself

concerning which Postal observes: 'there is apparently some mysterious, independent constraint which prevents the direct and indirect objects from being coreferential in such cases' (1971, 126). However dative movement is formulated, crossover accounts for the anomalous character of only one of these variants, that whose derivation involves movement. Postal, as we have seen, and following him Green, is thus led to propose a quite distinct constraint 'against co-referential noun phrase clause mates in the verb phrase or predicate of a sentence' (Green, 1974*a*, 184-5). Note too that if, as argued in the preceding sections, there is no rule of dative movement, the deviance of neither of (15) can be attributed to violation of the crossover constraint.

Jackendoff points out (1972, 157-8) that the deviance of (15.a) is predicted by the thematic hierarchy condition on reflexives (1972, 148), since the reflexive *to*-phrase, as a goal, is higher on the thematic hierarchy (*1*.28) than its antecedent object, which is theme. (15.b), on the other hand, is in accordance with the thematic hierarchy, but is excluded 'by appeal to the well-known constraint that dative shifts may not move definite pronouns out of post verbal position', as in (16.b):

(16) a. I gave it to John
      b.*I gave John it

or particularly in (17.b):

(17) a. I sold myself to the slave
      b.*I sold the slave myself

where the antecedent of the reflexive lies outside the verb phrase, and which therefore cannot be excluded by Postal's constraint. However, Jackendoff's explanation of the deviance of (15.b) is clearly inadequate, for the following reason. Definite pronouns can be 'moved' from post verbal position if that position is occupied by another such pronoun, as in (18):

(18) a. I gave him it
      b. I sold myself it

Accordingly, (19) are also well-formed:

(19) a. I sold him myself
      b. She gave me herself

But, unfortunately for Jackendoff's explanation, (20):

(20) a.*I sold him himself
      b.*She gave me myself

are not.

Thus, neither the crossover principle nor Jackendoff's account involving the thematic hierarchy condition will account for the double anomaly of (15). Rather, it looks as if Postal's 'mysterious' constraint on VPs is required after all, whichever of these is invoked otherwise. And such a conclusion receives some support from an observation of Green's, who notes that the passives of such sentences, 'where the co-referential noun phrases are no longer both in the predicate, are much more acceptable' (1974, 186). Compare:

(21) 1. a.*The slave-dealers sold Mary to herself
          b.*The slave-dealers sold Mary herself
      2. a. Mary was sold to herself by the slave-dealer

   b. Mary was sold herself by the slave-dealer

((b) is also OK, it seems, as a passive of the type of (2.150) for those speakers who allow such passives in general.) (21.2.a) constitutes yet another direct counter-example to the thematic hierarchy condition and (21.2.b) to the crossover principle (if the *to*-variant represents the basic order; otherwise, (2.a) is counter).

3.2.5. We find, then, that the crossover principle accounts for neither the well-formedness of (21.2.b) and (12.b) nor the deviance of (15.a), or more generally of prepositional examples where there appears to be no question of reordering:

   (22)   *The slave-dealers bought Mary from herself

On the other hand, we have accumulated a further counter-example to the thematic hierarchy condition, as well as discovering forms ((20)) whose deviance it fails to account for. It thus seems worth inquiring whether any formulation invoking grammatical or case relations can achieve greater generality.

   All of the (c) sentences in (5) appear indeed to violate a single condition which I give informally as (23):

   (23)   *Reflexivisation condition I:* the antecedent to a reflexive
        must not be an absolutive.

Whether or not the *about*-phrase in (5.1) originates in a sentence embedded in an absolutive, at the point at which reflexivisation occurs it must be a clause mate of the *to*-phrase; if it has a subordinate source, by coming to occupy the absolutive slot in the upper clause (so that it is eligible for passivisation etc.). Similarly, whether or not the derivation of (5.3.c) includes something like psych-movement, at the point at which reflexivisation occurs *I* is fairly uncontroversially absolutive. So too apparently *Charley* in (5.2.c); however, we shall have occasion to look again at both these assumptions below. Similarly the absolutive character of the subject in (6) excludes (6.d) as a reflexive sentence, though (6.b) remains deviant on account of a violation of the cyclic principle. Thus the absolutive character of an antecedent seems on the basis of such examples to underlie the kind of deviations which originally motivated the formulation of the crossover principle. It remains to be seen whether it is also relevant in those situations which were resistant to a crossover (or thematic hierarchy) account.

However, as far as the main theme of the present section is concerned, it is already clear that, however subject-formation is formulated, neither subject nor object status appears to be relevant in determining the well-formedness of reflexive sentences. Thus, the Reflexivisation Law of relational grammar will be necessarily relatively weak. It merely requires (Pullum, 1975*c*) 'that only terms can control Reflexivisation'. It follows from the range of examples that we have discussed that this is not a sufficient condition for reflexivisation: there are many instances of terms that do not control a viable reflexive. Unfortunately, as Pullum (1975*c*) observes, it is possible that it is not even a necessary condition: it may be false. If reflexivisation makes reference to 'cycle-final term structure' (i.e. the relevant terms are those at the end of the appropriate cycle), and if a sentence like *I was told lies by a beautiful girl about herself* is both well-formed and an example of ordinary reflexivisation, then the Reflexivisation Law must be weakened even further. Pullum (1975*c*, 4) suggests: 'Only a term can control the reflexivisation of a term'. However, this is fulfilled in most if not all cases quite trivially, taking together the requirement that, as Pullum puts it, 'The antecedent for Reflexivisation must precede the victim at the stage for which the process is defined', and the fact that almost universally (in English at least) only terms precede terms throughout the cycle. Indeed it is possible that the sentence containing the NP whose non-reflexivisability Pullum proposes to explain in part on the basis of his revised formulation of the Reflexivisation Law, is the only type of example where it applies non-trivially. And its relevance here is in doubt. He argues, as I understand it, that the sentence **I asked about the long-haired, somewhat eccentric young man who claimed he did the major part of the rescue work single-handed himself* is deviant because it requires that a non-term (*about . . . single-handed*) reflexivise a term (II → *himself*). But he does not argue for these termhood assignments. Moreover the argument depends upon complex NP shift being cycle-terminating rather than part of the shallow structure linearisation filter (cf. § 1.11). And, apart from this, such a sentence is excluded anyway by the constraint that also applies with dative shifts, such that simple objective pronouns cannot occupy such a position away from the verb. Thus, the existence of any 'reflexivisation law' that can be defined in terms of relational grammar is in doubt.

Principle (23), however, also accords with the deviance of (24):

(24) a.*The car is beside itself
b.*The castle occupies itself

with absolutive subject and locational phrase, and with that of the directionals in (25):

(25) a.*The marble rolled to itself
b.*The marble reached itself

as well as the absolutive locative subject sentence in (26):

(26) *The $\begin{Bmatrix} \text{bees} \\ \text{hive} \end{Bmatrix}$ swarm(s) with $\begin{Bmatrix} \text{themselves} \\ \text{itself} \end{Bmatrix}$

Such sentences, I suggest, reveal the semantic basis for the principle, viz. the avoidance of using an entity as its own reference object in a predication of location. By the principle this is widened to include all absolutive-antecedent reflexives. (It could however be argued (though I shall not pursue this) that all the deviant reflexives we have looked at involve not only an antecedent absolutive, but also as part of the same complex CR or as clause mate a locative: the principle then remains natural.) The crucial role of absolutive is again revealed by the well-formedness of directional sentences like (27):

(27) Fred received a $\begin{Bmatrix} \text{letter} \\ \text{present} \end{Bmatrix}$ from himself

with [loc, erg] subject. Let us return in the light of this to those examples resistant to the other accounts we have scrutinised.

3.2.6. We should note in the first place, with Jackendoff (1972, § 4.10.3), that while the well-formedness of (12.b) is difficult to square with an account which attributes the deviance of (5.3.c) to a movement which violates crossover (and we have seen that Postal's attempt to do so is not entirely successful), it is unproblematic in terms of the thematic condition or condition 1 in (23) which refer to the relations which the arguments contract. Under either account both *myself's* in (12) have a well-formed antecedent in the subject, which is an agent. However, the thematic hierarchy condition fails to predict the deviance of (15.b) which moreover, when a pronominal indirect object is involved, as in (20), cannot be attributed to an independent constraint on movement of pronouns. The thematic relations in (15.a) and (b) are the same, but whereas their order in (15.a) offends the thematic hierarchy condition (theme as antecedent, goal as reflexive), that in (15.b) and (20) is unexceptionable (goal as antecedent, theme as reflexive). In terms of the analysis of indirect objects developed in the immediately preceding sections, on the other hand, the relations in (15.a) and (15.b) differ; specifically, the goal (locative) in (15.b) is also absolutive once it has been raised out of the embedded directional sentence whose subject it is: cf. (2.188). Thus, (15.b) and (20), as well as (15.a), offend against reflexivisation condition 1, if this continues to apply throughout the derivation, in that the antecedent is in all these instances an absolutive.

3.2.7. Postal (1971, 36, 15) attributed the deviance of (5.b) to an infringement of ordering: they are excluded if *about*-movement, passive and psych-movement all precede reflexivisation. This does not conflict with the present analysis, except that it represents a quite arbitrary use of extrinsic ordering, for which Postal offers only the following motivation:

> The argument is the great difference in degree of syntactic deviance between [(5.c)] and [(5.b)]. While the sentences of [(5.c)] are only subtly deviant, those of [(5.b)] are crashingly unacceptable. Our explanation of this difference is that, while *both* of the examples involve some violation of a principle which excludes joint application of passive and reflexivisation to the same clause [(5.b)] involves, in addition, a violation of ordering. It is this extra violation that explains why the sentences of [(5.b)] type are so much further from well-formedness than those of the type [(5.c)]. Alternatively, we might say simply that ordering violations are much worse and yield more severe types of deviance than the types of violation illustrated by [(5.c)] (1971, 15).

Extrinsic ordering of cyclic rules is rather difficult to support (G. Lakoff, 1972*a*; Koutsoudas, 1972; Lehmann, 1972; Ringen, 1972; Postal, 1974, § 8.3). I assume here that rules apply simply whenever their structural description is satisfied, within the constraints of the cycle (though the principle of cyclic application may itself be contingent); and that if there are two or more rules whose structural indices are met simultaneously in a derivation, those rules will be applied simultaneously, unless some general principle supervenes. What is excluded, then, is a requirement that certain rules must apply arbitrarily in a certain order in order to account for varying acceptabilities. If such a position is tenable, as it promises to be, the ordering explanation for the deviance of (5.b) is excluded in principle. Moreover, in the present instance, it does not accord with the full range of relevant phenomena.

Notice that whereas (5.b) are excluded by Postal on the basis of a rule-ordering infringement, in the case of (6.c), 'the grammar predicts ... that [(6.c)] should be well-formed and the mystery is why it is not' (Postal, 1971, 31). And the mystery is resolved with reference to the crossover principle (1971, 63-4). However, it seems to me that (6.c) is fully as 'crashingly unacceptable' as (5.b), rather than displaying the 'subtle deviance' of (5.c). It is therefore unfortunate that whereas (6.b) are excluded with reference to rule-ordering (6.c) is grouped with (5.c) as representing an infringement of crossover. It is the more unfortunate in view of the fact that a simple generalisation serves to exclude both (6.c) and (5.b), one which I give informally as (28):

(28) *Reflexivisation condition 2:* the pronominal must not precede its antecedent

which holds up to shallow structure. As we have seen, it does not apply to such post-cyclic processes as *Y*-movement. The up-to-shallow-structure character of condition 2 also accounts for the fact that sentences like *Harry believes himself to be easy for John to please* lack a reading in which *himself* is coreferential with John. Lightfoot (1974, 154-5) points out, however, that given a rule of *tough*-movement, in terms of Jackendoff's cyclic inter-pretation rule for reflexives *himself* would be marked as coreferential with both *John* (on the *please*-cycle) and *Harry* (on the *believe*-cycle). (Of course Jackendoff's formulation can be saved in terms of an account involving *tough*-deletion rather than *tough*-movement (see below).)

3.2.8. Since (28) will also apply at the point at which reflexivisation occurs, and thus will account for the deviance of *Himself$_i$ killed John$_i$*, etc., the conditions for reflexivisation can simply be formulated as in (29):

(29) REFLEXIVISATION:
      S.D.:   case$_1$ $\leftrightarrow$ N$_1$, case$_2$ $\leftrightarrow$ N$_2$
      conditions: 1) case$_1$ $\neq$ [abs] (up to shallow structure; if N$_1$
               and N$_2$ are clausemates – i.e. if (4) holds)
            2) case$_1$ $\ll$ case$_2$ (up to shallow structure)

$$3) \ N_1 \text{ and } N_2 \text{ are coreferential}$$
$$4) \ \exists \ V_i (V_i \not\Rightarrow case_1 , V_i \not\Rightarrow case_2)$$

Condition (2) is as suggested above (28); condition (3) simply requires coreference; and (4) is the clausemate condition. We have in condition (1) added to the formulation in (23) the provision that it be met at least up to shallow structure, and also that it only holds at a particular point in a derivation if condition (4) also holds. So that (15.a) and (24) are excluded on the cycle on which reflexivisation occurs and (15.b) is excluded once the locative subject of the lower predication is raised into absolutive position and the lower V subjoined to the upper, with the result that *the slave* and *himself* are again clausemates.[40] However, a sentence like *Fred caused Bill to cut himself,* if it involves raising of *Bill* to absolutive, is not excluded in so far as *Bill* is at no point thereafter a clausemate of *himself.* All of the deviant possibilities discussed in the preceding involve an infringement of one or other of these conditions.

There are signs that the clausemate condition should be imposed on (29.2) as well as (1). I.e. derivations block as a consequence of an infringement of either (1) or (2) only if (4) is also met. In the latter instance, this is suggested by some observations of Postal's (1974, 275-6, n.6). Observe that complex NP shift (whether cyclic or part of shallow structure linearisation) can move an antecedent over its reflexive provided that they have ceased to be clausemates. In an example like Postal's *I believe to have talked about himself on the boat – the man who offered to sell me the rotten oats,* the antecedent subject of the lower clause has been raised into object position in the upper (thus, of course ceasing to be a clausemate of the reflexive), and thereby becomes eligible for complex NP shift, even though as a result (29.2) as it stands is infringed. It thus looks as if the up to shallow structure clausemate condition should apply to both (1) and (2) in (29). This revision does not detract from the account provided by (29) of the anomalies previously considered; it merely increases the plausibility of the condition we found it necessary to impose on (29.1). Accordingly, these reflexivisation phenomena provide strong support for the case grammar framework in which subject-formation is cycle-terminating, in that subject-formation itself destroys information crucial to (29), in particular (29.1).

3.2.9. There remain however, those instances of reflexivisation, illustrated by (21.2), which are unexpectedly well-formed (with respect

to the crossover or thematic hierarchy formulations). We have been able
to eliminate Postal's constraint on VPs (excluding coreferential NPs
therein) in favour of the more general reflexivisation condition 1.
However the VP constraint does at least predict the well-formedness of
(21.2), in which the reflexive's antecedent has been moved out of the
VP. Whereas, if passives share the same set of CRs as the corresponding
actives, prior to subject-formation, then the contrasting statuses of
(21.1) and (21.2) cannot be related to condition 1 in (29). Thus,
either Postal's constraint must be invoked after all, even more
'mysteriously', or passives differ in their CRs from the corresponding
actives. Moreover, they must differ in such a way that the acceptability
of (21.2) is allowed for but (5.2.b/c) continue to be marked by the
grammar as deviant. I suggest that an account which succeeds in doing
this in terms of independently motivated constraints is preferable,
other things being equal, to one which must invoke Postal's mysterious
constraint. Let us then consider what the set of CRs characterising
passive sentences must be, assuming the rules of (2.56-.57), and of
course envisaging that these CRs might differ from those in the
corresponding active. The section that follows will be devoted to
establishing this and to a consideration of some of the wider consequences
of adopting such a view of passives as is advocated there.

3.3 Reflexivisation, Passives and Equi

3.3.1. If sentences like (21.2) are not to fall foul of condition 1 in (29),
then their subjects must not be absolutive. But only absolutives and
ergatives occur as subjects. (This follows from the hierarchy of cases
and the necessary presence in any predication of an abs.) Therefore, the
subject of a passive must be an erg. However passives also can contain a
distinct agent, marked by *by*. Since only one erg is permitted per
predication, passive sentences must have a complex source. The subject
of the superordinate sentence in a passive configuration, we have
established, is an erg. It is however not agentive: in *John was carefully
smothered*, care is not being attributed to John. Erg is not agentive in
locational/directional sentences. The 'main verb' is dependent on the
auxiliary *be*, which has the passive ergative phrase as its subject. If the
passive *be* takes the main verb as a complement, this is in accordance
with natural serialisation (head + modifier), and also with
concord/government. Elsewhere (Anderson, 1975*a*) I try to show that
concord goes from dependent to governor (here, from subject to
auxiliary) whereas government is exercised by a governor of its
dependent (here, the participial form of the verb demanded by the

auxiliary). Also, the governing 'auxiliary' is optional; Anderson (1975*a*) again argues that such instances of apparently optional predicate governors involve an optional superordinate predication. The lower ('main') verb has thus undergone verb raising (*2.175.a*) to the 'auxiliary'. All such verbs originate in an absolutive phrase dependent on the upper V (see too the discussion of equi below). The position of the *by*-phrase in a passive is anomalous for an ergative, which is highest in the subject-forming hierarchy; its position is that to be expected of abl or loc, specifically a loc or abl that is dependent on *be*, if the passive is locational. In a predication which contains both an erg and a loc (+ abl), the erg is combined in a multiple CR with abs, abl, or loc. The subject erg in a passive is not absolutive (not to infringe reflexivisation condition 1, and because the lower sentence is embedded in abs). It is therefore also loc or abl. Conversely, the *by*-phrase is either abl or loc. Predications with locative ergative subjects are less complex (in terms of the set of features required to specify them) than those with ablative ergatives. Passives, then, to gather these observations together, are most easily allowed for if they involve a superordinate predication which is directional and ergative, and in which erg is combined with loc and a lower predication is embedded in the absolutive argument — i.e. if passives involve a structure such as is indicated in (30):

(30)

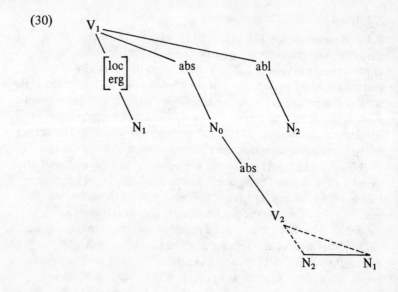

V_1 is exactly of the character suggested above ($(2.54.a)$) as a characterisation of *receive,* and thus permits a very natural notional characterisation of passives: 'N_1 receive (N_2 V N_1) from N_2'. Compare Gildersleeve & Lodge, 1897, 151: 'The Passive Voice denotes that the *subject receives the action* of the verb'.

Actually, the source of *be*-passives is slightly more complex, I would suggest, in that the *be* originates as the head of a predication superordinate to V_1 in (30), and V_1 is subjoined to this higher predicate: see Anderson, 1975*b*. (30) is probably more appropriate to the *get* passive. This is not crucial to the present discussion. Notice, however, that the appearance here of *get* is apparently natural (cf. § 3.4), and the occurrence of some such locative-subject verb is replicated in a number of languages (cf. Anderson, 1972, § II). However, this is not a simple matter to establish since discussions of passives often take them together with inchoative constructions (involving a 'become' verb) based on the 'passive participle' of the 'main verb'. And *get* apparently occurs as both an inchoative and a locative-subject verb. In the present instance, however, the locative-subject interpretation is favoured by the reflexivisation phenomena we have observed which require that the subject of a passive be non-absolutive. *By* in English, on the other hand, is not synchronically, it would appear, very natural as marker of an ablative argument. Other languages show more natural markers (Anderson, *ibid.*), though again such constructions are often collapsed in discussion with ('dative-agent') constructions like that proposed below for psych-movement verbs (on this cf. Benveniste, 1952). We return below in § 3.5 to a possible partial explanation for the English situation.

Such a source also permits a derivation from which the idiosyncratic passive transformation can be eliminated. All that is involved is a double application of equi (whereby the upper N_1 and N_2 delete the lower N_1 and N_2, respectively), verb raising, and subjunction of the empty, non-governing absolutive phrase to V_1, a process which I shall propose in a moment as a component of all derivations involving equi. Such a motivation (towards constraining the form of transformations) was also behind Hasegawa's (1968) proposal concerning the passive, which however retained an idiosyncratic NP-movement component whose role was to reorder the underlying subject of V_2. Here, this too is eliminated. I claim in general, as indicated above, that all apparent cyclic simplex NP-movement transformations involve raising or equi.

3.3.2. Chomsky (1970*a*, 219, note 29) professes some scepticism concerning Hasegawa's proposals. However, he provides no defence of the simplex, transformational account of passives, and his specific objections are uncompelling. Consider his first observation: 'A serious obection, it seems to me, is that there are phrases which can appear as subject only in the passive construction'. In support of this he adduces the triple in (31):

> (31) 1. a. A man to do the job was found by John
>   b. John found a man to do the job
>   2. A man to do the job came to see me

He describes (31.2), as compared with (31.1.a), in which the subject originates in object position (as in (31.1.b)), as 'highly unnatural'. Now, it seems to me that whatever difference in 'naturalness' there is between (31.1.a) and (31.2) provides rather a slim basis for rejecting the type of analysis for which Hasegawa argues. Moreover, the argument is loaded by the choice of examples. It is possible to discover instances with the phrase *a man to do the job* in subject position in a non-passive which are at least the equal of (31.1.a) in 'naturalness', as, say, in (32):

> (32) A man to do the job will always turn up

It is clear that whatever 'unnaturalness' can be attributed to (31.2) is not due simply to absence of passivisation. Chomsky's objection therefore does not go through.

The only other evidence he offers as a basis for his scepticism involves certain idiomatic expressions, concerning which he observes: 'there are certain idioms that undergo passivisation . . . although the phrase that appears as grammatical subject cannot normally appear as a deep subject'. And he offers the following examples:

> (33) a. I didn't expect that offence would be taken at that remark
>   b. Advantage was taken of John

Freidin (1975, 403) makes a general point concerning the use of data of this character: 'it does not seem advisable to try to justify the existence of a rule on the basis of constructions whose behavior is so idiosyncratic'. Moreover the restrictions involved are not well understood. As well as (33), for instance, which have a viable corresponding active, there are apparently transitive idiom structures which lack a passive:

(34) Fred kicked the bucket on Tuesday

and apparent passives without a corresponding active:

(35) A great time was had by all

But apart from this, despite the fact that Chomsky (1970*a*, 220) avers that 'such facts are difficult to reconcile with the proposal that the passive derives from a matrix proposition with an embedded complement', it is far from obvious what the force of his argument is intended to be. Chomsky cannot literally mean that the NPs that occur in subject position in the passives in (33) do not otherwise appear in subject position. For many of them, at least, this is untrue: consider, for instance, *Advantage lies with the aggressor*. If he means that they do not otherwise occur in such a position with the interpretation they receive in (33), this is because that interpretation depends on the NPs being in underlying representations the absolutive arguments of their respective verbs, together with which they constitute an idiom. But this does not preclude their also being subjects to the passive verb, particularly if lexicalisation is cyclic, in which case the insertion of the lexical forms that function as subject of the passive verb can follow its specification as abs by equi. Furthermore, there is no reason why equi itself should not perform the 'lexical insertion'. Equi is then simply a raising into a coreferential N rather than an empty one. Indeed, such a derivation expresses the generalisation that lexicalisation in the upper clause is not independent of the coreference relation holding between one of its arguments and an (already lexicalised) argument in the embedded sentence. At any rate, the whole issue can be decided only when we have a better understanding of the status of idioms.

3.3.3. The source for passives I have outlined differs from Freidin's (1975) 'lexicalist' treatment in one major respect: in the latter, N_1 and N_2 (cf. (30)) occur only once each in the underlying representation, in that the upper occurrence of N_2 and the lower of N_1 are absent and there is thus no equi. The structure is thus simplex, V_2 is the main predicate (an adjective) and V_1 is a quite distinct category, a 'copula'. Observe that this immediately destroys the generalisation concerning serialisation which is possible if V_1 and V_2 are predicates: the sequence is in accord with the natural serialisation for a centrifugal or right-modifying language in that V_2 originates in a modifier of V_1. It also seems to me that Freidin fails to overcome, for instance, what he

210   *On the Nature of Grammatical Relations*

admits to be 'the most serious drawback' (1975, 401) to a lexicalist analysis for the passive, namely the existence of passives like (36):

(36) The turtle was given an ear of corn (by the keeper)

If this is to be generated directly by the phrase structure rules, we require something of the character of (37):

(37) AP → A (NP) (PP)

(if passive verbs originate as the heads of adjective phrases). There is however only rather tenuous independent evidence for such a rule. Freidin offers such sentences as (38):

(38) a. This is too difficult a problem to give to a beginner
      b. Harold is so obnoxious a person that not even his
          analyst can stand listening to him

The obligatory presence of a submodifier (*so/too*) seems to be something of a problem here. But apart from this, for these to provide evidence for (37), Freidin has to show (a) that this is indeed an appropriate structure to suggest for the sentences in (38), and (b) that this structure is not derived. This he fails to do. Actually, I would have thought that sentences like *Fred is like Bill in adoring Wensleydale* were more promising than (38) with respect to (37). But this too requires to be motivated. The accommodation of (36) thus as it stands necessitates on a lexicalist analysis an otherwise unwarranted extension to the expansions for AP.

Freidin's arguments against non-lexicalist analyses (1975, § 2), on the other hand, prove to be rather insubstantial. One of these is directed against deriving 'non-statal' short (*by*-less) passives by deletion of pro-element. This, he claims, or so I understand it, is inadequate semantically (p. 387), in that sentences like those in (39):

(39) a. Germany was defeated
      b. Jane was elected president of the club

are more appropriately paraphrased by (40)

(40) a. Germany was defeated by her enemies
      b. Jane was elected president of the club by a majority of

the members.

than by sentences containing a pro-form *by*-phrase. But it is mistaken to attribute the same semantic characterisation to the corresponding sentences in (39) and (40). The fact, if it is a fact, that (39) are often understood in the same way as (40) is based on pragmatic considerations. It is, e.g., often the case that when someone is defeated it is by his enemies. However situations occur, as described in, say, (41):

(41) a. Germany was defeated by her own incompetence
      b. Jane was elected president of the club by the committee

where (39) but not (40) can be used appropriately. Thus (39) do not have the same semantic interpretation as either (40) or (41). Rather, they are often used in the same situation as one or the other. But this is irrelevant to the point at issue.

Freidin also notes that various verbs (like *resemble*), though apparently transitive, do not passivise; and he claims that this is not accounted for either by some independent constraint or by the form of the passive transformation. This is at best a rather inconclusive observation. Moreover, most if not all of the verbs listed by Freidin do indeed lack a property shared by verbs that passivise, i.e. a property which must be specified as in part determining whether a passive variant is viable. Namely, their subjects do not (before subject-formation) bear an ergative relation. This single generalisation accounts for the lack of a passive with *resemble* and for the failure of such reflexives as **Fred resembles himself,* in that the subject is an abs rather than erg.

3.3.4. If then, as seems reasonably plausible on the basis of the preceding, passive sentences are to be characterised in terms of an underlying structure containing the configuration in (30), the well-formedness of (21.2) is accounted for independently of Postal's constraint, as is the deviance of both (21.1) and (5.2.b/c). Let us now consider why this is so, in the first instance with (5.2.b/c).

Given an underlying structure of the character of (30), reflexivisation can occur on either the V_2 or the V_1 cycle, but since reflexivisation is obligatory, on the first cycle on which the SD is met. With (5.2.b/c), reflexivisation must apply on the first cycle, in that N_1 is coreferential with N_2, and all the other conditions are met. Now, if we interpret equi as suggested above (§ 2.7), i.e. as involving superimposing the lower identical N, with its CRs on to the upper N, then passivisation will involve an infringement of condition 2 on reflexivisation (29), as revealed in (5.2.b): thus there is no viable passive corresponding to (5.2.a). (5.2.c), on the other hand, would require that reflexivisation not occur (contrary to its obligatory character) on the lower cycle but only on the second (V_1).

There is, as we have seen, no reflexive of the character of (21.1). This is because the antecedent is absolute and thus violates condition 1 on reflexivisation. Similarly, with (21.2) there will be no reflexivisation on the first (V_2) cycle (ignoring the complex underlying *sell*). However, on the V_1 cycle, after V-raising the conditions for both reflexivisation and equi are met in both instances, and they can apply simultaneously:

(42) a.

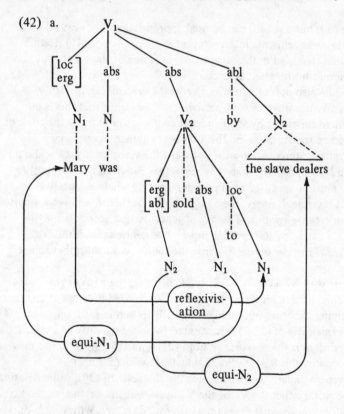

(42) b.

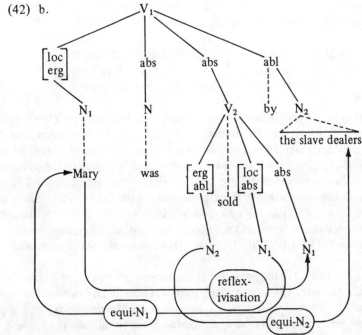

This requires that the sequence V-abs-V, as opposed to V-loc-V for non-auxiliary complement structures (cf. § 1.10), constitutes a simplex, i.e. is equivalent to V. (However, under the analysis alluded to above whereby *be* originates in another, superordinate (to V_1) predication, V_2 will be subjoined to V_1 anyway.) If this is a viable and plausible derivation, then all of the phenomena we have surveyed are accounted for by a formulation of reflexivisation which includes crucially a reference to the CR abs (in condition 1 in (29)) rather than to any grammatical relation.

It is possible moreover that the character of the antecedent can be even more narrowly constrained: almost all of the viable antecedents we have looked at have borne the CR erg (plus or minus some other non-absolutive CR). An exception, though, is (5.1.a), where the antecedent is a *to*-phrase (with no great claims on ergativity). However, it is possible that the situation exemplified by (5.1) can be allowed for otherwise. Specifically, suppose that *talk* is formed by incorporating a noun like 'information' into it from a dependent absolutive. The *about*-phrase is then originally a dependent of this noun. (5.1) in that case illustrates rather than 'ordinary reflexivisation' one kind of reflexivisation associated with 'picture-nouns' (Jackendoff, 1972,

§ 4.12; Postal, 1974, 64). That is, (5.1) is allowed for by the same principle, whatever its character, as allows for, say, (43):

(43) a.   I recounted to John a story about himself
     b. (*)I recounted a story about himself to John
     c.   *I recounted a story about John to himself

If such a derivation can be substantiated, then we can propose this even more specific form for reflexivisation condition 1. Notice too, however, that the viability of such a derivation would also mean that the argument of § 1.10 in favour of order in pre-shallow structures which was constructed on the basis of the interaction of psych-movement and passive with condition 2 on reflexivisation is invalid. This is because in all the instances that remain (if (5.1) are discounted) we can now associate with lack of ergativity of the antecede the deviance that was on the basis of (5.1) attributed to infringement of cond ition 2 of (29), i.e. to the fact of the reflexive preceding the antecedent.

3.3.5. Crucial to the preceding discussion of passives was the proposal that their derivation involves the application of equi (indeed two applications per passive). As such these derivations displayed properties which I am going to suggest are common to all applications of equi, specifically the following:

(44) *Equi properties:*

     a. Equi, like subject-raising, applies to the configuration produced by V-raising.
     b. Equi, like subject-raising, involves raising of an argument from an embedded sentence into the main clause.
     c. Equi, unlike subject-raising, does not utilise the absolutive N as a host.
     d. Equi, unlike subject-raising, utilises as a host a non-absolutive N identical to the raised N.
     e. Equi obeys the case hierarchy in selecting the argument(s) to be raised.
     f. Equi involves the subjunction of the main clause absolutive to its predicate.

What is most relevant to our present concerns is the generalisation, already noted in the course of previous discussions, that, in so far as reference is made to main clause relations, equi apparently involves reference to CRs (though as formulated in (44.c-.d) still rather trivially) whereas the relevant relations in the embedded sentence are post-subject-formation. And we must determine rather more precisely the character of the properties summarised in (44.c-.e); in particular, we must determine whether or not an attempt to render this characterisation if possible more specific continues to support the proposal that subject-formation is cycle-terminating. This we take up in the following section. (44.a-.b) I shall not pursue: their import is, I think, reasonably clear from the preceding discussion. I merely note here that we can associate with these shared operations a further common property: both raising and equi are linked with de-finitisation of the embedded S (Postal, 1974, 60, n.7). However (44.f) does require some further comment, I think, and I would like to dispose of it before proceeding with (44.c-.e).

3.3.6. The problem we encountered in ch.2 in connection with the indeterminacy of erg with respect to agency was resolved in § 2.8 by proposing a complex source for verbs like *buy* and *sell,* so that the agentive erg of examples (*2.*112.a/b) etc. originates in a non-locational upper predication, whereas the non-agentive erg associated with the subject of *receive* etc. is an original CR to the directional clause. So the generalisation is: erg is agentive in a non-locational clause. Clearly this requires that causative directional verbs like transitive *move* have a complex source. So that the case specification for *move* is as in (45):

(45)
$$\left(\begin{array}{c} \begin{bmatrix} V \\ erg \end{bmatrix} \\ | \\ abs \end{array}\right)$$
$$\begin{bmatrix} V \\ loc \\ abl \end{bmatrix}$$

the option including [V, erg] being associated with (*2.5.*c), *John moved the stone,* that lacking it with (*2.5.*a), *The stone moved.* However, the same considerations will require that the intransitive agentive *move* of (*2.5.*b), *John moved,* also have a complex source, of the character of (46) (which again ignores sequence):

(46)

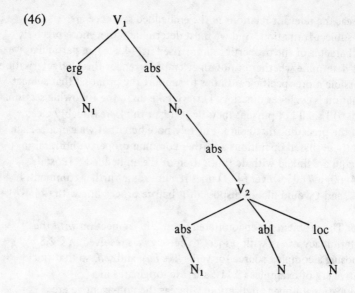

The derivation can proceed as with the passive, i.e. via verb-raising, subjunction of N_0 and equi; but also with subjunction of V_2 to V_1, resulting in (47):

(47)

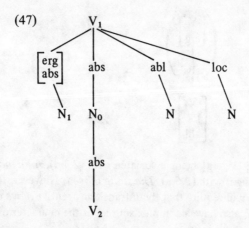

Thus, this possibility is allowed for if the specification in (45) is enlarged after the fashion of (48):

(48)

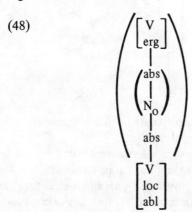

(The derivation of (47) involves a violation of the single argument subjunction condition (p.166): possibly this is allowed with an 'empty' node.)

Crawl, on the other hand, as necessarily causative intransitive, will require (49):

(49)

$$\begin{bmatrix} V \\ erg \end{bmatrix}$$
$$|$$
$$abs$$
$$|$$
$$N_o$$
$$|$$
$$abs$$
$$|$$
$$\begin{bmatrix} V \\ loc \\ abl \end{bmatrix}$$

with all components obligatory, whereas the transitive *throw* will be simply (50):

(50)

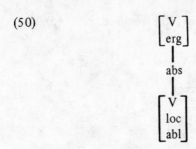

(Of course these latter will also incorporate further components specifying manner of locomotion/projection.)

Various considerations favour such a derivation (apart from the fact that it involves only processes also required for passives and conventional instances of equi). Notice that intransitive causatives thereby end up, like intransitive non-causatives such as *work,* via equi, with a [abs, erg] argument. This is important in determining the morphology of a language like Basque, in which all absolutives, whether or not they are also ergative, are given the same (nominative) marker. If, however, intransitive agentives like *move* involved a derivation including raising, rather than equi, followed by deletion of a reflexive object, a new rule transferring the abs of the deleted object to the ergative subject would have to be introduced for these languages, in order to achieve the appropriate assignment of cases. (But see § 3.5.6.)

Such a (raising) derivation would also require us to mark *move* as a verb that permits deletion of a reflexive object, whereas *crawl* requires (that its object be reflexive and) that the reflexive be deleted, whereas *throw* forbids deletion of a reflexive:

(51) a. John moved (himself)
      b. John crawled (*himself)   } towards the window
      c. John threw himself

But this distribution of reflexives follows from the specifications of (48), (49) and (50) respectively. *Crawl* (49) is inserted with respect to a subjunction tree which contains an absolutive N, so that there cannot be an absolutive available on which to form the reflexive; in other words the derivation of *crawl* is required by the lexical specification of (49) to have undergone equi and not raising. The converse is true of *throw,* whose lexical specification does not include abs-N_0 and which therefore must result from a derivation involving raising and not equi: it cannot thus be intransitive. *Move,* however, allows both derivations by virtue of the optional abs-N_O of (48).

Some further, marginal support for the positing of a transitive superordinate as underlying these agentive intransitives derives from the occasional reflex (as *it*) of the posited N_O in notionally intransitive sentences such as *We hot-footed it to the border* or *They made it to the border*. However, more interesting is the consequences of the immediately preceding discussion for the analysis of passives.

3.3.7. Above I proposed a derivation for English passives which involved a double application of equi. Suppose we substitute raising for one of these. In the case of N_2 such a possibility is blocked, in that if the lower N_2 in (30) is raised into the upper absolutive, it simply becomes the illegitimate (absolutive) antecedent to an ablative reflexive. However, suppose that, moving down the hierarchy, N_1 is raised into the upper absolutive. All the conditions for reflexivisation are thereby satisfied. Now, if the English *get*-passive shares at least the configuration in (30) with the *be*-passive, then the normal development via equi results in such sentences as (52):

(52) Fred got flattened by a bus

But *get* seems also to allow the raising possibility predicted for a structure such as (30), as illustrated by (the non-agentive-subject interpretion of) (53):

(52) Fred got himself flattened by a bus

So whatever else characterises the difference between *get* and *be*-passives (Hasegawa, 1968; R. Lakoff, 1971; Matthews, 1973; Gee, 1974b), one distinction seems to be that whereas the *be*-derivation is like that for *crawl*, in requiring equi and rejecting raising, the *get*-passive allows, like *move*, either equi or raising (for N_1).

Clearly, too, the raising derivation will underly the reflexive passives in, for example, Icelandic, or the Romance languages (for discussion, see Hadley, 1867; Key, 1851, 1874; Anderson, 1972). The last of these discussions shows (§ II) that all that need be added to the above account of reflexive *get*-passives in English to allow for a reflexive passive like Portuguese *Louva-se o capitão* ('The captain praises himself' = 'The captain is praised') is subjunction of the 'main verb' to the passive (as I suggested for the derivation of the *be*-passive). There too it is observed that reflexive passives also display both 'short' (agentiveless) and 'long' forms, and that passive (or impersonal) intransitives like Latin *pugnabatur,* ('It was fought') (Gray, 1939, 218-20; on Sanskrit see too Gonda, 1951) are matched by reflexive impersonals like Romanian forms such as *Se pleacă mîine* ('It is being left tomorrow' = 'They (indefinite) are leaving tomorrow'; Sandfeld & Olsen, 1936, § 125). All this is unsurprising in the light of the analysis sketched out here.

Notice finally on the subject of (44.f) as a property of equi that there are more traditional equi verbs, like *expect* or *want,* which show the two derivational possibilities we have associated with *move* and with the *get*-passive, as illustrated by (54):

    (54) a. Mario wants (himself) to be elected
           b. Melvin expected (himself) to do better than that

(For discussion of such verbs, see Postal, 1974, § 4.16.) This is again allowed for if the lexical specification for these verbs contains an optional abs-N_o component.

3.3.8. Before proceeding with our main theme, let us note that the kind of extension of equi analyses to passives and intransitive causatives that was proposed above can also encompass rather plausibly psych-movement variants. Postal (1971, chs. 6 and 22) and others have argued that sentences such as those in (55):

    (55) a. Schwarz is loathsome to me
           b. Billy is irritating to me
           c. Fred seems to me to be a fool
           d. It is lucky for you that Bill won

have undergone the rule of psych-movement, which 'is formally similar to passive in that it moves an NP from a grammatical subject position into the predicate and causes it to be supplied with a preposition, usually *to* but occasionally *for* . . . At the same time, the rule moves an NP from the predicate into grammatical subject position' (Postal, 1971, 39). Thus, the corresponding sentences in (56) indicate more accurately, on this view, the underlying grammatical relations:

    (56) a. I loathe Schwarz
           b. I am irritated at/with Billy
           c. I believe Fred to be a fool
           d. You are lucky that Bill won

These differ in various ways from the examples in (55), apart from in interpretation, and Postal is careful to avoid suggesting a simple transformational relationship, except perhaps in the case of the (d) examples. The others differ in word class of the main predicate (adjective/noun – (a)), in adjective-suffix (b) and even lexically (c). However, if lexical insertion is cyclic, then all of these distinctions can be contingent upon the respective presences of the configurations resulting from application *v.* non-application of the rule. If, further, there is involved here, as in the case of passive, not just a rule but the presence of a superordinate predication of some sort, then the differences (including that in interpretation) can be related to this or to the presence of the CRs which the superordinate introduces. I return to this in a moment.

Postal observes in justification of psych-movement the shared grammatical relations and selectional restrictions of (55)/(56) – cf. *Schwarz is loathsome to the rock / *The rock loathes Schwarz* – and the crossover violations associated with the psych-movement variants that we have discussed. Recall distributions like:

(57) 1. a.*Schwarz is loathsome to himself
      b.*Billy is irritating to himself
      c.*Fred seems to himself to be a fool
   2. a. I loathe myself
      b. I am irritated at/with myself
      c. I believe myself to be a fool

((57.1.a) is acceptable to some under the irrelevant agentive interpretation 'Schwarz behaves towards himself in a loathsome fashion'.) An argument from shared selectional restrictions is in itself, of course, not conclusive for Postal's proposal. They can, for instance, be mediated through the common thematic relations rather than via a common deep stucture (cf. e.g. Jackendoff, 1972, §§ 2.5, 4.10.2). And we have seen (§ 1.3) that the argument involving the distribution of *personally* that Postal invokes in support of his proposed deep structure identifications is inconclusive. Moreover, we found in the course of the discussion in § 3.2 that the deviance of (57.1) can be predicted without reference to a crossover violation, if the subject is in each instance an absolutive (rather than say agentive).

However, within a framework like the present one in which there are no deep structure relations distinct from the case (or thematic) relations, it behoves us to seek an explanation in terms of CRs and/or derivational history of the correlation in restrictions between such pairs as are illustrated by (55) and (56). Two main possibilities present themselves: either the difference between these sentences is simplex, a question of a movement transformation like psych-movement; or a complex source like that we envisaged for passives is appropriate. It seems to me that such evidence as we have favours the latter alternative. As a simplex movement transformation psych-movement would be, like passive, idiosyncratic and non-unitary; it would also, apparently, be neither sequence- nor structure-preserving. It is frequently associated with particular morphological characteristics or with lexical uniqueness (*seem*, for example, which does not occur in configurations that have failed to undergo psych-movement). The application of the putative transformation is associated with the introduction or retention of a particular preposition, usually *to*, whose occurrence in post-psych-movement structures is apparently idiosyncratic, on a movement analysis. The observable properties accord more naturally with a complex source, as I shall now try to show.

However, we must reckon with one difference between passive structures and psyched structures which might give us pause. One advantage of the proposed complex source for passives is that the *be* verb that occurs in such can be allowed for like any other verb that takes a complement. The evidence of serialisation, in that English is a head + modifier (centrifugal) language, and of concord confirms this. Elsewhere (Anderson, 1975*a*) I argue (as noted above) that concord is an anti-dependency phenomenon; it goes from argument to predicate, whereas rection or government is con-dependency. And this supports Ross's analysis of auxiliaries in English, in that they show concord with the subject but require a particular form (rection) of the following verb. So that a sentence like *John has been sleeping* possesses, at a superficial level at least, a dependency configuration like that indicated in (58):

(58)

CONCORD
(person/number)

RECTION

The passive auxiliary is like the others in this and other respects. But in the examples involving psyched verbs we have considered there is no such reflex of a higher verb. Fortunately, however, there are active sentences containing some verbs which 'correspond to' both a psyched and a passive variant, as exemplified in (59):

(59) 1. Lots of people know the answer
    2. a. The answer is known by lots of people
       b. The answer is known to lots of people

and in the psych-movement sentence there does occur a *be* as reflex of the predicate in the superordinate clause, as well as the *to* which is associated with psyched variants. This means that either *seem* differs from *know* in requiring subjunction of the main verb to this upper predicate whereas *know* simply lacks such a requirement; or both *seem* and the psyched *known* undergo subjunction to the psych predicate but *known* is associated in addition with another higher predication (realised as *be*), just as I suggested the *be*-passive differed from the *get*-passive in involving a *be*-predication in addition to the passive ('receive') predication. A decision concerning these alternatives is, however, not crucial to the present discussion. Let us rather give some consideration to the character of the psych-predication.

We can immediately make a number of tentative proposals concerning this. We have already encountered in §§ 2.6-.8 an example of an apparently independent, idiosyncratic use of *to* concerning which there were motivations for proposing a lexically more natural source, such that *to*-datives, like other *to*-phrases, mark instances of goal or allative phrases. Again, the psych-movement *to* is natural if it marks a locative in a directional predication. Suppose that this is so: what are the other arguments in this predication? Once more we can presume that the proposition associated with the main verb is embedded, like other sentences showing non-gerundive equi or raising, in an absolutive phrase. As in the derivation of passives and intransitive causatives, this absolutive will come to be subjoined to the upper V. The subject must then be ablative (since the predication is directional) and either absolutive or ergative (in order for it to be occupying subject-position). This last alternative can be settled, I suggest with reference to the kind of example we looked at (in § 1.11) in another context, namely one like (60):

(60) I am impressed by Bill

in whose derivation both passive and psych-movement have applied. Under the proposals made here, such a sentence comes from a structure such as is roughly indicated (in its relevant respects) in (61):

(61)

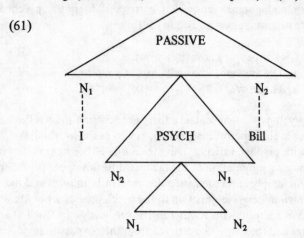

That is, passivisation applies to the output from the cycle referring to the psych-sentence. Now, we have found that a necessary condition for passivisation was that the predicate embedded in the passive be ergative. In that case, the subject in a psych-predication like that contained in (61), i.e. N_2, must be ergative. And this accords with the well-formedness of *Bill impresses himself*, in that the antecedent is non-absolutive (indeed, ergative). However, a psych predicate like *seem* does not allow a reflexive in its *to*-phrase. Thus, rather than simply differing from *impress* by lacking abs in its specification (so preventing object-formation with the locative), it lacks erg; and its subject is [abl, abs] . We have indeed no motivation for suggesting an equi rather than a raising source for the subject of *seem*. And indeed the latter (as compared with equi) requires a simpler predication-type for such a psych verb, lacking both the abs and erg of *impress*. The psych predicate is then [abs, loc, abl, abl (erg)], where the extra abl allows, in accordance with (2.56/57) for the conjunction of [abs, abl] or [erg, abl] for the argument in subject position. That is, it is the same as the passive predication except for the presence of abs rather than (or in addition to) erg and of the extra ablative component, which changes the 'orientation' of the predication: locative subject for passive, ablative for psych. Thus, a psych-movement verb like *impress* differs from *seem* in also being specified as [erg] , and thus requiring the

maximum array of case features allowed for by (2.56/57). The abs is attached
to the locative argument, which as an object undergoes passivisation. There is
no passivisation with *seem* etc., in that it is non-ergative.

This means, then, that whereas *believe* etc. are simple [loc, erg]
verbs, psych verbs like *seem* and *impress* must be inserted with respect to
respective configurations like those in (62):

(62) a.
$$\begin{bmatrix} V \\ loc \\ abl \\ abl \\ abs \end{bmatrix}$$
$$|$$
$$\begin{bmatrix} V \\ loc \\ erg \end{bmatrix}$$

b.
$$\begin{bmatrix} V \\ loc \\ abl \\ erg \\ abl \\ abs \end{bmatrix}$$
$$|$$
$$N_0$$
$$|$$
$$\begin{bmatrix} V \\ loc \\ erg \end{bmatrix}$$

seem   *impress*

Moreover the subject ablative argument in the (upper) predication
associated with such verbs as *impress* will be marked as also abs by the
application of equi (cf. the discussion of *buy/sell* above, and further on
equi in general below).

Notice finally that such a derivation, involving equi and subjunction,
for intransitive causatives and for [loc, erg] subject verbs like *intend*
accounts for the observation of Robin Lakoff's 'that no single lexical
item may take a *for-to* complementiser and undergo both the Passive
transformation and Equi-NP-Deletion' (G. Lakoff, 1970*b*, § V).

Such a treatment of passives and psych-movement sentences means
that we can allow for these 'movements' by a structure-preserving rule
which does not have a recourse to 'empty nodes'. Within the present
framework the only lexically empty node we have invoked is the
absolutive N that serves as the host in raising. However, its 'emptiness'
only arises, in a sense, in the course of the derivation, as a result of
V-raising. Say we define a N that is empty simply as 'either
non-coreferential or as having no dependents' — a not unnatural
interpretation given that the lexical content for Ns derives from a
dependent predicate, and that 'co-referential Ns' include personal and

relative pronouns. Then there are no empty Ns in underlying representations.

If such an analysis of passives is maintainable, it suggests too that the notion 'chômeur' may not be a primitive concept: the 'chômeur' in these instances at least is simply an erg that becomes a (non-ergative) loc or abl by equi. However, let us now turn to some considerations more directly relevant to the theme of the present chapter, namely those properties of equi noted under (c-e) in (44). (44.c) as such is, as observed above, relatively trivial: it merely states that the controller for equi will be a coreferential N other than the (absolutive) N that governs the complement sentence containing the subject N to be deleted, and that the controller will not also be absolutive. It becomes potentially rather more interesting in those instances where there is apparently an obligatory controller.

3.4 Case Relations and Grammatical Relations 2: Equi

3.4.1. Postal (1970, § V.D; and Appendix) discusses the 'control problem' at some length. It appears that for many predicates any NP or NPs in the main clause can act as controller in accordance with pronominalisation constraints. Postal (1970, 470) observes of (63), for instance:

(63)   Harry talked to Bill about kissing Greta

that 'the erased subject of *kissing* can be understood as either *Harry* or *Bill';* moreover, there is a reading wherein 'the deleted subject is a coreferent of *Harry* and *Bill* jointly'. However there are other main clause predicates which require a unique controller.

Rosenbaum (1970) proposed a principle for determining the controller, the 'minimal distance principle', concerning which he says (p.26): 'the noun phrase in the main sentence which is relevant . . . is also that noun phrase which is least distant from the initial noun phrase of the complement', where 'distance here naturally can be defined in terms of the underlying phrase structure itself by making reference to the number of branches in the path which separates the NP nodes in the main sentence from the initial NP node in the complement'. In terms of such a principle (for a rather more formal characterisation, cf. Rosenbaum, 1970, 27), the controllers in (64) are correctly predicted:

(64)   a.   Fred permitted Bill to leave
         b.   Joe tried to leave

as *Bill* and *Joe,* respectively. Thus, if the application of the principle is limited to instances where control is not free (within the pronominalisation constraints), in these and many other cases it serves to select the appropriate controller. However, it is not universally adequate. With verbs like *promise,* for instance, it makes the wrong prediction:

(65)   Fred promised (Bill) to leave

Here the controller is *Fred* not *Bill,* whether or not a NP like *Bill* intervenes (cf. (64.a)). Notice too, on the other hand, that the controller apparently cannot be uniquely specified on the basis of grammatical relations. There is certainly no general requirement that the controller, if obligatory, always be an object, for instance. Nor do individual verbs always uniquely select either subject or object as controller, as Jackendoff (1972, 214) points out with reference to a verb like *get:*

(66)   a. John got to leave
       b. John got Bill to leave

In this instance, the minimal distance principle makes the correct selection: *John* is controller in (66.a) but *Bill* in (b). However the controller is subject in (a) and object in (b).

Jackendoff goes on (1972, § 5.11), as we have already described in § 1.4, to try to show that in all these and other instances what is constant for a particular verb is the thematic relation of the controller. Unfortunately, his argumentation occasionally leaves something to be desired. He argues, for instance, that *John* in (66.a) and *Bill* in (66.b) are both themes on the basis of corresponding pairs like those in (67):

(67)   1. a. Joe got to Philadelphia
           b. Frank got Joe to Philadelphia
       2. a. Frank got furious at Henry
           b. Frank got Joe furious at Henry

However it is not at all clear that (66) should be 'analogised' to these rather than to, say, (68):

(68)   a. Joe got a present (from his aunt)
       b. Frank got Joe a present

where, in Gruberian terms, *Joe* appears to be a goal. Or even that (66.a) should not be analogised to (68.a) but (66.b) to (67.b), in which case the thematic constant hypothesis for obligatory controllers is disconfirmed, it would appear. However, even the resolution of this indeterminacy is quite beside the point, in the present context, unless it is firmly established that the derivation of (66.b) does involve equi rather than raising. This, as far as I am aware, Jackendoff does not attempt to do. The same is true of the other example, *keep,* that Jackendoff cites (1972, 215) along with *get.*

Postal (1974, 318-20, 360-2) discusses Huddleston's (1971, 158) observation that sentences like (69) can be understood in two rather different ways:

(69) I allowed Bob to leave

which he paraphrases as 'I gave permission for Bob to leave' *v.* 'I gave permission to Bob to leave.' My intuitions are uncertain here, but it seems to me that two such understandings also characterise (70):

(70) a. I got Bobo expelled by the college authorities
      b. I got the college authorities to expel Bobo

That is, there is a reading which (70) share, but they each also have a distinct interpretation. Huddleston (1971) allows for the contrast in (69) by positing two different sources: one in which an extra NP is present in the main clause, controlling equi; one in which this is lacking and which develops by raising. We can allow for the situation illustrated by (66) in the same way, in which case (66.b) does involve (at least on one reading) the application of equi. However, as Postal shows, such an assumption is not necessarily the best way to provide for this contrast in understanding.

Since the interpretation of these crucial examples is (at least) in doubt, it looks as if we should accede to Jackendoff's (1972, 217) conclusion that 'if all verbs with an optional NP behaved like *promise,* maintaining a fixed control position when the optional object is added, this would argue that grammatical relations determine control.' Actually, however, both the grammatical relations and the thematic relations (or CRs) are in this situation capable of determining control, since both remain constant. Moreover, it is even conceivable that a restricted variant of the minimal distance principle can be maintained, if we specify the controller as the nearest obligatory NP to the complement subject in the configuration associated with the particular main clause

verb, thus accommodating the major class of counter-examples, namely
that illustrated by (65). In the absence of a well-motivated analysis of
the *get* sentences in (66), the resolution of the control problem seems
to be indecisive in selecting among these competing theories of
semantico-syntactic structure(s).

At this point two possible strategies seem appropriate, before we
abandon equi as irrelevant to the point at issue. Either we can try to
develop some greater understanding of the (rather complex) syntax and
semantics of *get*, or we can try to arrive at a more general account of
control. For instance, is it possible to arrive at a principle of
controller-selection that is generally applicable rather than one which is
idiosyncratic to particular verbs? If so, this might in turn throw some
light back on the problem with *get*. Let us take the latter course,
particularly since there already exist some suggestions in this direction
which will help us along the way.

3.4.2. Postal (1970, § V.D) tried to relate controller selection in many
cases to 'one or other independently required constraint on
pronominalisation processes' (p.470). He observes, for instance, that
whereas *he* in (276.a) can be coreferential with either *Harry* or *Max:*

(71) a. Harry told Max that he was sick

   b. Harry told Max that he $\left\{ \begin{array}{l} \text{should} \\ \text{ought to} \end{array} \right\}$ visit Greta

(71.b) (under the 'embedded imperative' interpretation) allows
coreference with only *Max,* i.e. the equivalent of the controller for
equi in (72):

(72) Harry told Max to visit Greta

The coreference constraints in (71.b) and (72) are reducible to a single
principle (the *'ought* modal constraint') if they contain embedded Ss of
the same underlying character, i.e. crucially containing a modal. And
Postal shows that other shared restrictions can be associated with the
presence of such a modal element (p.471) and that other instances of
selection of indirect objects as controller for equi can plausibly be
related to the *ought* modal constraint (pp.471-3). Other cases of control
where the indirect object is selected are rather to be associated with the
would modal constraint, as in (73):

(73) Bill asked Tom to fire the cannon

in which the deleted lower subject is coreferential with *Tom,* and which is paraphraseable by (74):

(74) Bill asked Tom if he would fire the cannon

However there are other apparent cases of the *would* modal constraint where the subject is selected, as in (75):

(75) Harry promised Bill to visit Greta

Cf. (76):

(76) Harry promised Bill that he would visit Greta

He in (76) can be taken as coreferential with *Bill* only on a simple epistemic (prediction) interpretation of *will,* rather than the volitional/intentional use appropriate to (76) with *Harry* and *he* coreferential and, *ex hypothesi,* to (75). Further examples, which apparently show selection of subject (rather than the indirect object) as controller by the *ought* modal constraint, as in (77):

(77) a. Bill asked Tom when to fire the cannon
      b. Bill asked Tom when he should fire the cannon

are, however, on the other hand, fairly plausibly disposed of by invoking 'an extra layer of embedding', roughly of the character of (78):

(78) Bill asked Tom to tell him when $\left\{ \begin{array}{l} \text{he should go} \\ \text{to go} \end{array} \right.$

where the *he* and the deleted subject of *go* are coreferential, as elsewhere, with the indirect object, *him.* There remains, however, the discrepancy with the *would* modal constraint, which allows selection of either subject or indirect object.

Postal goes on (1970, app.) to observe that the verbs we have been concerned with are all 'non-declarative linguistic verbs', and that the constraints he has formulated can be unified with reference to the corresponding direct discourse variants of the sentences involved. He formulates the generalisation as in (79):[41]

(79) Given an Indirect Discourse linguistic sentence [such as those
      we have been considering – JMA], call it S_{ID}, in which EQUI
      has applied, the following principle describes whether EQUI
      deletes an NP which is a coreferent of the subject or of the
      indirect object:
      Take the Direct Discourse 'version' of S_{ID}, call it S_{DD}.
      Then:
      a. If the subject of the complement sentence in S_{DD} is FIRST
         PERSON, EQUI operation in S_{ID} deletes an NP *which is a*
         coreferent of the main clause subject.
      b. If the subject of the complement sentence in S_{DD} is
         SECOND PERSON, then EQUI operation in S_{ID} deletes an
         NP *which is a coreferent of the main clause indirect object.*

The correlations are illustrated by the pairs in (80):

(80) 1. a. Harry$_i$ told Betty to marry him$_i$
         b. (You) marry me, Harry told Betty
      2. a. Harry$_i$ asked Betty to marry him$_i$
         b. Will you (please) marry me, (Betty), Harry asked Betty
      3. a. Harry asked Betty when to leave
         b. When should I leave, Harry asked Betty
      4. a. Harry promised Betty to leave
         b. I will leave, Harry promised Betty
      5. a. Harry shouted to Betty to leave
         b. (You) leave, Harry shouted to Betty
      6. a. Harry warned Betty not to leave
         b. Don't (you) leave, Harry warned Betty
      7. a. Harry ordered Betty to leave
         b. (You) leave, Harry ordered Betty

Postal notes some problems with (79); but more important for our
present concerns is that the selection of controller, though now correlated
with a much wider range of facts, still remains at least in part apparently
idiosyncratic to particular verbs, as illustrated by (80.4) *v.* (80.1).

3.4.3. Given the discussion in the previous chapter, in which we arrived
at a complex source for indirect objects, and where specifically I
suggested that prepositionless indirect objects derive from underlying
(locative) ergatives, thus derivatively subjects, it is appropriate that we
should consider whether such a more abstract analysis might lead to a

more general principle of controller selection. And indeed Postal elsewhere (1974, 255-7) argues that provided verbs like *persuade* etc., as exemplified in (81):

(81) I $\left\{ \begin{array}{l} \text{forced} \\ \text{persuaded} \end{array} \right\}$ Bob to leave

can be decomposed, via predicate raising, into some such structure (for the *persuade* sentence) as (82):

(82) I CASE (Bob $\left\{ \begin{array}{l} \text{AGREE} \\ \text{INTEND} \end{array} \right\}$ (Bob leave))

then control by objects can be reduced to a case of subject control. He proposes the selection principle of (83):

(83) The controller NP for Equi is always a cyclic subject at the point when control is checked, which is at the end of the lowest cycle covering the controller.

He does not, however, develop this notion. Let us now examine its adequacy with respect to such sentences as (82) against the background of the analysis of indirect objects proposed in § 2.8.

Tell appears to be an indirect object verb like *give*. Like *thank* and *help* it differs from *give* in incorporating the absolutive argument (GIVE *someone help* ⇒ *help someone*: GIVE *someone* INFORMATION ⇒ *tell someone*). Unlike *help,* the absolutive frequently contains a complement S, and this S is left behind when the absolutive head noun (INFORMATION) is incorporated, thus giving (80.1.a) or (71) or (72). Thus, underlying (71.a) is, schematically, (84):

(84) Harry CAUSE (Max RECEIVE INFO ($\left\{ \begin{array}{l} \text{Harry} \\ \text{Max} \end{array} \right\}$ sick))

whereas (71.b) requires at least (85):

(85)

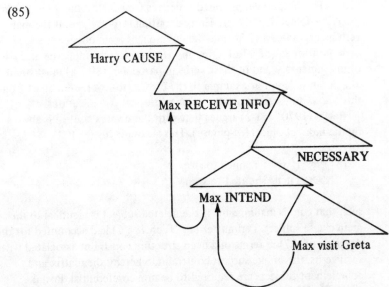

where equi in both instances involves the cyclic subject of the main clause. However, again such examples are indecisive as to whether grammatical relations or CRs must be invoked. The two upper *Max*'s are both subjects, but they are also both [loc, erg] . Thus alternatively to (83) we might have (86):

(86) *Controller selection:* The controller NP for equi is always an erg.

Again I assume that control is established in the lowest cycle covering the controller, and thus in the present framework before subject selection on that cycle. So (86) is a tighter constraint than (83): it excludes NPs that are subject but are not underlying ergs. Moreover, either formulation is incompatible with an account whereby indirect object is a primitive.

Either (83) or (86) will thus provide for (72) and (80.1.a), and for (80.6/7.a), given that similar analyses are appropriate; they are also both compatible, trivially, with the derivation of intransitive causatives like those in (50), as well as, of course, of 'traditional' subject-controller equi verbs like *intend*. If intransitive *get* (as in (66.a)) takes a [loc, erg] subject (like *receive*), and if the object of the transitive (if at least on one interpretation it is not due simply to raising) originates as the [loc, erg] subject of an embedded directional (cf. *persuade*), then selection of controller is in its case too in accord with (83)/(86). Moreover, even

(80.5.a) is compatible, provided it derives from a structure like that in (85) *plus* something like 'by Harry shouting to Betty', i.e. if the main verb incorporates an instrumental component from outside the configuration in (85). But, given my ignorance concerning the analysis of instrumentals, and of these verbs in particular, (80.5.a) must stand as a potential counter-example to (83)/(86). However, even apart from this, *shout* and *scream* present some additional complications.

Postal (1970, 471-2) argues that with these verbs control is always by the indirect object (*to*-phrase). This accounts for (87):

(87) a.*Harry screamed to stop
      b.*Lucile shouted to stop

such that equi is inadmissible if the deleted subject is identical to the main clause subject. Perlmutter (1971, ch.1, § 1) had accounted for the deviance of (87) in terms of a deep structure constraint associated with such verbs, the unlike-subject constraint, whereby the matrix and complement subjects are required to be non-coreferential. Postal argues that this is unnecessary, given the restriction of control to the *to*-phrase; and moreover undesirable, given that (88):

(88) I screamed to myself to stop

is non-deviant (or at least is much better than (87.a)). However he fails to take account of the crucial kind of example adduced by Perlmutter (1971), illustrated in the first place by (89.a):

(89) a. I screamed to be allowed to shave myself
      b.*I screamed for Frank to be allowed by me to shave himself

which now seems to show equi under the control of the subject. But if this is so, we cannot, as Postal suggested, relate the anomalous character of (87) to obligatory selection on the part of *scream* of a *to*-phrase as controller. Rather, we seem to require still some kind of non-coreferentiality constraint, either a deep structure unlike-subject requirement, or, in the present framework, a semantic constraint against a coreferential agent in the next lowest sentence, thus excluding both (87) and (89.b). But Perlmutter, following Ross, notes (1971, 6-8, n.5) that this latter sentence is excluded anyway by a restriction whereby 'in sentences in which the subject of the embedded sentence is identical to the subject of the matrix sentence, the passive transformation cannot apply in the embedded sentence without producing an ungrammatical sentence', as illustrated by *I expected Fred to be allowed by me to shave himself*. However, as stated, this is clearly too general, in that it would equally exclude the perfectly viable *The doctor$_i$ expected Fred to be examined by him$_i$* (Shaw, 1974, 212). Instead, the crucial factor in the non-acceptability of (89.b) is the presence of *allow*, as Shaw further points out; substitute another verb and a much higher degree of acceptability results:

(90) I screamed for Fred to be examined by me

(90) shows that it is not simply a 'deep structure' constraint that is involved here, if passives are given a simplex transformational analysis. Shaw claims that what is required is a global constraint ruling out these sentences with *scream* as a matrix verb if both in deep structure and at the point at which equi applies the subjects are identical. However, this fails to account for the well-formedness of (88), with identity at both relevant levels, although it predicts that of *I screamed to myself to be examined by Fred*.

If, on the other hand, the *to*-phrase in (88) etc. originates in a subordinate directional predication ((88) = 'CAUSE BY screaming (REQUEST GO to myself . . .)') and if passives have the complex source advocated above, then something like Perlmutter's constraint seems still appropriate; say: 'in the structure underlying these surface verbs the ergative argument of CAUSE may not be identical with an immediately subordinate agent' (thus permitting identity to the subject of passives). Note that if some such independent referential non-identity constraint is required, then we can regard *scream* as showing free rather than obligatory control; and such verbs thus cease to stand as a potential counter-example to (83)/(86). (To look at it another way, they illustrate obligatory non-control by an ergative.)

3.4.4. Whatever the resolution to the problem of the syntax of *scream*, more direct difficulties for such formulations of control selection as are represented by (83)/(86) are presented in (80.2/3.a) and (80.4.a). Consider firstly *promise*. This is again a *give* verb, so that something like (91) is appropriate as an underlying schema for (80.4.a).

(91)

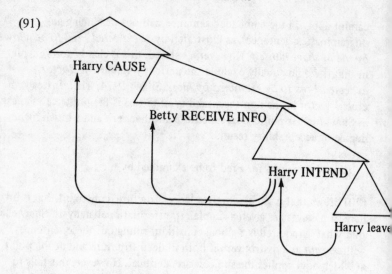

Now, whereas equi on the INTEND cycle occurs as predicted (as indicated by the arrow), the controller for the next application is not the subject/erg in the sentence immediately superordinate to the term to be deleted but apparently rather that in the one above. With (80.2.a), on the other hand, we have (92):

(92)

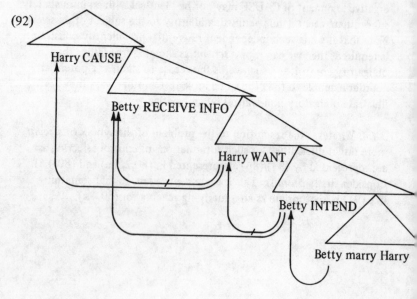

Here there are three applications of equi, the latter two of which 'skip'
a predication. And (80.3.a) is worse still, even if (93) is only
approximately accurate:

(93)

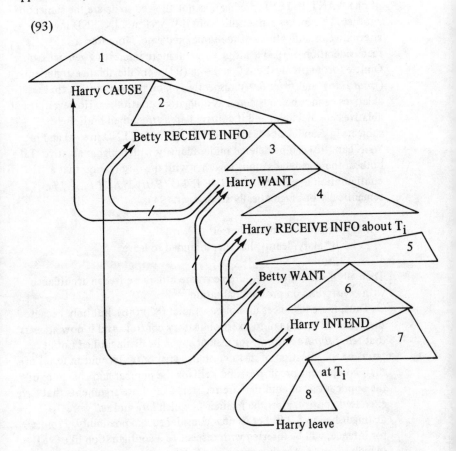

Here potential controllers are skipped on cycles 5 and 4 and 3
respectively, and on cycle 2 the eventual controller involves the bypassing
of two potential ones on cycles 4 and 3. Certainly, all the applications
involve control by a subject/erg, but it looks as if we now have to mark
predicates as to whether they require or permit a potential controller to
be skipped.

However, there is a generalisation governing all the instances we have considered; viz. a controller can be skipped only above the WANT/INTEND predicate(s). This is in part allowed for if the subject of one WANT/INTEND predicate is not allowed to delete the subject of another. This makes sense notionally if WANT and INTEND involve alternative modifications of the same predicate. Moreover, a reconsideration of (93) leads us to a still more interesting generalisation. Omitted from predications 2 and 4 in (93) were the ablative arguments (*from Harry* and *from Betty* respectively), on the assumption that ablatives cannot be considered as obligatory controllers. However, if such ablatives are included, and if control here is free, then both the subjects in 5 and 3 of (93) and the subject of INTEND in (91) and of WANT in (92) can be deleted under identity with a higher ablative. Take both of these generalisations together with the observation that a configuration like *Betty* RECEIVE INFO *(Betty* WANT *(. . .))* is semantically or pragmatically strange; cf. (94):

(94) a.*Mary promised herself to leave
      b.*Mary$_i$ learnt that she$_i$ intended to leave

Then all of the control requirements are otherwise free in accordance with constraints on pronominalisation.

Thus, these instances do not contradict (83)/(86), but only because they (and all verbs) fail to exert obligatory control. And it now appears that *tell, promise* and *ask,* for instance, will be distinguished not in terms of specification of distinct obligatory controllers but in terms of their component predicates, and perhaps the number and character of the applications of equi that are registered on those arguments that have exercised control, after the manner in which *buy* and *sell* were distinguished in § 2.8. Let us now consider such a possibility. *Promise,* for intance, will be inserted with respect to a configuration like (95) (which suppresses each intervening abs):

(95)

$$
\begin{bmatrix} V \\ erg \end{bmatrix}
$$
$$
|
$$
$$
\begin{bmatrix} V \\ loc \\ abl \\ erg \end{bmatrix}
$$
$$
|
$$
$$
\begin{bmatrix} V \\ loc \\ erg \end{bmatrix}
$$
$$
|
$$
$$
N_o
$$

Compare *ask:*

(96)

$$
\begin{bmatrix} V \\ erg \end{bmatrix}
$$
$$
|
$$
$$
\begin{bmatrix} V \\ loc \\ abl \\ erg \end{bmatrix}
$$
$$
|
$$
$$
\begin{bmatrix} V \\ loc \\ erg \end{bmatrix}
$$
$$
|
$$
$$
N_o
$$
$$
\left(
\begin{bmatrix} V \\ loc \\ abl \\ erg \end{bmatrix}
\right.
$$
$$
|
$$
$$
\begin{bmatrix} V \\ loc \\ erg \end{bmatrix}
$$
$$
|
$$
$$
\left. N_o \right)
$$
$$
\begin{bmatrix} V \\ loc \\ erg \end{bmatrix}
$$
$$
|
$$
$$
N_o
$$

(where the optional subparts allow for (93) *v.* (92)). If a verb with a derivation like *promise* is uniquely specified by the subjunction tree alone, then it is obviously possible to make a much stronger hypothesis than otherwise concerning the information that must be available to control lexical insertion. This is possible in particular if all verbs characterised by such a subjunction tree share the same control possibilities for equi. Recall that the *buy/sell* distinction (and the derivation of intransitive agentive *move* (§ 3.3)) required in addition only that the CRs raised by equi on the current cycle be available for determining lexical insertion. Indeed, more specifically, they require simply that the erg in the main clause be marked with the CR(s) of the NP it deletes under equi. Perhaps this is as far as a hypothesis concerning the case information available to lexical insertion need be weakened (to include information outside the subjunction tree). Certainly it looks as if the kinds of example we have been dealing with involve free selection of controller, and lexical insertion controlled by the subjunction tree alone. At most, information concerning erg-controlled equi may have to be taken into account. This means that instead of principles (83)/(86) governing selection of obligatory controller, we can turn the generalisation around, determining lexical insertion on the basis of the application of equi. *Buy* and *sell* are distinguished on the basis of whether equi has deleted an ablative or an allative phrase and thus whether abl or loc is registered on the erg of the main clause. If this is the only kind of control that is required, then we can substitute for (83)/(86) the principle (97):

(97)   Only erg has registered on it the CR of the NP deleted under equi.

Thus, only in instances involving control by erg will case information about the deleted NP be available in determining lexical insertion. Rather than a condition on obligatory control we have a further constraint on the information available to lexical insertion. (97) may be an instance of a still more general principle whereby in general when an argument in a complement is removed (rather than simply raised) an upper erg is marked with the CR of the deleted argument. Recall, for instance, the derivation suggested in § 2.8 for verbs like *obey* and *refuse* whereby the lower directional V has subjoined to it the absolutive argument (which would otherwise turn up as *refusal* etc.). Again an absolutive argument is removed and the surface verb takes only one object. However, the corresponding nominalisations behave like those corresponding to [abs, erg] -subject verbs such as *depart* in allowing either *of* or *by* as marker of the erg argument (§ 3.5): cf. *the departure of/by the enemy* and *the refusal of/by the enemy v. the destruction of (*by) the town by (*of) the enemy.* This suggests that the erg argument with *refuse* is marked with abs on removal of the lower abs argument. Such an operation also ensures that the array of cases is well-formed after subjunction: only if the erg argument in the same predication is also abs can a locative be itself abs (cf. § 2.1). It remains to be seen, however, to what extent this hypothesis and its instantiation as (97) is viable.

3.4.5. However that may be, the important point for our present declared concerns is that control of equi offers no support for pre-cyclic subject-formation; rather, a minimal generalisation is that the controller cannot be absolutive, which supports the cycle-terminating position on subject-formation. The support is of course even more striking if something like (97) can be maintained. Similarly, if our observations concerning the syntax of *scream* are accurate the same conclusion follows, in that crucially involved is an unlike-agent constraint. And the formulation of the unlikeness constraint on the RECEIVE INFO predication (cf. (94)) depends upon an analysis whereby once again 'indirect object' is rejected as a primitive notion. Accordingly, I conclude that the phenomena we have surveyed in this and the preceding sections select the theory of cycle-final subject-formation (i.e. case grammar) over a theory whereby subjects are selected prior to the application of the cyclic rules. The syntactic rule of raising involves crucial reference to main clause absolutives (whether or not they subsequently become subjects). The same is true, negatively, of equi and reflexivisation (if they are syntactic rules). Reflexivisation and principle (97) may indeed require an even tighter specification in terms of CRs. Even if it is claimed that these latter are not syntactic rules but semantic (Jackendoff, 1972; Helke, 1972) then again we have semantic generalisations, like that involving 'holisticness' (§§ 1.8-.9), which invoke CRs rather than 'deep' grammatical relations.

3.4.6. It remains to consider point (e) among the set of characteristics attributed by (44) to equi: viz. that the element selected for deletion is in accordance with the case-hierarchy. As far as the examples we have been involved with in this section are concerned, this is satisfied rather trivially, in that it is always the subject (i.e. erg after subject-formation) of the complement sentence that is deleted. However, recall the derivations proposed above for *buy/sell* verbs and for sentences involving passive or psych-movement. *Buy* involves deletion of a lower locative coreferential with the upper erg; *sell* a similar ablative. In neither instance is the lower absolutive deleted, even when it occupies subject position. However, this is allowed for if the verbs involved are specified as raising verbs rather than simple equi verbs: that is, they lack the subjoined abs ____ N_o characteristic of simple equi verbs. In that case the lower subject is pre-empted for raising, and thus must be passed over as a candidate for equi.

More problematical apparently (both with regard to (44.e) and to control) are passives and psych-sentences of the *impress* variety. In these instances we have two applications of equi. With passive the lower subject is deleted under coreference with the upper ablative, whereas the upper [loc, erg] deletes the 'object'. In a psych-sentence the only relevant difference is in the distribution of loc and abl in the upper sentence. The problem here, as far as control is concerned, is that the other possibility for each of them, deletion of the lower subject by the upper erg phrase and the object by the other upper phrase, is not realised. However, this can be allowed for by requiring that in the specification for a passive or psych-verb the ergative phrase is also marked as abs (thus requiring that equi apply only in the desired manner), just as the ergative phrase with *buy* is also marked as loc and that with *sell* as abl. Moreover, apart from being permitted by (97), this remains consistent with (44.e), since it is only if the subject is deleted by equi that the object can also be so deleted.

Similarly, deletion of the objects of complements is possible only if the subject of the complement is absent, as in (98):

   (98)   a. This problem is too abstract to solve
          b. Mary is pretty to look at

(Lasnik & Fiengo, 1974, § 1). Apparent subjects in complements showing object deletion are not so. Compare (99):

   (99)   a. This problem is too abstract for Bill to solve
          b. For Bill, this problem is too abstract to solve
          c. This problem is too abstract to solve, for Bill

with object deletion, and where the *for*-phrase is, like a main clause adjunct, preposeable (as in (b)), with (100):

   (100)   a. This problem is too abstract for Bill to solve it

       b.*For Bill, this problem is too abstract to solve it

       c.*This problem is too abstract to solve it, for Bill

where the *for*-phrase, as subject of the complement, does not prepose with respect to the main clause (Lasnik & Fiengo, 1974, 538). Thus such derivations are again compatible with (44.e), in that the complement object is deletable only in the absence of the subject.

    Lasnik & Fiengo also argue (1974, § 2) that the derivation of *tough*-sentences like those we considered above in our discussion of reflexivisation involves COMPLEMENT OBJECT DELETION (cf. Ross, 1967) rather than a movement rule (i.e. essentially an equi rather than a raising derivation) such as was assumed above (following Rosenbaum, 1967; Postal, 1971). However, whether equi or raising is involved,[42] in either case, it is again true that, as we observed in § 3.2, it is only in the absence of the complement subject that the object undergoes the rule. Once more (44.e) is to that extent maintained, though we should note that a non-object (non-abs) can be affected even in the presence of an object: *John isn't easy to tell the truth to*, etc. Here, (44.e) should be restricted to respect for subjecthood. We turn in the section that follows to a reconsideration of the status and character of the case hierarchy in relation to a range of typological considerations.

3.5 Case Relations and Grammatical Relations 3: Typological remarks

3.5.1. In so far as raising etc. are universal rules, our conclusions concerning the respective roles of the (underlying) CRs and of derived ('grammatical') CRs are universally valid. That is, subject-formation (in particular) is universally cycle-terminating. We return to one refinement of such a proposal in a moment. At this point I merely want to indicate that such a conclusion is also quite compatible with typological studies like that by Keenan & Comrie (to appear) on 'noun phrase accessibility' in relativisation. Indeed the resolution of some problems with their formulation, for example, will lend some additional support to (a refinement of) this proposal.

    Keenan & Comrie propose the accessibility hierarchy (henceforth AH) replicated in (101):

(101)   *Accessibility hierarchy*

        Subj > DObj > IObj > Obl > Gen > OComp

(where 'Subj' = 'subject', 'DObj' = 'direct object', 'IObj' = 'indirect object', 'Obl' = 'other oblique case NPs', 'Gen' = 'adnominal genitives', and 'Ocomp' = 'object of comparison'. Not all NP positions in any language are accessible to relativisation; in terms of the AH, Keenan & Comrie formulate what they refer to as 'the case constraint' which specifies the necessary conditions under which a particular NP is accessible:

(102) *Case constraint*
       For unmarked simplex sentences,
       a. any relative clause forming strategy in any language must operate on a continuous segment of the accessibility hierarchy   and
       b. for each NP position on the AH there are relative clause forming strategies that relativise it but no others lower than it.

And they embody a further hierarchy-bound claim in the 'absolute subject condition':

(103) *Absolute subject condition*
       Subjects are universally the easiest position on the AH to relativise. That is, if a language can relativise any NP position on the AH it can relativise subjects, but this is not true of any other position of the AH.

Neither of these generalisations, nor indeed the AH itself is in conflict with the cycle-terminating hypothesis for subject-formation, provided that relativisation is either cyclic or post-cyclic. Equally, of course, they are in that event also compatible with pre-cyclic subject-formation. But there is an apparent exception to (103) which is of some interest in any discussion of the place of subject-formation, in that, I am going to suggest, a resolution of the anomaly favours cycle-terminating subject-formation. However, before we proceed on these lines, one other aspect of the AH reproduced in (101) requires a comment or two. This is the role of 'indirect objects', in that it is appropriate that we should establish whether it is compatible with the analysis of these that we developed in §§ 2.7-.8.

3.5.2. Keenan & Comrie observe that (§ 1.2.3) 'the indirect object is perhaps the most subtle one on the AH. For purposes of relative clause formation it appears that many languages either assimilate indirect

objects to the other oblique cases . . . or to direct objects . . .' This is
perfectly natural in terms of the proposals made above whereby (in
English) prepositionless indirect objects originate as embedded (locative)
subjects which are raised into object position whereas prepositionful
'indirect objects' are, as is transparent in many languages, simply
(allative) locational phrases. But there are, they go on to say,
languages which 'appear to discriminate indirect objects from both its
immediate neighbours on the AH', as an example of which Keenan &
Comrie cite Basque. This situation again is quite natural, given that
those 'indirect objects' which originate as embedded subjects come to
have a derived [loc, abs] specification, the abs being in common with
simple (direct) objects but the [loc] with other 'oblique' case phrases.
(Though, as we have seen, the subject-forming hierarchy ranks [loc,
abs] above [abs] rather than below it.) And I conjecture that 'indirect
objects' will behave distinctively with respect to relativisation only when
they are provided, as we noted (§ 3.3) was true for Basque, with a
distinctive marker. In Basque ergative and absolutive arguments,
including the 'indirect object' [loc, abs] , are 'registered' on the verb,
such that an absolutive, an ergative where it is distinct from the
absolutive and a (dative) [loc, abs] where there is another abs are each
given distinctive representation in the form of the verb. And any of
these arguments can be relativised; but in the 'restricted dialect'
described by de Rijk (1972) no others can without difficulty. This is
quite consistent with the analysis we have developed.

   However, Keenan & Comrie in fact fail to show that Basque 'indirect
objects' behave distinctively (i.e. in any way differently from other
absolutives) with respect to relativisation as such (rather than concord, say).
So relativisation in Basque, as discussed by them, does not provide us with
any motivation for establishing 'IObj' as a distinct position on the AH. They
mention two further languages which they claim discriminate 'indirect
objects' with respect to the AH, viz. Tamil and Roviana. I am unable to
comment on the situation in Roviana (a language of New Georgia), due to
my lack of a grammar, let alone a speaker of that language. However, it is
clear that in the light of my observations concerning Basque, and those I
shall make concerning Tamil, the data they present are insufficient to
establish their point. Consider, however, Tamil.

   Keenan & Comrie do not distinguish which variety of Tamil they
want to refer to; and there are differences between varieties with
respect to relativisation. But, I think the following is accurate for some
familiar varieties, at least. The inflexion which serves as 'indirect object'
marker, *-kki/-kku,* has a wider range of 'uses' than is traditionally

associated with such a term. Admittedly, there are operational difficulties in applying the traditional term and consequent variations in usage. Indeed, the worthy Meiklejohn (1892, 93), in discussing the syntax of English, cautions his readers as follows:

> Special care is needed in dealing with the Indirect Object. There is a tendency on the part of many young students to put down any word or phrase which they cannot easily classify as 'Indirect Object'. Thus words or phrases which are Extensions of the Predicate or Enlargements of the Object are often wrongly classed as Indirect Object.

But few of Meiklejohn's students would, I think, be tempted to label all the uses of -*kki*/-*kku* as 'IObj'. For instance, it can mark the (non-animate) concrete spatial goal with verbs of movement. And such arguments can also be relativised using the same strategy as with 'indirect objects' in some narrower traditional sense. Keenan & Comrie do not explain their usage concerning 'indirect object' (etc.); so it may be that they do intend that it be given a rather broad interpretation.[42] But if this is so, then it is proper that they should specify what characteristics they are requiring of an argument if it is to count as such a creature. But even if all instances involving -*kki*-/-*kku* are to be treated as 'indirect objects', it is simply not the case that the same relative-forming strategy cannot be employed with other (oblique) cases. Thus whereas the distinct strategy that Keenan & Comrie illustrate with reference to relativisation of an instrumental is perfectly in order; it is equally possible to relativise instrumentals utilising the strategy they attribute to subjects, direct and indirect objects. Compare with their example [(104.a)] the instrumental in (104.b):

(104)   a.   Anta manitan aṭi-cc-a peṇmani(y)-
             'that' 'man' 'hit'-'past'-rel 'woman'-
             ai jaan kaṇ-ṭ-aan
             acc 'John' 'see'-past-concord
    b.   Naan avan-e aṭi-cc-a perampu . . .
             'I' 'he'-acc 'hit'-past-rel 'stick'

        (a. = 'John saw the woman whom that man hit';
         b. = '. . . the stick with which I hit him';
        rel = relative participle marker; acc = accusative).

As it stands, the Tamil evidence does not seem to provide support for distinguishing (with respect to the AH) 'indirect objects' from the oblique cases (if these latter include spatial goals or even instrumentals, etc.). Accordingly, it is not clear that the notion 'indirect object' is at all relevant to the AH (at least as far as relativisation is concerned).

3.5.3. There is, on the other hand, an observation concerning indirect objects relevant to our present concerns which arises from Keenan & Comrie's attempt (§ 2.3.2) to extend the applicability of the AH to the phenomenon of verb agreement, concerning which they claim:

> Verb-agreement follows the AH in the sense that the easiest noun phrases for verbs to agree with are their subjects, then direct objects, then indirect objects, then other oblique constituents. Some languages have no verb-agreement . . . others have agreement with subjects only . . . Yet others . . . have subject and direct object agreement. Further, such languages as Chinook . . . and Abaza . . . have agreement with subject, direct and indirect object.

Again, if agreement as a rule (or rather the feature-copying part – see below) can apply after subject-formation (Pullum (1975*d*) suggests it is post-cyclic), such phenomena are compatible with either pre-cyclic or cyclic subject-formation. Keenan & Comrie, however, note two kinds of exception to this generalisation, the second of which is, as I have anticipated, particularly germane to the concerns of the present section. But even the first exception which they observe is rather suggestive, to put it no more strongly. The exception is represented by Tzeltal, 'where verbs overtly agree with subjects and indirect objects but not, apparently, with direct objects'. Now this is explicable if Tzeltal is a language which allows only subject agreement and if indirect objects have their source in embedded subjects, provided that agreement involves not only a post-cyclic feature-copying operation but also the cyclic establishment of a co-referential link between a subject (or whatever) and its predicate (Fauconnier, 1971). I am assuming that agreement is 'global' in the sense that it involves two components: a cyclic indexing of a predicate with respect to certain arguments (arguments e.g. which bear the basic CR in the sense discussed below – i.e. abs or erg (as subject)), and a postcyclic feature-copying rule (or the like). In the present instance the indirect object as a cyclic subject has its predicate indexed accordingly, though the actual form of the agreement (the feature-copying) is determined post-cyclically. (There will also have to be no agreement if an embedded subject becomes an object — cf. § 2.8 on quantifier movement.) Unfortunately, it is not at all clear that it is after all necessary to allow for such a pattern of agreement, since, as far as I can determine, the situation in Tzeltal is not as Keenan & Comrie portray it. Keenan & Comrie do not give a source for their observations; but a perusal of ch.7 of Kaufman (1971), at least, reveals no evidence for indirect object agreement in Tzeltal. Rather, Tzeltal is an 'ergative' language in which the agreement markers fall into two sets, such that those for intransitive 'subjects' are identical to those for the 'patient' in transitive sentences and the transitive agent requires a distinct set.

However, this does lead on to the other kind of exception to the accessibility hierarchy as far as agreement is concerned. And the same kind of exception occurs with respect to relativisation. We shall find that the relevant phenomena have an important bearing on our ongoing concern with the status of subject-formation. However, before proceeding, let us note that there are languages which by their pattern of agreement do reflect a relationship between ergative NPs and dative. Specifically, there are a number of languages which display identical or near identical marking of concord for ergative and dative. Such a language is Basque. (For some discussion, see, e.g. Lafon, 1961.) Consider, for example, some forms of the 'analytic verb'. In this case, the tense and concord marking is carried by an 'auxiliary verb' and the 'main verb' is participal in form. The ordinary transitive auxiliary is the *tu* in (105):

(105)   zi - tu - t
         'you' 'I'   (= 'I (verb) you')
         abs - stem - erg

to which the absolute index, in this instance *zi*, is pre-fixed and the ergative, *t*, suffixed. The third person absolute index merges with the stem:

(106)   a. du - zu   b. du - t
            'him' 'you'   'him' 'I'
            abs + stem - erg   abs + stem - erg

as does the first person singular:

(107)   a. nu - zu   b. nu - ∅
            'me' 'you'   'me' 'he'
            abs + stem - erg   abs + stem - erg

In all these singular indices each member of the absolutive series is distinct from the corresponding ergative:

(108)

persons	absolutive	ergative
I	tu → nu	-t
II	zi-	-zu
III	tu → du	-∅

Only the second person markers show any resemblance. (There is a greater degree of resemblance in the plural, but since the series nevertheless remain distinct and since a description of the plural forms would involve us in additional morphological complexities (see e.g. (112)), I leave these aside. Also, the paradigm of the 'intransitive auxiliary' is rather less regular, but is most readily seen as involving a variant of the (prefixed) absolutive series: cf. e.g. *zire* 'you (abs) are'.)

Now, the 'auxiliary' used with verbs like 'give', which take abs, erg and 'dative', has two forms relevant here, one for when the dative is third person and one for when it is not (keeping the absolutive constant as third person); cf.:

(109) a. dio - ∅ - t
   'him' 'to him' 'I' (= 'I (verb) him to him')
   abs + stem - dat - erg
  b. dau - t - ∅
   'him' 'to me' 'he'
   abs + stem - dat - erg

(109) also already reveals identity of marker for first person erg and dat; also that they are both suffixed, thus distinguished only in that the dative markers precede the erg. Similarly, as again shown by (109), and by (110):

(110) dio - ∅ - ∅
  'him' 'to him' 'he'
  abs + stem - dat - erg

third person datives and ergatives are both -∅. The second person dative is suffixed -*tzu*. We accordingly have the series shown in (111):

(111)   persons   dative

                        I   -t

                        II   -tzu

                       III   -∅

The affinity with the ergative series is striking, as is also the case with the plural forms, despite minor discrepancies similar to the *-zu/-tzu* of the second person singular. Indeed, this parallelism and the zero-markings for third person dative and ergative lead to the occurrence of ambiguous forms like *diote* which can be parsed in the three ways shown in (112):

(112)   a. dio - ∅ - te - ∅
              'him' 'to them' 'he'
              abs + stem - dat - pl - erg
         b. dio - ∅ - ∅ - te
              'him' 'to him' 'they'
              abs + stem - dat - erg - pl
         c. dio - ∅ - te - ∅ - te
              'him' 'to them' 'they'
              abs + stem - dat - pl - erg - pl

(*-te-te* simplifies to *-te*.)

Such a situation (whereby indices of concord reveal an affinity between ergative and dative) is not restricted to Basque. Similar observations have often been made concerning the North-West Caucasian group, for example. In discussing Abaza, Allen (1956) distinguishes three concord series — let us call them simply 1, 2 and 3 — of which 2 and 3 are almost identical. Abaza is also at least in part morphologically ergative, and series one accordingly concords with the absolutive argument with intransitives such as that in (113):

(113)   d-θád
          'he/she' - 'has gone'

(Allen, 1956, 152) and transitives like that in (114):

(114)   a. d -1 - ʃʸə́d
            'him/her'-'she'-'killed'

        b. d - y - bád
            'him/her'-'he'-'saw'

(Allen, 1956, 154) while the *l* of series 2 in (114) agrees with the ergative. A series 2 marker also occurs in (115):

(115)   a. y -1 - ə́ - s - d
            'it'-'to her'-prefix-'I'-'gave'
        b. y - 1 - ə́ - y - td
            'it'-'to her'-prefix-'he'-'gave'

(Allen, 1956, 156-7) but here indicating the 'dative' whereas the ergative 'I' is marked by a series 3 element (which, however, as we have observed, differs minimally from series 2: cf. e.g. the ergative *y* for third person singular human masculine in both (114.b) and (115.b)). Of particular interest here is that the three-marker complexes we find with a verb like 'give' in (115), i.e. series 1 +series 2 +series 3, identical to those associated with the causatives of transitive verbs like 'kill' in (114):

(116)   y - 1 - s - r - ʃʸə́d
        'it'-'to her'-'I'-prefix-'made-kill'

(though they are distinguished by the sequence of the arguments with which the indices are in concord). This and similar phenomena in the other languages of the group,[44] though apparently not in the rest of the North Caucasian group (Dumézil, 1933, ch.1), follow quite naturally from a source for 'datives' such as was argued for in ch.2, whereby they originate as embedded (locative) ergatives, just like the argument in the case of 'make-kill' in (116) which takes the same concord series 2. Of course there are many further complexities in a description of the verb morphology of these languages. The incorporation of various prefixes into the verb, for instance, allows agreement where otherwise there would be none (Dumézil's (1932, ch.7) classes F-H). Moreover, beside 'transitives' like 'kill' in (114) there is another class (Dumézil's class B, Allen's (1956) class 2) in which the 'agent' takes a series 1 marker (i.e. like an absolutive) whereas the other argument takes a series 2 (*d-l-ə́sd* 'He/she *(d)* hit her *(l)*'). But in all these instances this other argument is apparently a goal, and indeed such sentences could be argued to be reductions from the same kind of structure as underlies 'give' ('give blow to' ⇒ 'hit'). However that may be, the similarities with the Basque situation are clear. And such a situation is quite inexplicable if datives or indirect objects are atomic primitives.

3.5.4. However, both these languages and Tzeltal, to return to our main theme, illustrate another kind of exception in agreement to what is predictable from the principles associated with the AH, one which Keenan & Comrie are in part aware of. But it seems to me that they frame the character of the discrepancy rather misleadingly. In various 'ergative languages' as they put it, 'transitive verb agreement is with the direct object rather than the subject'. But as we have noted with respect to Tzeltal, Basque etc., the discrepancy is even more significant than that. It is not just that what Keenan & Comrie call the 'direct object' shows agreement while the transitive 'subject' does not; the markers of agreement are also identical to the agreement markers for intransitive 'subjects'. Compare the Avar examples in (117):

(117) a.   emén   v-ač-ula
         'the father' concord-'come'-present
    b.   ebel-ica   emén   v-a č-ula
         'the mother'-erg 'the father' concord-'bring'-present

where in both instances the v marks agreement with *emén*.[45] Moreover in Tzeltal and other languages the transitive 'subject' does require agreement, but the markers of that agreement, as we have observed, are distinct from the set shared by transitive 'objects' and intransitive 'subjects'. Such systems of agreement and of noun morphology have been studied for some time.[46] This pattern of agreement (and noun-inflexion) is exactly what we would expect if subject-formation has not applied. The 'transitive object' and 'intransitive subject' are both (in the absence of subject-formation) absolutive (whether or not the 'intransitive subject' is also ergative), while the 'transitive subject' is ergative (and not absolutive). What is shown by languages like Avar, then, is that when subject-formation is lacking the absolutive is the highest relation on the hierarchy. Whereas, as we have seen, if subject-formation occurs, the ergative (on the interpretation of subject-formation as substitution of an erg — § 2.8) is the highest relation. A simple generalisation governs both situations: the CR — let us call it the BASIC CR — that is obligatory in any predication at a certain point in a derivation is highest in the hierarchy at that point. In the absence of subject-formation, abs is the obligatory CR (as argued in §§ 1.9-.10). The result of subject-formation is to introduce an erg into any predication which lacks it, at the expense of the obligatory status

of abs (some instances of which become ergs): erg thus is obligatory
after subject-formation. Naturally, 'obligatory' is not intended to refer
to necessary manifestation in surface structure or the like. Rather abs
(and possibly erg) are obligatory in the sense that they must be present
in any predication at some point in the derivation of sentences containing
the predication. (However, there is a correlation in some languages with
(non-elliptical) obligatory overt occurrence: see below.)

Of course, it is possible (as we have noted in § 3.1) to introduce into
a deep subject/object grammar an ad hoc definition for absolutives
which singles out the 'transitive object' and the 'intransitive subject'.
But such definitions, apart from being quite adventitious within such a
framework, beg the crucial question: what motivations are there for
labelling these arguments 'subject' and 'object' in the first place, rather
than as the semantically relevant abs and erg? On the other hand, it
follows naturally within a framework in which subject-formation is a
cycle-terminating rule that where the arguments in a language show no
sign of subject-formation, the pattern of agreement will similarly reflect
the obligatory status of abs rather than erg. (Though we shall refine on
this below.) And likewise, if we return now to relativisation, if
relativisation or a relativisation strategy is limited to a single position in
the case of a language of this kind, it will again be that characterised
by the basic relation in the absence of subject-formation, viz. absolutive.
Such a language is Dyirbal.

3.5.5. Dixon (1969; 1972, § 4.10) provides quite extensive documentation
of the restriction of relativisation to absolutives in Dyirbal. As he
observes (1972, 100), 'The "common NP" of a constituent sentence
must be in nominative case [the unmarked marker for absolutives – JMA]
for the sentence to be embedded on to the "common NP" of the matrix
sentence'. And he shows that there exists a construction (the '*ŋay*' or
'anti-passive' construction) whereby in a transitive simple sentence
'ergative is substituted for the nominative inflexion of the NP in O
function, and nominative for the ergative inflexion of the A NP' and
'the verbal stems are put into -*ŋay* form' (1972, 65); and that in order
for an A NP to be relativised it must appear in the -*ŋay* construction,
i.e. it must be marked as nominative (§§ 4.10, 5.5; see too 1969, 36-7).
Compare, in a language apparently showing subject-formation, the 'voices'
of Tagalog, which enable a range of NPs otherwise bearing distinct
relations to occupy subject position (Schachter & Otanes, 1972) and so
be eligible for relativisation (which is limited to subjects – Keenan &
Comrie, to appear: § 1.1). Thus Dyirbal *d̠ugumbil* ('woman') in both

of (118) is absolutive in the embedded (relative) sentence and thus relativises straight-forwardly:

(118) a. ŋadⱼa balan dⱼugumbil ɲinaŋu buṛan
        'I' classifier 'woman' 'sit'-rel 'look'
        (= 'I am watching the woman who is sitting down')
    b. balan dⱼugumbil ŋadⱼa buṛaŋu ɲinaŋu
        classifier 'woman' 'I' 'watch'-rel 'sit'
        (= 'The woman who I am watching is sitting down')

(Dixon, 1972, 100). Whereas the ergative *yaɣaŋgu* of a sentence like (119):

(119) bayi yuṛi baŋgul yaṛaŋgu bagan
        classifier 'kangaroo' 'spear' 'man'-erg classifier
        (= 'Man speared kangaroo')

(*ibid.*), must, in order to undergo relativisation, be 'converted' into an absolutive in a *ŋay*-construction, ín which this suffix is attached to the verb:

(120) bayi yaṛa bagalŋaŋu bagul yuṛigu
        classifier 'man' 'spear'-ŋay-rel classifier 'kangaroo'-erg
        banagaɲu
        'return' (= 'Man who speared kangaroo is returning')

(Dixon, 1972, 101). The significance of this is discussed by Johnson (1974, 277 ff), who also points out that absolutives are invoked by other rules in Dyirbal whose equivalents in subject-forming languages refer to subjects.

So, for example, in the formation of what Dixon (1972, §§ 4.5.2, 5.2.2) calls 'topic chains' the NPs in common must be absolutive, as in (121):

(121) bayi yaṛi baniɲu baŋgun dⱼugumbiṛu balgan
        classifier 'man' 'came-here' classifier 'woman'-erg 'hit'
        (= 'Man came here and was hit by woman')

If the second instance of the common NP is ergative, then the second sentence must assume the *-ŋay* form:

(122)   bayi yaṛa baniɲu bagun dⱼugumbilgu
         classifier 'man' 'came-here' classifier 'woman'-erg
         balgalŋaɲu
         'hit'-ŋay (= 'Man came here and hit woman')

In order for a 'topic chain' to be formed in which the ergative NP of the
first sentence is identical to the absolutive of the second, the second
sentence must assume the -ŋura construction (§§ 4.5.5, 5.6):

(123)   balan dⱼugumbil baŋgul yaṛaŋgu balgan baniɲura
         classifier 'woman' classifier 'man'-erg'hit' 'came-here'-ŋura
         (= 'Man hit woman and then immediately came here')

(The 'then immediately' part of the gloss is intended to indicate the
component of meaning which Dixon (1972, 77) describes the -ŋura
construction as adding.) Thus, the 'unmarked' 'topic chain' involves
absolutives in common. And the same is true of 'implicated topic
chains' (Dixon, 1972, § 5.4.4) involving 'lower topic deletion' (equi)
such as are illustrated by (124):

(124)   ŋadⱼa bayi yaṛa gigan bagun dⱼugumbilgu
         'I' classifier 'man' 'told' classifier 'woman'
         wawulŋaygu ŋinungu undalŋaygu bagu
         'fetch'-ŋay-comp 'you' 'bring'-ŋay-comp classifier
         midⱼagu wambalŋaygu
         'house' 'build'-ŋay-comp (= 'I told the man to fetch
         the woman to bring you to build the house')

Each embedded sentence appears in the -ŋay construction, so that the
(underlying) ergative can be deleted (as a derived absolutive). Again abs,
as the basic, or obligatory CR in a language lacking subject-formation,
occupies the special place occupied by subject, the obligatory derived
CR, in subject-forming languages.

3.5.6. A final instance of this. Perlmutter (1971, ch.4) proposed for
French and English (languages with subject-formation) a constraint of
the character of: 'Any sentence other than an Imperative in which there
is an S that does not contain a subject in surface structure is
ungrammatical' (p.100). Languages which include this constraint in
their grammars are 'type A languages'. It is not clear whether a language
which expresses relativisation and anaphora in part by deletion is

automatically excluded as Type A. In other respects, however, it seems
likely from Dixon's description (1972, § 4.5.1.) that Dyirbal may be a
type A language (though the status of subordinate subjects is unclear (to
me, at least)), but only if for 'subject' in Perlmutter's formulation we
can read 'absolutive'. However that may be, absolutives in Dyirbal
are again unique in that 'any sentence . . . must contain a topic
[= absolutive – JMA] NP'. In other languages a preference for
sentences which contain an overt absolutive is provided for in another
way. Comrie observes (1973, § 1) that when an absolutive phrase is
'removed' as such from a transitive predication in Chukchee, e.g. by
'absolutive-incorporation', the underlying erg CR comes to be marked
as abs (i.e. like English *offer, advise,* etc. (§ 3.4.4) it is a derived
agentive intransitive), even though in simple transitive sentences which
lack 'absolutive-incorporation' the morphology follows the usual
'ergative' pattern.

3.5.7. Confronted with such phenomena from Dyirbal as we have just
surveyed, Keenan & Comrie (n.1) concede that 'Dyirbal may be a
partial counterexample to the Absolute Subject Condition' (103), but
suggest that 'the constituent that Dixon wants to identify as the object
of transitive sentences has several properties that we normally expect
subjects to have (e.g. it often occurs initially, it gets control-deleted in
CONJUNCTION-REDUCTION and EQUI)'. However, to introduce
'subject' and 'object' here is simply inappropriate. The properties
which 'the object of transitive sentences' shares with 'subjects' in other
languages are those attributable to the basic (obligatory) CR: in
non-subject-forming languages it is the absolutive throughout; in
subject-forming languages whereas abs is obligatory before subject-
formation, erg (subject) is after. In a language with subject-formation,
conjunction-reduction and equi (which follow the relevant subject-
formation cycle, and may be the same rule – Anderson, 1974*a*)
delete subjects as the basic CR; otherwise abs is deleted. The
inappropriateness of equating 'the object of transitive sentences' with
subjects is underlined by those properties that it fails to share with
subjects, like (the subject's) being the repository for the agent in
unmarked action sentences. Such an inconsistent extension of the
term 'subject', indeed, serves only to confuse: as an extended exercise
in such confusion I recommend to the reader the use of 'sujet apparent'
v. 'sujet réel' etc. followed in works like Marr & Brière, 1931, part II.
However, it should be clear from the preceding discussion that what is
required is not an abandonment of (103) (and its equivalent for

processes other than relativisation), but rather simply the substitution for
'subjects' in its occurrences therein of 'the obligatory CR for the
predication at that point in the derivation': i.e. basic CR. (One can, of
course, label such a CR 'subject' but only by perpetrating what seems to
me, as I have indicated, an abuse of terminology.) Similarly, Pullum
(1975e) found that the only examples of OSV, i.e. object-initial
languages that he could substantiate were 'ergative' languages in whose
description O was being equated with abs and S with erg. These
languages are not exceptional with respect to the generalisation that
subjects either precede or are more peripheral than their objects if
the generalisation is reframed in terms of basic CR (S in subject-forming
languages, abs otherwise) *v.* non-basic (rather than simply S *v.* O).
We must now, however, take into consideration some related phenomena
which, I think, will lead to a further sharpening of our understanding of
the character and status of subject-formation.

3.5.8. We need, in the first place, to take account of the fact that a
large number of languages are PARTIALLY SUBJECT-FORMING, in
the sense that subject-formation either only occurs or only fails to
occur in certain predication types. Georgian, for instance, is often cited as
a language which, depending on the 'tense', displays either an 'ergative'
or 'subject' structure with active verbs. (For a brief description, see
e.g. Lafon, 1963, 1971.) Consider Lafon's examples (1971, 342):

(125) 1. a. mama   rbi-s
               'father' 'run' -concord (= 'father runs')
        b. mama c'er-s c'eril-s
               'father' 'write' -concord 'a letter'-dat/acc
        2.   mama-m dac'er-a c'erili
               'father'-erg 'wrote' -concord 'the letter'

The -*s* suffixed to the verbs in (125.1) agrees in both instances with the
subject *mama*, whereas the -*a* of *dac'era* concords with the ergative NP.[47]
That is, more generally, rather than there being a simple SUBJECT-
FORMING *v.* NON-SUBJECT-FORMING dichotomy (English, say, *v.*
Dyirbal) languages can vary in the extent (measured in construction-types)
to which subject-formation is applied. Indeed, we shall find that there is
evidence that both English and Dyirbal are partially subject-forming.
Consider firstly the case of Dyirbal, since an investigation of the status
of subject-formation there will uncover the further main respect in
which our notion of this process requires refinement.

Dixon (1972, §§ 3.3.1, 4.1.2) notes that 'superficially, pronouns in [the Dyirbal and Mamu dialects] follow a "nominative-accusative" pattern'. For example, there is a single form, *ŋad̡a,* for the 'first person singular' whether it 'corresponds to' an ergative noun in a transitive sentence or the single argument of an intransitive verb, whereas the absolute in a transitive sentence has a different form, *ŋayguna:*

> (126) a. ŋad̡a baniɲu 'I'm coming'
> b. ŋad̡a ɲinuna balgan 'I'm hitting you'
> c. ɲinda ŋayguna balgan 'You're hitting me'

(Dixon, 1972, 60). This is most naturally allowed for if subject-formation applies here, so that *ŋad̡a* is a subject pronoun and *ŋayguna* is an absolutive that has failed to undergo subject-formation in a construction to which subject-formation applies, i.e. it is an object. Such a situation is typical of the Australian languages. However, a more detailed consideration of the status of subject-formation in such cases will now require us to modify the formulation of this process arrived at above.

Dixon goes on (§ 5.2.2.) to 'give syntactic reasons suggesting that pronouns, like nouns, follow an underlying nominative-ergative pattern' (p.60). This is unsurprising, given the argument of this chapter. But the character of the evidence he provides is incompatible with either the formulation or the derivational status suggested above for subject-formation. I proposed in ch.2 on the basis of evidence from English that subject-formation involves the substitution of erg for the hierarchically highest CR in a predication; I re-state the formulation here as (127):

$$(127) \quad \text{abs} \rightarrow \text{erg, where} \begin{bmatrix} \text{abs} \\ \text{case} \end{bmatrix} > \text{abs}$$

In this chapter we have surveyed various pieces of evidence in the syntax of English for locating (127) at the end of the cycle, i.e. as applying at the termination of each cycle. Notice in Dyirbal, however, that though the pronouns are subject/object in character, it is nevertheless still only an absolutive pronoun that undergoes deletion under identity in a 'topic-chain', whether or not it is subjective or objective in form. Thus (128):

> (128) ŋad̡a baniɲun baŋgun d̡ugumbiɾu balgan
> 'I' 'came-here' classifier 'woman'-erg 'hit'

= 'I came here and was hit by woman'

is a well-formed 'topic-chain', even though the pronouns involved are respectively subjective and objective in the 'corresponding' simplex sentences:

(129) a. ŋadja baniɲu 'I came here'
       b. ŋayguna baŋgun dⱼugumbiʈu balgan 'woman hit me'

And, on the other hand, (130):

(130) *ŋadja baniɲu balan dⱼugumbil balgan
      'I' 'came-here' classifier 'woman' 'hit'

is not such, even though the pronouns in the corresponding simplexes are identical in form; compare with (129.a) the sentence in (131);

(131) ŋadja balan dⱼugumbil balgan 'I hit woman'

Rather, the second sentence in the chain must assume the *-ŋay* construction:

(132) ŋadja baniɲu bagun dⱼugumbilgu balgalŋaɲu
      'I' 'came-here' classifier 'woman'-erg 'hit'-*ŋay*

If subject-formation as expressed in (127) applies at the end of each cycle then it would have destroyed the information on which the respective well-formedness and deviance of (128) and (130) depends, viz. whether the NP to be deleted is absolutive or not. In order to express this generalisation, subject-formation in Dyirbal must be weakened in one of two obvious ways: either subject-formation is post-cyclic in Dyirbal, or it differs from (127) in involving addition of erg rather than substitution. In the latter case, both erg and abs thereby become basic CRs. That is, rather than (127), subject-formation in Dyirbal involves (133):

(133) SEMI-SUBJECT-FORMATION:
$$\text{case} \rightarrow \begin{bmatrix} \text{case} \\ \text{erg} \end{bmatrix}, \text{ where erg} > \begin{bmatrix} \text{abs} \\ \text{case} \end{bmatrix} > \text{abs.}$$

whereby subject-formation does not, as in English, destroy the case information of the argument that is subjectivised. Rather, both its casehood and its subjecthood are available to subsequent cycles. Erg in this instance thus corresponds to Dixon's (1972, § 5.8.2) '+actor' feature, in terms of which he accounts for Dyirbal pronoun morphology. However, he also requires imperatives to include a [+ actor] NP, whereas it is rather the case that it is only underlying ergs that correlate with imperativisation: not all intransitive verbs permit unmarked imperativisation.

Now, the formation of 'topic-chains' in Dyirbal refers, as we have seen, to abs as basic. Accordingly the second possible modification to subject-formation [(133)] is supported (rather than post-cyclic application) if we can show that there are aspects of Dyirbal syntax or there are languages which make the other choice, i.e. take erg as basic, where both are available. There do appear to be such languages. Moreover, there is evidence of the other choice internal to Dyirbal.

As Dixon observes: 'There is one respect in which pronouns seem to have slightly wider syntactic possibilities than nouns' (1972, 134). And from his discussion it seems clear that these 'wider syntactic possibilities' depend upon subject-formation. A 'subject' pronoun like $\eta ad_j a$, as well as being the link in a 'topic-chain' involving absolutives, can also, unlike full NPs, 'run through a sequence of transitive simple sentences' (Dixon, 1972, 73), such as (134):

(134) $\eta ad_j a$ bala yugu yuban/balan $d_j$ugumbil $d_j$ilwan
'I' classifier 'stick' 'put-down' classifier 'woman' 'kicked'
(= 'I put down the stick and kicked the woman')

So a non-initial 'subject' pronoun can be deleted in the formation of a 'simple chain' if the pronoun and its 'controller' share their (underlying) CR (both abs or both simple erg). It is significant that this hierarchical equivalence of abs and erg is attributable only to those forms that show a subject/object morphology. Erg is permissible as a deletee only with forms to which (133) has applied, i.e. to which an erg has been added. The generalisation seems to be this: abs is always deletable under identity with a controller abs; however simple erg is deletable if it is a subject (it is marked by an extra erg). Observe too that 'in the "norm" word order, a non-pronominal NP in ergative inflexion comes after any (nominative) topic NP [in agreement with the generalisation suggested above — JMA]; but an NP involving a pronoun in [subject] form . . . will precede any other NP' (again in conformity with Pullum's proposals (1975e)) (Dixon, 1972, 134). Now, such phenomena do not necessarily show that (127) or (133) (as the case may be) are in the cycle: that depends on the status of the principles governing deletion in 'topic-chains' and the establishment of word order in Dyirbal. However, they do suggest that at some point information concerning both underlying CRs and subjecthood must be available to certain syntactic processes. Thus (127) must be weakened to (133) anyway; and it is therefore (at least) unnecessary to demote subject-formation further to a post-cyclic status.

If this is so, then it looks as if we need to recognise not only that languages may be partially subject-forming, in that subject-formation occurs only in certain construction-types, but also that subject-formation itself may involve either substitution (127) or addition (133). In view of the fact that (133) does not destroy information concerning underlying CRs, I shall term the languages showing this SEMI-SUBJECT-FORMING. Dyirbal, then, is partially subject-forming (only pronouns) and also semi-subject-forming ((133) rather than (127) is appropriate). English is not semi-subject-forming ((127) can be maintained); but we shall in a moment consider some indications that it is only partially subject-forming, i.e. that there are constructions in English which apparently lack subject-formation. Dyirbal owes its semi-subject-forming status to the fact that despite its pronominal subject-object morphology, information concerning CRs clearly must remain available throughout the cycle. It also appears to be the case that there are languages with an ergative morphology whose syntax nevertheless invokes the notion 'subject'.

3.5.9. Heath (1974) argues that this is true of Basque, for instance, concerning which he cites such generalisations as (p.250): 'the choice between perfective . . . and subjunctive . . . complements depends on whether the main-clause controller NP is coreferential with the lower-clause *subject'* (i.e. erg in transitives, abs in intransitives). Since, however, the subjects referred to by the rules he discusses are in embedded clauses, his observations are quite compatible with the hypothesis of cycle-terminating subject-formation. However, not only the nominal morphology but also, as we have seen, the markers of agreement on the verb are in Basque of an 'ergative' character. If at least the feature-copying part of agreement is late (post-cyclic), this suggests that Basque is semi-subject-forming in that the distribution of underlying CRs (rather than subjects) must be available to the rules of agreement. Alternatively, Basque has full subject-formation, and agreement is on the basis of case forms rather than relations; but this fails to account for the erg/dat parallel noted above. And it may be excluded in principle.

Unlike the Dyirbal pronouns, the 'ergative' morphology is retained in Basque; conversely syntactic reference to subjecthood is apparently more extensive. And other Australian languages appear to be like Basque in this respect. Hale claims that 'in the majority of [ergative] languages in Australia, the rules and constraints in the grammar which make reference to the relation "subject-of" show that the subject of a non-transitive sentence is the NOMINATIVE NP and that the subject of a transitive sentence is the ERGATIVE NP' (1970, 771-2). But either reference is once again to embedded subjects (in e.g. complementiser insertion) or is post-cyclic (agreement) or his claim is unjustified. As an instance of the last, we can note imperativisation, which Hale includes as subject-dependent but which clearly does not involve subjects but simply agents, whether simple (in a transitive sentence) or in combination with abs (intransitive agentives). It seems to me that this is typical of situations where it has been claimed that a morphologically 'ergative' language is underlying 'subjective' in character. References to 'subject' are compatible with the assumption of cycle-terminating semi-subject-formation.

Some of Comrie's discussion of the 'ergative' (1973) is devoted to showing that 'subject and direct object are relevant categories in describing the syntax of [many ergative] languages' (p.242). But once more the phenomena concerning morphology, agreement and word order are not incompatible with cycle-terminating (semi-) subject-formation, as is his demonstration that the choice of ergative v. subject morphology can be based on quite superficial syntactic considerations (cf. e.g. the phenomena from Chukchee noted above). On the other hand, his assumption of underlying subject-object structures for these languages (as for any others) is quite a prioristic. They are, for instance, as we have seen, in conflict with generalisations concerning raising etc. Moreover, attaching ergativity to such structures, such that the ergative is essentially the marker of a 'transitive subject', means that (1973, 252) 'the ergative may appear as a totally arbitrary rule for a language to have'. Comrie's suggested explanation, 'in terms of a measure of closeness of nodes', requires the importation of a notion (node-counting) which is, as far as I am aware, required by no other generalisation. (Rosenbaum's (1970) similar 'minimal distance principle' for equi controllers is also inappropriate.)

Another problem in such an approach to 'ergativity' is that it is not clear how one is to recognise a 'transitive verb' and a 'transitive subject'. Recall, for instance, the situation in Abaza, or consider Georgian, where

there are certain verbal forms that take two arguments neither of which
is, in either the 'present' or the 'aorist', marked as 'ergative': rather one
is 'dative-accusative', the other 'nominative':

> (135)   a.   Ḳoṭe   m-dzul-s
>   'Ḳoṭe' 'I-hate-her' (= 'I hate Ḳoṭe')
>   b.   Ḳeto-s Ḳoṭe s-dzul-s
>   'Ḳeto'-dat/acc 'Ḳoṭe' 'he-hate-her'
>   (= 'Ḳeto hates Ḳoṭe')

(cf. (125)). Other verbs incorporate the absolutive:

> (136)   a.   m-acxeleb-s
>   'I'-'fever'-'it' (= 'I fever/have fever')
>   b.   Luarsab-s gaexard-a
>   'Luarsab'-dat/acc 'rejoice'-'is-it'
>   (= 'Luarsab rejoices')

(examples from Chanidze, 1963). On the 'transitive subject' account,
either (135) are, for some reason, exceptional with respect to the rule
placing ergative markers or the verb forms are, for some reason, not
transitive. (They cannot, on grounds of circularity, be excluded as
transitive only because they do not show the ergative marker.) Notice,
however, that these are all [loc, erg] (experiencer) verbs, and thus
their exceptionality as well as regular 'ergativity', is, on the other hand,
perfectly natural on the basis of the representations and derivations
proposed on independent grounds within a case grammar such as we
have been discussing here.

     The CRs also throw some light on semantic extensions of ergativity
which Comrie's 'syntactic' account leaves untouched, indeed apparently
inexplicable in a non-arbitrary way. Comrie discusses, for example, the
situation in Bats (North-East Caucasian) where the ergative form in
transitive sentences like (137):

> (137)   As   jopsṭ   axo
>   'I'-erg 'plough' 'the land'

is also used in an intransitive like (138):

> (138)   As wože
>   'I'-erg 'fell'

in contrast with (139):

(139)   So wože
           'I'-abs 'fell'

The contrast however is apparently not simply one of non-agentive *v.* agentive (i.e. [abs] *v.* [abs, erg]), as in 'active' languages like Dakota (see below); rather, (138) also imputes responsibility: 'it was my own fault that I fell'. But this is not unnatural, given a semantic status for erg and abs, since 'responsibility', 'fault' are contingent upon agency. What seems to be happening in Bats is that since in intransitive predications the erg marker is not needed to distinguish the (absolutive) ergative phrase as such (in contrast with transitives, where there is a distinct absolutive) it is utilised only when it is required to emphasize the ergativity of the argument in order to impute blame. A definition of the ergative as 'syntactic expression of a transitive subject' offers on Comrie's own account no explanation for such a situation.

Similarly, it is unnecessary to attribute the 'active' morphology of Siouan languages to some surface aberration even if references to subjects are required by the syntax. Again, as I understand it, the syntax of these languages is not in conflict with the hypothesis concerning subject-formation formulated here. And they are morphologically rather transparent with respect to (underlying) CRs. In morphologically 'ergative' languages a simple ergative is opposed to an absolutive, whether or not this absolutive is also ergative: crudely, the argument in all 'intransitive' sentences is marked by abs, as well as the non-ergative argument in transitives. In Dakota, on the other hand, one can distinguish an 'active' pronoun series from a 'non-active'. 'Active' pronouns are ergative, either alone or in combination with abs, whereas 'inactive' are simply abs. Thus in most cases the morphology correlates well with the distribution of CRs we established above on independent grounds. Compare (140):

(140)   a. ma-čéka   'I stagger'
           b. ma-yá-kte 'You killed me'
           c. wa-lową   'I sing'
           d. ča-wá-pa   'I stab him'

(from Wolff, 1951), where *ma* is the non-active first person marker and *wa* the active. Matthews (1965, 142-7) rejects such a natural explanation for the morphology of Dakota, on the basis once more of a priori assumptions concerning underlying structures and the citing of a few lexical exceptions, concerning which he says himself: 'Actually, the actual number of exceptions is small: the use of the ergative relation [he only discusses the 'active' morphology as an exception to the 'ergative' situation – JMA] explanation does account for the form of most subjects and goals in Hidatsa sentences' (p.147). However, he goes on,

> it is important to note that although the performance of the ergative explanation is a close approximation to that desired, it differs radically from the present explanation in terms of subjects, goals, and objects, active and stative verb phrases, and the causative construction. In no sense is the ergative explanation a close approximation of the correct explanation.

The 'present explanation', which is presumably to be identified with the 'correct explanation', constitutes another example of arbitrary syntax in which the semantically natural (and its syntactic relevance) is not distinguished from the lexically exceptional, and in which the positing of 'deep structures' is irrelevant to the expression of the semantic generalisations embodied in a case grammar account, and indeed is otherwise unmotivated. And again the possible natural basis for some of the exceptions is obscured. Matthews notes, for instance, that whereas the verb 'hear' takes a 'goal' subject, that for 'see' does not. Observe, however, that it is possible to make a case that notionally the orientation of these two verbs may also be opposed. Gruber (1967) has argued for English, for example, that the 'object' of *see* is allative; i.e. in terms of the present framework the 'subject' of *see* is the ablative term in a directional relationship. Now, rather the reverse orientation is appropriate for *hear:* contrast with *see into* etc. sentences like *He heard from his sister that* . . . However that may be, a more adequate account of the full range of phenomena, semantic, syntactic, morphological, lexical, will, it seems to me, have to be one which has a place for the hypothesis that Matthews rejects, whereby the distribution of the person markers in Hidatsa is not arbitrary.

References to CRs and subjecthood can thus interrelate in an intricate fashion, particularly in semi-subject-forming languages. This is well illustrated by Itkonen's discussion (1974-5) of ergativity in Finnish. He notes, for instance, that though in general subject-formation is evident in Finnish (on the basis of concord etc.), the formation of certain 'deverbal adverbs' is on a partially ergative basis (1974-5, § 1.3). He also illustrates (§ 2.5) how an earlier ergative system in 'necessive infinitival clauses' is in process of transformation into a subject-based one. Formerly

only a transitive ergative was marked by the (dative) genitive inflexion
in sentences like *Pojan pitäisi syödä puuro* ('The boy (gen. sg.) should eat
porridge'); cf. *Poika pitäisi mahtua tälle penkille* ('The boy (acc. sg.)
should sit on this bench'). However, the genitive inflexion is spreading
to the latter non-agentive kind of sentence as well, thus bringing this
construction type in line with the position in simple finite clauses. This
is a restricted instance of a development that it is sometimes suggested
has occurred more generally in the history of the Indo-European
languages: i.e. the development of subject-formation and the taking
over of the former ergative marker for subjects in general.

Most striking perhaps as a consequence of the simultaneous
availability of the CRs and the subjecthood status of a single argument
such as is allowed by semi-subject-formation is the phenomenon of
'existential sentences' (Itkonen, 1974-5, § 1.4) and the development of
partitive subjects in intransitive sentences (§ 2.4). In 'normal sentences'
the subject is in the nominative case and, if transitive, the object may be
either accusative or partitive (the latter expressing 'an indefinite
quantity of a divisible object concept' (p.395)); concord is with the
subject. However, in a subset of intransitives, 'existential sentences', i.e.
in which the main propositions are themselves existential (denote being
in, coming into or going out of a location or existence) or contain
quantified arguments which originate in a superordinate existential (cf.
Anderson, 1974*a*), there is an alternation in the inflexion of the
'subject' between nominative and partitive (on the same basis as with
transitive objects). And there is no concord. (The alternation in
intransitive existential sentences is a later development than that in the
object and seems to have originated with intransitive verbs which also
have a transitive use.) Thus concord, for instance, is appropriately
formulated as depending on both subjecthood and casehood as well as
other factors. And the possibility of having a partitive inflexion depends
on the CR (absolutive) and information some of which originates
outside the main proposition (in e.g. a superordinate existential) and
thus accessible only after subject-formation in the main proposition.
All these observations, however, remain compatible with
cycle-terminating (semi-) subject-formation.

None of the phenomena we have surveyed, then, are in conflict with
the hypothesis of cycle-terminating subject-formation, provided we
allow this to be partial, and provided we admit semi-subject-formation
(133) as well as (127). Indeed, the observations concerning 'ergative'
and 'active' languages that we have taken account of are naturally
allowed for in terms of the distribution of CRs that was argued for

largely on the basis of the fully subject-forming language English. On
the other hand, for the hypothesis of 'subject'-'object' 'deep structures'
these phenomena constitute arbitrary elaborations upon the underlying
structural relations, in part syntactically defined, in part semantically
distinctive (Comrie, 1973). Worse, perhaps, they constitute morphological
partial correlates of the 'thematic relations' which are interpreted at
'deep structure'. If, on the other hand, these are not interpreted at 'deep
structure' (Jackendoff, 1975), then even that slim 'motivation' for the
positing of such a level disappears. And the status of the 'ergative'/'active'
markers (how are they introduced? etc.) remains uncertain.

If there are (non-semi-)subject-forming languages, like English, which
have developed from an earlier non-subject-forming language, like
perhaps Indo-European (Uhlenbeck, 1901; Kretschmer, 1947), then the
semi-subject-forming situation constitutes a plausible middle stage, to
the extent that the existence of such a possibility is well attested in
extant languages. We have seen that languages can maintain an 'ergative'
morphology while incorporating a rule of semi-subject-formation,
which can serve as the basis for full subject-formation, perhaps initially
only in certain constructions.[48] It is, however, not my concern to
pursue such questions of history, which introduce a host of issues we
cannot adequately deal with here. Instead I would like to conclude this
section by indicating certain features of contemporary English which
can be attributed to its being (? still) only partially subject-forming.

3.5.10. Chomsky (1970*a*) discusses, among other things, passive
nominalisations such as that in (141):

(141)   The city's destruction by the enemy

corresponding to the active (142):

(142)   The enemy's destruction of the city

I am not concerned here with these pairs in relation to the 'lexicalist
hypothesis'. My interest is focussed on another 'variant' of (141) noted
by Chomsky, viz. (143):

(143)   (The) destruction of the city by the enemy

This last can be allowed for if the passive transformation is broken down
into two components, agent-postposing, which alone has applied

in (143), and NP-preposing, which has also, together with agent-postposing, applied in (141). If agent-postposing can apply even in the absence of a post-verbal object, then the same rule has operated in the derivation of (144):

(144) a. The advance by the enemy
       b. The offer by the enemy to spare the city

but not of (145):

(145) a. The enemy's advance
       b. The enemy's offer to spare the city

The capacity for agent-postposing to apply without consequent NP-preposing (143) and in the absence of an object is limited to nominalisations, however:

(146) a.*Destroy(ed) (of) the city by the enemy
       b.*Advanc(ed) by the enemy

though this can be allowed for, perhaps, in a non-ad hoc way in terms of Perlmutter's (1971, ch.4, (9)) constraint (English is a type A language). But it seems to me that a rather different conclusion might be drawn from this range of phenomena, one which indeed accords better with some related observations.

Notice in the first instance that as well as (144) and (145) we can have (147):

(147) a. The advance of the enemy
       b. The offer of the enemy to spare the city

Whereas to (148):

(148)   The enemy's tendency to destroy cities

there corresponds no (149):

(149)   *The tendency by the enemy to destroy cities

though we do find (150):

On the Nature of Grammatical Relations

269

(150)   The tendency of the enemy to destroy cities

How are we in a non-arbitrary way to prevent agent-postposing from
applying to (148)? And why does *of* alternate with *by* in (144)/(147)?
There is, indeed, one obvious correlation: *of* in such examples manifests
the CR abs (provided subject-formation has not applied), whereas *by*
marks erg. The sentences in (144)/(147) involve agentive intransitives, and
in them *the enemy* is thus both abs and erg. I tabulate these
correlations in (151):

(151)   a. *of*   = abs; in (143), (150)
         b. *by*   = erg; in (143)
         c. *of, by*   = abs, erg; in (144), (147)

If, however, subject-formation had applied in the case of (150), we
would expect it to be marked as *by* also. The distribution of markers in
(151. a/b) is precisely what we would expect of an 'ergative' language, i.e.
they correlate with the underlying CRs rather than showing any sign of
subject-formation. And this is confirmed by (144)/(147), which reveal
that, quite naturally, a NP which is [abs, erg] can be marked by either
of, the reflex of abs, or *by*, the reflex of erg. I suggest then that (143),
(144), (147) and (150) simply lack subject-formation. And this correlates
with sequence; they show no sign of subject-preposing, which depends
on subject-formation, in that they all follow the nominalised predicate
they depend on.

(141), (142), (145) and (148) show subject-preposing, apparently,
and the putative subject has a special marker, -*s*. Abs continues to be
marked by *of*, as in (142), but in (141), (145) and (148) the underlying
abs argument has undergone subject-formation, in (141) in a passive.
We can allow for all of these sentences, and the restrictions we have
noted, by allowing subject-formation to be optional in nominalisations,
and by requiring that subject-preposing and passivisation be contingent
upon subject-formation.

As a confirmation of this we should note that there are
nominalisations like (143) which lack subject-formation variants like
(141)/(142), such as (152):

(152)   Knowledge of these facts by unauthorised persons

Cf. (153):

(153)   a. *These facts' knowledge by unauthorised persons
        b. *Unauthorised persons' knowledge of these facts

This situation can be allowed for by restricting subject-formation (and thus also passivisation) in nominalisations to agentive ergs (and absolutives), i.e. by excluding e.g. [loc, erg] NPs from subject-formation. (We should note, however, that this is overridden in an 'extent' nominalisation like that in *My uncle's knowledge of French astounded me;* and clearly there exist other subregularities not dealt with here. However even in such a case a variant parallel to (141) is excluded.) In an account involving NP-preposing and agent-postposing, however, the latter will have to be made to apply obligatorily with *knowledge* whereas the former will have to be obligatorily excluded, two instances of an arbitrary exception. Notice further that there are also nominalisations containing an *of-* and a *by*-phrase which have a related nominalisation structure like that in (142) but not one like (141), and whose unnominalised congener lacks a passive, because it is adjectival; compare:

(154)   Awareness of these facts by the appropriate authorities

with both (155):

(155)   a.*These facts' awareness by the appropriate authorities
        b. The appropriate authorities' awareness of these facts

and (156):

(156)   *These facts are aware(d) by the appropriate authorities

Thus, the adjective nominalisation permits subject-formation but lacks a passive, as does the unnominalised form. Here, if we are to invoke pre-and post-posing, agentive postposing is optional for the nominalisation (but is excluded altogether in the unnominalised variant), but NP-preposing remains impossible. In the non-nominalised congener there is, however, no passive possibility at all.

It seems clear, then, that the occurrence of the *by*-phrase in such sentences as (143), (152) and (154) has nothing to do with the application of (one component in) the passive transformation. *By* simply marks ergative NPs. It is removed by subject-preposing. It thus turns up, as expected, where subject-formation (and thus subject-preposing) is lacking, as the marker of underlying ergative NPs, and also in instances where a subject is moved out of subject position before preposing occurs (at shallow structure), as in passives. We noted in ch.2 that the occurrence of *by* as marker of the 'agent' in passives is unnatural given the source for passives proposed there, whereby the 'agent' is an ablative phrase. This is less anomalous if *by* is simply the idiosyncratic marker of all ergative phrases which in this instance is carried up into the ablative in passives by the operation of equi. In other languages it is the abl of the passive predication that is given overt expression; in English the *by* of the lower erg. On the other hand, under psych-movement, as in *That was known to many people,* the *to* of the allative phrase in the psych-predication is expressed, rather than the *by* marking [loc, erg] in the basic predication. (Indeed, otherwise such passives and psych-variants would collapse in expression: *That was known by many people.*) If the *to* in psych-movement variants with *know* derives from the psych-predication, and this latter requires subject-formation to occur in the basic predication, we would predict that there will be no nominalised equivalent to (152) containing *to,* since we have established that *knowledge* rejects subject-formation. And this is indeed the case:

(157)   a.*Knowledge of these facts to unauthorised persons
         b.*These facts' knowledge to unauthorised persons

It seems to me that the phenomena we have surveyed point to the conclusion that English is only partially subject-forming, in that this applies optionally in nominalisations, and indeed for a subset of such it is excluded. I shall not pursue further here the question of determining the domain of subject-formation in English and elsewhere; preliminary work indicates that there is a hierarchy of constructions with respect to eligibility for subject-formation (as was suggested to me by Dave Roberts). We also now need to reformulate this process.

3.6 Postscript

3.6.1. Let us now turn in the light of these phenomena and other observations we have made to a final formulation of subject-formation and subject-preposing. Another property of the nominalisations lacking subject-formation is also relevant here. In all of (143), (152) and (154), which contain both an *of-* and a *by*-phrase, the *of*-phrase comes first. However, the reverse order is equally viable. I accordingly interpret subject-formation as having the character of (158):

(158)   a. *subject-formation*
   $case_i \rightarrow erg$
   b. *argument-ordering*   , where for $i \neq j$ $erg >$ $\begin{bmatrix} (case_j) \\ abs \end{bmatrix}$ $>$
   $> \quad \supset \quad \ll$

The second part serialises arguments in accordance with the case hierarchy for subject-forming languages, on the assumption that up to subject-formation the arguments are unsequenced with respect to each other and merely all depend to the left (centripetal) or right (centrifugal) of their predicate. In § 1.11 we hypothesised that serialisation depended on two sets of information, (a) the modifier-head (dependency) relationships, and (b) the relational hierarchy. However such evidence as we have found to support the hypothesis that underlying representations are invariant rather than unordered (like the typology of extraposition) applies only to the factors under (a). (The reflexivisation phenomena discussed in § 1.11 are doubtful in the light of the discussion in the present chapter.) So that it is possible that, as the nominalisations evidence suggests, sequencing of the arguments of a predicate relative to each other is determined only cycle-finally (i.e. along with subject-formation in languages which show this). Notice too, incidentally, that if this is so, the question of whether or not a predicate can have subjoined to it non-contiguous arguments has no content.

If such sequencing of arguments also occurs at this point in non-subject-forming languages, then the hierarchy will have abs at the top as the basic CR in the absence of subject-formation (158.a). This gives e.g. abs erg V languages (i.e.'apparent' OSV – Pullum, 1975*e*). In subject-forming languages (158.b) allows for VSO and SOV. In English there is a post-cyclic subject-preposing rule (→ SVO), while in other languages there is, according to Pullum (1975*e*), a subject-postposing rule (→ VOS). There are also both V-initial (centrifugal – e.g. Nass-Gitskan) and V-final (centripetal – Dyirbal) ergative languages. However, in Nass-Gitskan at least, according to Rigsby (1975), the order is V erg abs and V erg form a constituent (VP). We can again attribute this to subject-postposing, if this is generalised to postposing of the basic case.

The equivalent of SVO in 'ergative' languages would be abs V erg, which possibility does not, however, seem to be well represented in the languages of the world. It is possible that we can relate this to the notion 'basic CR' (as defined in § 3.5). A basic case phrase is 'unmarked' vis-à-vis other case phrases. If any member of a paradigmatic opposition is to be given zero expression it will tend to be the unmarked ones (Greenberg, 1963), in this instance the basic CR. In subject-forming languages both erg (as subject) and abs (as object and complement – see below) are basic, respectively after and before subject-formation. If both, as unmarked CRs, are given zero expression then SVO order is optional for discrimination. However, 'ergative' languages have only one basic CR, and only absolutes tend to be given zero expression. Thus the situation especially favouring an equivalent of SVO order does not arise.

We are now in a position to look a little more carefully at the formulation of subject pre- and post-posing (I shall not pursue here the possibility that some SVO sequences derive from SOV, since the status of this is in even more doubt than other typological aspects of serialisation; moreover a formulation is not difficult to arrive at.) In ch.2 we formulated subject-preposing as reproduced in (159):

$$(159) \quad \text{erg} \lesseqgtr V \supset \text{erg} \ll V$$

This would require that subject-postposing must be given a rather different type of formulation, in that by it erg comes to follow all the case phrases dependent on the same predicate. Moreover, Pullum suggests that there is evidence that in SVO and VOS languages VO form a constituent. We can allow for all of this in terms of a formulation such as (160):

$$(160) \quad \textit{subject-positioning}$$
$$V_0 \ll \text{erg}_1 \ll X(\text{case}_1) \supset \text{erg}_1 \lesseqgtr V_{0,1} \ll X(\text{case}_2)$$

where the subscripts indicate degree of dependency, such that on the left of the rule both erg and case (as degree one) depend on V (degree zero); and X is any (possibly null) sequence of dependents of V.[49] By (160), (a) the V is assigned two degrees (zero and one) of dependency and all its original dependents except erg are weakened to degree two, and (b) erg comes to precede or follow ($\gtrless$) V_0. Thus, from such a structure as (161), which includes case$_1$ but takes X to be null:

(161)

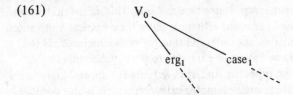

we get either of (162):

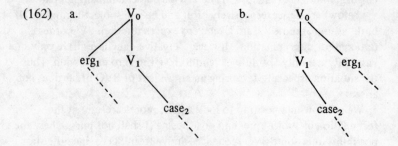

(162)   a.   b.

Note that in (162.b) erg will come to follow not just the V but any dependents of V_1; otherwise non-projectivity would result. Throughout the application of the cyclic rules we have made the assumption that a predicate which has another subjoined to it also has assigned to it the original dependents of the subjoined predicate. Thus schematically:

(163)

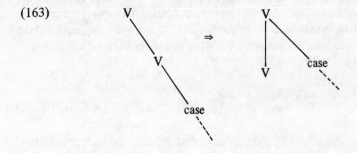

However, the postcyclic rule of subject-positioning introduces just such a configuration as is denied pre-shallow structures. These are structures in which the elements in a subjunction tree can take independent arguments, rather than only the governor of the subjunction tree having the capacity for having (adjoined) arguments. Moreover, in (162) it is a single element which occupies both positions in the subjunction tree, i.e. is of both dependency degree zero and one. This means that, on the one hand, we should examine rather carefully the empirical motivations for such a formulation as (160) (and thus for such structures as (162)); but on the other, we have now extended to post-cyclic syntax configurations of a type that Anderson & Jones (to appear) argue are appropriate to characterise phonological structures. It is also possible that abs-/object-incorporation involves just such a process (without (re-) sequencing), and perhaps cyclically. In this instance, however, only the abs is reattached to the equivalent of V_1 and all other arguments remain attached to V_0.

We have found it necessary, to sum up, to propose that subject-formation (158.a) can apply only partially in a language, i.e. only in certain specific circumstances; specifically, it can apply only in certain constructions (pronominal predications in Dyirbal), or optionally in certain constructions (nominalisations in English). Indeed, I am uncertain whether there are any languages which are completely non-subject-forming or the reverse. Moreover, though we can maintain that full subject-formation (as in (158)) occurs in English, there is in Dyirbal, or Basque, perhaps, only semi-subject-formation, in that rather than the rule involving substitution we have simply addition (133): thus information concerning both (underlying) casehood and subjecthood remain available on subsequent cycles. We have, however, been able to maintain in § 3.5 the position originally established in previous sections for English specifically, that subject-formation is cycle-terminating.

3.6.2. We have otherwise not found it necessary to introduce rules which change the CRs associated with a given NP (and 'changes' of this character are all contingent upon processes like raising). That is, either the derived relations alluded to in derivations are (with the exception of subjecthood) the same as underlying CRs or, perhaps, they are definable in terms of these. For instance, it is possible that we require in English, at least, to refer to a relational notion 'object' which includes the two post-verbal arguments in (164):

(164)   Frederick gave his granny the loot

but only the first of those in (165):

(165)   a. Frederick gave the loot to his granny
         b. Frederick loaded the truck with the loot

For one thing, only the 'objects' normally (i.e. unless overruled lexically) have no overt case marker. Now if objects are limited to abs then the final argument in (165.a) is excluded as a potential object. But the final argument in (165.b) *is* absolutive, according to the analysis offered above. It may be that that particular aspect of the analysis requires modification anyway. However, this is unnecessary merely to provide an appropriate basis for defining objects. These we can define without modification as in (166):

(166)   *Object:* An absolutive is an object if it is at some point the hierarchically highest absolutive argument in a predication which prior to subject-formation also contains a separate ergative argument.

Given the schematic underlying representation for (164) shown in (167):

(167)

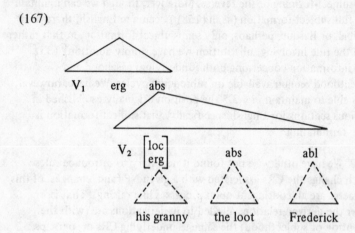

then on the V_2 cycle *the loot* meets the conditions specified in (166) and is thus an object, whereas on the V_1 cycle:

(168)

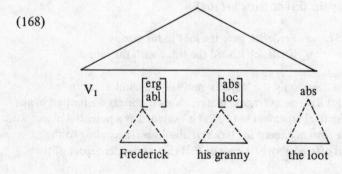

his granny meets these same conditions. Both post-verbal arguments in
(164) are objects. Clearly, on the other hand, only the first of the two
post-verbal arguments in (165.a) does so, in that the second is not
absolutive. The final argument in (165.b) is, as we have recalled, an
absolutive. But at no point in the derivation does it meet the
conditions specified in (166): at no time is it the hierarchically highest
absolutive in a predication also containing (before subject-formation) a
separate erg. Cf. (169):

(169)   a.

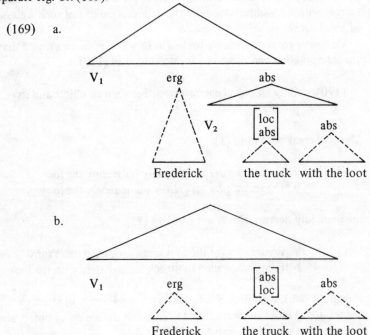

    b.

On the V₂ cycle ((169.a)), *the loot* is subordinate to *the truck,* which
latter is moreover non-ergative: neither argument is an object. And on
the V₁ cycle ((169.b)) *the loot* remains subordinate to *the truck;* but they

are now, however, in a predication which also contains a separate ergative phrase, and *the truck* is thus an object.

We can thus formulate objecthood as involving the cyclic introduction (simultaneous with subject-formation) of (in English) the null (or, alternatively, lexically determined) case marker with respect to an absolutive which meets the definition in (166). Other absolutives have *with* introduced. Such a formulation is supported to the extent that other syntactic generalisations (apart from the distribution of the null marker with non-subjects) require the delimitation of just such a class of absolutives.

One such generalisation we looked at in § 2.8, where we found that the interpolation ban should be formulated as in (170):

(170)   Only an object can intervene between an object and its predicate

Thus, whereas both of (171):

(171)   a.*Frederick gave immediately his granny the loot
         b.*Frederick gave his granny immediately the loot

are markedly deviant, this is not true of (172):

(172)   a. Frederick gave the loot immediately to his granny
         b.?Frederick loaded the truck immediately with the loot

though (172.b), with final absolutive, is (in the absence of stress on *immediately*) more awkward than (172.a). Our definition of object also excluded the second argument in (173):

(173)   The person you love is the one you hurt most

since prior to subject-formation both arguments are absolutive, and thus correctly predicts that (174) is well-formed:

(174)   The person you love is frequently the one you hurt most

On the other hand, the second argument apparently has, like the object in English, the null marker. This is thus also inserted with respect to a simple abs which prior to subject-formation is in the same predication as another simple absolutive argument. In other languages,

of course, this correspondence between object and complement to *be*
is not found and indeed in more formal English the two are distinguished
by the pronominal morphology (*I v. me* etc). This suggests that even
in English objecthood involves not simply the introduction of the null
marker but also perhaps the addition of some surface relation, unless it
is simply the case that, say, interpolation is disallowed before a
null-marked absolutive after any element but *be*. Alternatively the
second abs in (173)/(174) is deleted (as part of subject-preposing), just
as subject-preposing removed the erg CR; and it is thus not realised by
the null object marker. This accords with the fact that in many
languages (and marginally in English) the subject and complement
both bear the non-oblique inflexion, whereas that for the object as
defined by something like (166) is distinct, oblique, an accusative. The
crucial thing is that the absolutives in equative predications fail to meet
the definition for objects ((166)) and therefore fail to receive the object
marker (which happens to be null in English). The zero expression for
the CR in their case is due to the distinct process (whatever its
character) that in English removes case nodes after subject-preposing, or
in other languages introduces a nominative inflexion. This would enable
us to maintain a formulation of the interpolation ban like (170) which
refers to objects characterised by presence of the null (object) marker.
If too sentences like ?*His plays have very frequently a sad ending* are
markedly better than those in (171) this would confirm the notion of
object formulated in (166) as far as expression of the interpolation ban
is concerned, in that these sentences have a [loc, abs] subject and [abs]
postverbally. However, in many languages this postverbal abs in 'have'
sentences bears an accusative inflexion. Is there a different criterion for
objecthood required for different generalisations (and different
languages)? Perhaps this is unsurprising given the epiphenomenal status
of objecthood suggested by the account developed here. However that
may be, it seems plain that whereas subject-formation involves a
neutralisation of CRs, 'object-formation', whatever its character,
introduces a diversification amongst the class of absolutives.

3.6.3. Thus, if we return to the question with which this whole
discussion started, we have in the course of the discussion arrived at
what appears to be part of an answer, at least. In § 1.1 we broached
the traditional problem of arriving at a non-arbitrary articulation of the
relationship between CRs and the elements that mark them. We have on
the whole been able to maintain that this is a natural relationship, at
least, for such parts of English that we have looked at: the distribution

of case markers is far from arbitrary in terms of the semantically relevant localist case grammar that we have elaborated. Moreover, though underlying case relations may be collapsed as a result of the operation of such rules as raising and equi, we have found it necessary to propose only one process (and that, as we have seen, of limited distribution), viz. subject-formation ((158.a)), whose formulation involves as an essential part the neutralisation of case relations.

NOTES

1. For discussion of notions of 'case', 'subject', etc. see e.g. Havers, 1911; Sandmann, 1959; Lyons, 1968*a*, §§ 7.4.2, 8.1; Anderson, 1969, 1971*b*, ch.1; Starosta, 1973*a*.
2. On some problems arising from such a proposal, see e.g. G. Lakoff, 1970*a*, App. F.1; McCawley, 1973*a*, § 2.2.2; Freidin, 1975. On the other hand, difficulties with Hasegawa's analysis are raised by Chomsky (1970*a*, 212; 1970*b*, 85, fn. 36) — see too, McCawley, 1970, note 6; and § 3.3 below.
3. Principally 1965, 1966*a*, 1966*a*, 1968*a*, 1968*b*, 1971*a*, 1971*b*, 1971*c*, 1972. For related but distinct suggestions put forward over about the same period see e.g. Anderson, 1968*a*, 1969*a*; Brekle, 1970. Nilsen provides in the course of two recent discussions (1972, 1973) a range of references to further related work.
4. Cf. the introduction to Stockwell, Schachter & Partee, 1973. And much of Fillmore's work has indeed been concerned with such questions: see particularly 1966*b*, 1968*b*, 1970, 1971*a*, 1971*b*.
5. Cf. Anderson, 1970, 1971*b*; Huddleston, 1970, 1971, § 3.1; Mellema, 1974, § III; and on *see* and *show* specifically, Contreras, 1970. We return to some of these questions below.
6. For further discussion of such matters, see e.g. Gruber, 1965; Jackendoff, 1972, § 2.2; Cruse, 1973; D. Lee, 1973; Schachter, 1973, § 1.23. See too below.
7. This emerges from discussions by e.g. Dougherty, 1970*b*, 1971, 1973; Teng, 1970, § 2; Andrews, 1971; and Anderson, 1973*a*, § 2; despite the argument partly in its favour in Quang (1969), which is however inconclusive (Wang, 1971; Bang-Bang, 1974).
8. I note in passing that the passive corresponding to (67.a), if the *by*-phrase is in Jackendoff's terms 'theme' and the subject a 'location', constitutes another counter-example to the Thematic Hierarchy Condition, which ranks 'location' above 'theme'.
9. For other problems with I, see Walmsley, 1971; Nilsen, 1972: 21ff, 1973; Buckingham, 1973; Seiler, 1973.
10. Cf. of late e.g. Partee, 1971; Fraser, 1971; Chomsky, 1972*a*; Kilby, 1973*b*; Vestergaard, 1973.
11. See further Ljung, 1970, 54-5; Partee, 1971, 21; Huddleston, 1971, 116; Vestergaard, 1973, 85-6.
12. Cf. e.g. Abraham, 1971*a*; Cook, 1971*a, b*, 1973; Fillmore, 1971*c*, 1972; Kirkwood, 1973; Langendoen, 1969, 1970*a*; McCoy, 1969; Marino, 1972; Nilsen, 1972, 1973; Platt, 1971; Stockwell, Schachter & Partee, 1973; Vestergaard, 1973; Walmsley, 1971.
13. E.g. Günther, 1975; Heger, 1966, 1971; Helbig, 1971; Helbig & Schenkel, 1973; Heringer, 1973.
14. E.g. Halliday, 1967-8; Hudson, 1971
15. Such as are represented by Chafe, 1970; Ikegami, 1970, 1973; Inoue, 1970; Leech, 1969; Schank, 1972; Sgall *et al.*, 1969; Panevová, 1974.
16. For general discussion, see e.g. Bever, 1970; Grosu, 1971, 1974; Morgan, 1973; Green, 1974*b*; Hankamer, 1974.
17. Apart from in Starosta's own work, such an approach is exemplified by discussions including Manley, 1972; Taylor, 1972; P. Li, 1973; Ramos, 1973; Kullavanijaya, 1974.

18. Take as a sample (even a subset of) the sets of derivations proposed in Ross, 1967; Postal, 1971, 1974.
19. Notice, for instance, with respect even to the generalisation concerning raising formulated in § 1.9.2. that a framework whereby information concerning CRs and grammatical relations is equally available throughout derivations provides no explanation for the interaction between CRs and (derived) grammatical relations described in that section. Why is the host for raising specified as absolutive (i.e. as a CR) but the source as a subject (a grammatical relation)? This is perfectly natural if subject-formation is cyclic.
20. Similar considerations apply to Starosta's appeal (as analogous) to the distinction between natural and grammatical gender, as to Katz's (1967, § vi) discussion of the same. Only if semantic and grammatical gender are described in terms of the same alphabet (of semantic elements) can we give expression to the naturalness or otherwise of some grammatical form. A masculine form is natural if it is semantically masculine; it is unnatural (grammatical) if it is masculine only by lexical convention and it is semantically of some other gender. Cf. here e.g. Givón, 1970.
21. On simplex features, cf. Sanders, 1971.
22. Clearly (ii, iii, iv) can be further collapsed, given that each merely specifies that a particular case feature entails the presence of the corresponding CR in certain environments, however I preserve the more extended notation in the interests of clarity.
23. If we impose the additional requirement that CRs are preferably introduced as an additional component to an already present argument, then even the subparts of (iii) and (iv) need not be ordered with respect to each other.
24. Cf. here Carnap's (1958, § 18) 'functions'; and see further the discussions in McCoy, 1969; Nilsen, 1972; Cook, 1973.
25. For discussion see e.g. Hays, 1964; Robinson, 1970b. Cf. too Tesnière, 1959. On dependency structures in phonology, see Anderson & Jones, 1974, to appear.
26. On the perceptual basis for such a principle, see e.g. Kuno, 1974; Anderson, 1975a.
27. Cf. Seuren, 1969; Miller, 1973a, for arguments in favour of such a view of selectional restrictions even within a deep subject/object grammar.
28. See G. Lakoff, 1966, 1970a, for a similar position; and cf. Lyons, 1966; Anderson, 1969a.
29. For one suggestion of an appropriate classification, see again Anderson, 1973a.
30. Cf. e.g. Chomsky, 1970a; Bowers, 1969, 1975; Newmeyer, 1971; Baker 1975.
31. The intimate relationship between case markers and complementisers (particularly in linguistic elaboration) is well illustrated by such discussions as Ferguson, 1970; Moravcsik, 1972; Hinds, 1973; Joseph, 1975; and Washabaugh, 1975.
32. On Planudes, see too Robins, 1974. Hjelmslev (1935) provides a concise history of the localist debate, culminating in terms of number of contributions and general interest aroused in the controversies of the late nineteenth century. (This is but one of many areas of debate obscured by the standard histories of the period (like Pedersen's (1931)) with their concentration on the development of theories of genetic comparison and reconstruction.)
33. For discussion, see e.g. Catford, 1959; Cooper, 1968; Teller, 1969; Leech, 1969; Bennett, 1972; Clark, 1973; Jessen, 1974, chs. 2 & 3; Dreike, 1974.
34. This variety is described by e.g. Jackendoff & Culicover, 1971. On the history of such passives see Visser, 1973, §§ 1976-7.
35. Cf. e.g. Johnson, 1974; Bell, ?1974; Keenan, 1975; Shimizu, 1975; Trithart, 1975.
36. For a related observation, see Morin & O'Malley, 1969, 184, footnote 2.

37. For some discussion, consider van der Gaaf, 1929; Vendryes, 1921, 125-6; Anderson, 1971*b*, §9.5.
38. Carden, 1968, app. B, 1973; Hudson, 1970; Dougherty, 1970*b*, 876-7; Postal, 1974, § 4.5; Anderson, 1974*a*. The character of the movement processes is unimportant for the present discussion, which is concerned with the nature of the NPs that a quantifier can move from.
39. See however the works referred to in note 35 above.
40. The antecedent apparently can bear an abs relation as a result of raising or equi and still be viable: the abs referred to by (29.1) is cycle-initial. Otherwise such psych-movement sentences (§ 3.3.8) as *Bill impressed himself* would be excluded.
41. I have changed Postal's 'Direct Discourse' in the first line of (79) − cf. 1970, 495 − to 'Indirect Discourse', since otherwise the formulation fails to make any sense.
42. For other contributions to the debate, see e.g. Postal & Ross, 1971; Akmajian, 1972; Postal, 1972, 217-8, n.10; Lightfoot, 1974; Langacker, 1974; Jackendoff, 1975.
43. For an example of such an extended usage, see Reece, 1970. Vagueness concerning the criteria for indirect-objecthood also vitiates Moravcsik's (1974) otherwise informative discussion of object agreement.
44. Cf. e.g. Dumézil, 1932, ch.7; 1931, 94-7, 119-30; Paris, 1969 (the last two on Ubykh); Allen, 1964.
45. Examples from Tchekhoff, 1973, 257-9.
46. Cf. for discussion, illustration and references to earlier work, Allen, 1950-1; Meščaninov, 1967; Comrie, 1973.
47. On a similar discrepancy in other languages see e.g. Allen, 1950-1 (Hindi); 1960 (Rājasthānī) Comrie, 1973, §§ 2-3 (Georgian, Pānjabi).
48. On a mechanism for the reverse development, via a 'passive' construction, see e.g. Allen, 1950-1, 71-3; Pirejko, 1968.
49. It may be that for particular languages X does not contain all dependents of a V but only some subset up to some cut-off point on the relational hierarchy.

BIBLIOGRAPHY

Abbreviations

AL	Acta Linguistica (Hafniensia)
ArchL	Archivum Linguisticum
BGDSL	Beiträge zur Geschichte der deutschen Sprache und Literatur
BSL	Bulletin de la société de linguistique de Paris
BS³	Berkeley Studies in Syntax and Semantics
CJL	Canadian Journal of Linguistics
CLS	(Papers from the annual regional meeting of the) Chicago Linguistic Society
ES	English Studies
EWPL	Edinburgh Working Papers in Linguistics
FL	Foundations of Language
FoL	Folia Linguistica
IF	Indogermanische Forschungen
IJAL	International Journal of American Linguistics
IL	Indian Linguistics
IULC	(distributed by) Indiana University Linguistics Club
JL	Journal of Linguistics
LAUT	(distributed by) Linguistics Agency, University of Trier
Lg.	Language
LIn	Linguistic Inquiry
LLWP	Languages and Linguistics Working Papers, Georgetown University
MSLL	Monograph series on Languages and Linguistics, Georgetown University
PBML	Prague Bulletin of Mathematical Linguistics
PIL	Papers in Linguistics
POLA	Project on Linguistic Analysis, Ohio State University
PPhS	Proceedings of the Philological Society of London
RRLing	Revue roumaine de linguistique
SL	Studia Linguistica
TCLP	Travaux du cercle linguistique de Prague
TPhS	Transactions of the Philological Society of London
WPL	Working Papers in Linguistics, Ohio State University
YPL	York Papers in Linguistics
ZRPh	Zeitschrift für romanische Philologie

Abraham, Werner (1971*a*), 'Nachwort', to Abraham (1971*b*), 185-205
—— (ed.) (1971*b*), *Kasustheorie*. Frankfurt/M, Athenäum
Akmajian, Adrian (1972), 'Getting tough', *LIn* 3, 373-7
Allen, W. Sidney (1950-1), 'A study in the analysis of Hindi
    sentence-structure', *AL* 6, 68-86
—— (1956), 'Structure and system in the Abaza verbal complex', *TPhS*,
    127-76
—— (1960), 'Notes on the Rājasthānī verb', *IL* 21, 4-13
—— (1964), 'Transitivity and possession', *Lg*. 40, 337-43
Anderson, John M. (1968*a*), 'Ergative and nominative in English', *JL* 4,
    1-32
—— (1968*b*), 'On the status of "lexical formatives" ', *FL* 4, 308-18
—— (1969*a*), 'Adjectives, datives and ergativisation', *FL* 5, 301-23
—— (1969*b*), 'A note on "rank" and "delicacy" ', *JL* 5, 129-35
—— (1970), 'The case for cause: a preliminary enquiry', *JL* 6, 99-104
—— (1971*a*), 'Dependency and grammatical functions', *FL* 7, 30-7
—— (1971*b*), *The Grammar of Case: Towards a Localistic Theory*,
    London & New York, Cambridge University Press
—— (1971*c*), 'A proposal concerning the lexicalisation of complex
    structures', *SL* 25, 1-8
—— (1972), 'Remarks on the hierarchy of quasi-predications',
    RRLing 17, 23-44, 121-40, 193-202, 319-35
—— (1973*a*), 'Some speculations concerning meetings, matrimony,
    family resemblances and related matters', *YPL* 3, 7-29
—— (1973*b*), 'Maximi Planudis in memoriam', in Kiefer & Ruwet,
    20-47
—— (1973*c*), *An Essay concerning Aspect: Some Considerations of a
    General Character arising from the Abbé Darrigol's Analysis of the
    Basque Verb*, The Hague, Mouton
—— (1973*d*), 'Universal quantifiers', *Lingua* 31, 125-76
—— (1973*e*), Review of Geneviève N'Dyaie, *Structure du dialecte
    basque de Maya*, Mouton, The Hague, 1970, *Lingua* 32, 344-55
—— (1974*a*), 'Concerning quantifiers and coordination', LAUT
—— (1974*b*), 'Existential quantifiers', *AL* 15, 1-27
—— (1975*a*), 'Noun phrases as adjectives: Serialisation in seven parts',
LAUT
—— (1975*b*), 'A note on the placement of universal quantifiers',
    FoL 7, 317-38
—— (1975*c*), 'La grammaire casuelle', in Anderson & Dubois-Charlier,
    18-64
—— (1975*d*), 'A non-argument for deep structure', *YPL* 5, 87-96

——— & Françoise Dubois-Charlier (eds.) (1975), *La grammaire des cas,
(= Langages* 38) Paris, Didier-Larousse

——— & Marilyn E. Jessen (1973), 'Some time, I', *EWPL* 3, 123-40.

——— & Charles Jones (1974), 'Three theses concerning phonological
representations', *JL* 10, 1-26.

——— & Charles Jones (forthcoming), *Phonological Structure and the
History of English,* Amsterdam, North-Holland

Anderson, Stephen R. (1971), 'On the role of deep structure in
semantic interpretation', *FL* 7, 387-96

——— & Paul Kiparsky (eds.) (1973), *A Festschrift for Morris Halle,*
New York, Holt, Rinehart & Winston

Andrews, Avery (1971), 'Against conjunct movement', *LIn* 2, 250-2

Bach, Emmon (1968), 'Nouns and noun phrases', in Bach & Harms, 90-122

——— (1971), 'Questions', *LIn* 2, 153-66

——— (1974), *Syntactic Theory,* New York, Holt, Rinehart & Winston

——— (1975), 'Order in base structures', In Li, 307-43

——— & Robert T. Harms (eds.) (1968), *Universals in Linguistic Theory,*
New York, Holt, Rinehart & Winston

Baker, C. Leroy (1975), 'The role of part-of-speech distinctions in
generative grammar', *Theoretical Linguistics* 2, 113-31

Baltin, Mark (1975), 'On the cyclicity of extraposition', *LIn* 6, 465-8

Bang-Bang, C.C. (1974), 'The grammar of sexual inequality', LAUT

Bartsch, Renate & Theo Vennemann (1972), *Semantic Structures,*
Frankfurt am Main, Athenäum

Becker, Donald A. (1971), 'Case grammar and German *be*', *Glossa* 5,
125-45

Bedell, George (1973), 'The arguments *for* deep structure', in Schachter
& Bedell, 1-33

Bell, Sarah J. (?1974), 'Two consequences of advancement rules in
Cebuano', mimeo

Bennett, David C. (1972), 'Some observations concerning the
locative-directional distinction', *Semiotica* 5, 58-88

——— (1975), *The Spatial and Temporal Uses of Prepositions in English,*
London, Longman

Benveniste, E. (1952), 'La construction passive du parfait transitif',
BSL 48, 52-62

Berman, Arlene (1974), 'On the VSO hypothesis', *LIn* 5, 1-38

Bever, Thomas G. (1970), 'The cognitive basis for linguistic structures',
in John R. Hayes (ed.), *Cognition and the Development of Language,*
New York, John Wiley & Sons, 279-362

Bierwisch, M. & K.E. Heidolph (eds.) (1970), *Progress in Linguistics,*

The Hague, Mouton

Binnick, Robert I. (1971), 'Bring and come', *LIn* 2, 260-5

Boas, Franz (ed.) (1922), *Handbook of American Indian Languages*, 2 (= Smithsonian Institution Bureau of American Ethnology Bulletin 40), Washington

Bogoras, Waldemar (1922), 'Chukchee', in Boas, 631-903

Bowers, John S. (1969), 'Adjectives and adverbs in English', IULC

—— (1975), 'Some adjectival nominalisations in English', *Lingua* 37, 341-61

Brecht, Richard D. & Catherine V. Chvany (eds.) (1974), *Slavic Transformational Syntax*, Ann Arbor, University of Michigan

Brekle, Herbert E. (1970), *Generative Satzsemantik und transformationelle Syntax im System der englischen Nominalkomposition*, Munich

Bresnan, Joan W. (1970), 'On complementisers: Toward a syntactic theory of complement types', *FL* 6, 297-321

Browne, E. Wayles (1972), 'Conjoined question words and a limitation on English surface structures', *LIn* 3, 223-6

Buckingham, Hugh W. (1973), 'The comitative and case grammar', *FL* 10, 111-21

Carden, Guy (1968), 'English quantifiers', in Kuno

—— (1973), *English Quantifiers: Logical structure and Linguistic Variation*, Tokyo, Taishukan

Carnap, Rudolf (1958), *Introduction to Symbolic Logic and its Applications*, New York, Dover

Chafe, Wallace L. (1970), *Meaning and the Structure of Language*, Chicago, Chicago University Press

Chanidze, A. (1963), 'Le sujet grammatical de quelques verbes intransitifs en géorgien', *BSL* 58, 27-40

Chomsky, Noam (1957), *Syntactic Structures*, The Hague, Mouton

—— (1965), *Aspects of the Theory of Syntax*, Cambridge, Mass, MIT Press

—— (1970*a*), 'Remarks on nominalization', in Jacobs & Rosenbaum, 184-221; reprinted in Chomsky (1972*b*)

—— (1970*b*), 'Deep structure, surface structure and semantic interpretation', in Jakobson & Kawamoto, 52-91; reprinted in Chomsky (1972*b*)

—— (1972*a*), 'Some empirical issues in the theory of transformational grammar', in Peters, 63-130; also in Chomsky (1972*b*)

—— (1972*b*), *Studies on Semantics in Generative Grammar*, The Hague, Mouton

—— (1973), 'Conditions on transformations', in Anderson & Kiparsky, 232-86

Chvany, Catherine V. (1974), 'The grammar of *dolžen:* Lexical entries as a function of theory', in Brecht & Chvany, 78-122

Clark, Herbert H. (1973), 'Space, time, semantics and the child', in T.E. Moore (ed.), *Cognitive Development and the Acquisition of Language*, 27-63, New York, Academic Press

Comrie, Bernard (1973), 'The ergative: Variations on a theme', *Lingua* 32, 239-53

Contreras, Heles (1970), Review of Goldin (1968), *Lingua* 25, 12-29

Cook, Walter A. (1971*a*), 'Case grammar as deep structure in tagmemic analysis', *LLWP* 2, 1-9

—— (1971*b*), 'Improvements in case grammar 1970', *LLWP* 2, 10-22

—— (1973), 'A set of postulates for case grammar analysis', *LLWP* 4, 35-49

Cooper, C.S. (1968), 'A semantic analysis of English locative prepositions', AFCRL-68-0056 U.S.A.F., Bedford, Mass., Report No. 1587, Bolt, Beranek & Newman,

Cruse, D.A. (1973), 'Some thought on agentivity', *JL* 9, 11-23

Curry, H.B. (1961), 'Some logical aspects of grammatical structure', in Jakobson, 56-68

Daneš, F. (1968), 'Some thoughts on the semantic structure of the sentence', *Lingua* 21, 55-69

Darrigol, J.-P. (1829), *Dissertation critique et apologétique sur la langue basque,* Bayonne

Davidson, Donald A. & Gilbert H. Harman (eds.) (1972), *Semantics of Natural Language,* Dordrecht, Reidel

Dillon, George L. (1974), 'Passives and reflexives as quasi-predications', Ms.

Dirr, A. (1905), 'Grammatičeskij očerk tabasaranskogo jazyka', *Sbornik materialov dlja opisanja mestinostej i plemen kavkaza* 35, 3, Tbilisi

Dixon, R.M.W. (1969), 'Relative clauses and possessive phrases in two Australian languages', *Lg.* 45, 35-44

—— (1972), *The Dyirbal Language of North Queensland,* London & New York, Cambridge University Press

—— (1973), 'The semantics of giving', in Gross, Halle & Schützenberger, 205-23

Dougherty, Ray C. (1970*a*), 'Recent studies on language universals', Review of Bach & Harms (1968), *FL* 6, 505-61

—— (1970*b*), 'A grammar of coordinate conjunction, I', *Lg.* 46, 850-98

—— (1971), 'A grammar of coordinate conjunction, II', *Lg.* 47, 298-339

—— (1973), 'A survey of linguistic methods and arguments', Review of Reibel & Schane (1969), *FL* 10, 423-90

Dreike, Beate (1974), 'What is the "sense" of prepositions?', *EWPL* 4, 1-13

Dumézil, Georges (1931), *La langue des oubykhs*, Paris, Champion

—— (1932), *Etudes comparatives sur les langues caucasiennes du nord-ouest*, Paris, Adrien-Maisonneuve

—— (1933), *Introduction à la grammaire comparée des langues caucasiennes du nord*, Paris, Champion

Emonds, Joseph (1969), 'A structure-preserving constraint on NP-movement transformations', *CLS* 5, 60-5

—— (1970), *Root and Structure Preserving Transformations*, IULC

—— (1972), 'Evidence that Indirect Object Movement is a structure-preserving rule', *FL* 8, 546-61

Evers, Arnoldus (1975), *The Transformational Cycle in Dutch and German*, Doctoral dissertation, University of Utrecht

Fauconnier, Gilles R. (1971), *Theoretical Implications of some Global Phenomena in Syntax*, Ph.D. dissertation, University of California, San Diego (available from IULC)

Ferguson, Charles (1970), 'Grammatical categories in data collection', *WPLU* 4, F1-F15

Fillmore, Charles J. (1965), 'Toward a modern theory of case', *POLA* 13, 1-24; reprinted in Reibel & Schane, 361-75

—— (1966a) 'A proposal concerning English prepositions', *MSLL* 19, 19-33

—— (1966b), 'Deictic categories in the semantics of "come" ', *FL* 2, 219-26

—— (1968a), 'The case for case', in Bach & Harms, 1-88

—— (1968b), 'Lexical entries for verbs', *FL* 4, 373-93

—— (1970), 'The grammar of hitting and breaking', in Jacobs & Rosenbaum, 120-33

—— (1971a), 'Types of lexical information', in Steinberg & Jacobovitz, 370-92; also in Kiefer, 109-37

—— (1971b), 'Verbs of judging', in Fillmore & Langendoen, 273-89

—— (1971c), 'Some problems for case grammar', *WPL* 10, 245-65 (also in *MSLL* 23, 35-6)

—— (1972), 'Subjects, speakers and roles', in Davidson & Harman, 1-24

—— & D. Terence Langendoen (eds.) (1971), *Studies in Linguistic Semantics*, New York, Holt, Rinehart & Winston

Fischer, Susan D. & Byron Marshall (1969), 'The examination and abandonment of the theory of begin of D.M. Perlmutter as carried out by two of the inmates of room twenty-E-two-fifteen, under the direction of divine providence', IULC

Fletcher, Paul (1971), 'Case grammar: Its viability as an alternative grammatical model', *Lingua* 28, 237-50

Fodor, Jerry A. (1970), 'Three reasons for not deriving "kill" from "cause to die" ', *LIn* 1, 429-38

Frajzyngier, Zygmunt (1975), 'Against the universality of spatial source and goal', *FL* 13, 349-60

Fraser, Bruce (1971), 'A note on the *spray paint* cases', *LIn* 2, 604-7

Freidin, Robert (1972a), 'On the analysis of passives', mimeo (published version: *Lg.* 51 (1975), 384-405)

—— (1972b), 'Transformations and interpretive semantics', mimeo

Fujimura, Osamu (ed.) (1973), *Three Dimensions of Linguistic Theory*, Tokyo, TEC

van der Gaaf, W. (1929), 'The conversion of the indirect personal object into the subject of a passive construction', *ES* 11, 1-11, 58-67

Gee, James Paul (1974a), 'Jackendoff's thematic hierarchy condition and the passive construction', *LIn* 5, 304-8

—— (1974b), 'Get passive', IULC

Gildersleeve, B.L. & G. Lodge (1897), *Latin Grammar*, 3rd edn, London, Macmillan

Givón, Talmy (1970), 'The resolution of gender conflicts in Bantu conjunction: When syntax and semantics clash', *CLS* 6, 250-61

Gleitman, Lila R. (1965), 'Coordinating conjunctions in English', *Lg.* 41, 260-93; reprinted in Reibel & Schane, 80-112

Goldin, Mark G. (1968), *Spanish Case and Function*, Georgetown University Press

Gonda, J. (1951), *Remarks on the Sanskrit Passive*, Leiden, Brill

Gray, Louis H. (1939), *Foundations of Language*, New York, Macmillan

Green, Georgia M. (1974a), *Semantics and Syntactic Regularity*, Bloomington & London, Indiana University Press

—— (1974b), 'The function of form and the form of function', *CLS* 10, 186-97

Greenberg, Joseph H. (1963), 'Some universals of grammar with particular reference to the order of meaningful elements', in Joseph H. Greenberg (ed.), *Universals of Language*, 58-90, Cambridge, Mass., MIT Press

Grinder, John T. (1970), 'Super Equi-NP Deletion', CLS 6

—— (1972), 'On the cycle in syntax', in Kimball (1972), 81-111

Gross, Maurice, Morris Halle & M.P. Schützenberger (eds.) (1973), *The Formal Analysis of Natural Languages*, The Hague, Mouton

Grosu, Alexander (1971), 'On perceptual and grammatical constraints', *CLS* 7, 416-27

—— (1974), 'On reordering elements of clause non-final constituents', *CLS* 10, 198-215

Gruber, Jeffrey S. (1965), *Studies in Lexical Relations*, Ph.D. dissertation, MIT (available from IULC)

—— (1967), 'Look and see', *Lg.* 43, 937-47

Gundel, Jeanette K. (1975), 'Left dislocation and the role of topic-comment structure in linguistic theory', *WPL* 18, 72-131

Günther, Hartmut (1974), 'Valency, case forms, and case relations', Ms.

Hadley, J. (1867a), *Essays Philological and Critical*, London, Macmillan

—— (1867b), 'On passive formations', in Hadley (1867a), 199-214

Hale, Kenneth L. (1970), 'The passive and ergative in language change: The Australian case', in Wurm & Laycock, 757-83

Hall, Barbara (1964), Review of Šaumjan & Soboleva (1963), *Lg.* 40, 397-410

Halliday, M.A.K. (1967-8), 'Notes on transitivity and theme', *JL* 3, 37-81, 199-244; 4, 179-215

Hankamer, Jorge (1973), 'Unacceptable ambiguity', *LIn* 4, 17-68

—— (1974), 'On the non-cyclic nature of WH-clefting', *CLS* 10, 221-33

Hanmagomedov, Bejdullach hadji Kurbanovič (1958), *Sistema mestnych padežej v tabasaranskom jazyke*, Machačkala

Hasegawa, Kinsuke (1968), 'The passive construction in English', *Lg.* 44, 230-43

Haudry, Jean (1968), 'Les emplois doubles du datif et la fonction du datif indo-européen', *BSL* 63, 141-59

—— (1970), 'L' instrumental et la structure de la phrase simple en indo-européen', *BSL* 65, 44-84

Hays, David G. (1964), 'Dependency theory: A formalism and some observations', *Lg.* 40, 511-25

Heath, Jeffrey (1974), 'Some related transformations in Basque', *CLS.* 10, 248-58

Heger, Klaus (1966), 'Valenz, Diathese und Kasus' *ZRPh* 82, 138-70

—— (1971), *Monem, Wort und Satz*, Tübingen, Niemeyer

Helbig, Gerhard (ed.) (1971), *Beiträge zur Valenztheorie*, The Hague, Mouton

—— & Wolfgang Schenkel (1973), *Wörterbuch zur Valenz und Distribution deutscher Verben*, 2nd edn, Leipzig, VEB Bibliographischer Verlag

Helke, Michael (1972), 'On reflexives in English', *Linguistics* 106, 5-23
Heringer, Hans J. (1973), *Theorie der deutschen Syntax*, 2nd edn,
    Munich, Hueber
Hinds, John (1973), 'Case markers and complementizers', *WPLU* 13, 93-6
Hjelmslev, Louis (1935/7), 'La catégorie des cas', *Acta Jutlandica* 7, i-xii,
    1-184; 9, i-vii, 1-78, reprinted 1972 by Willhelm Fink Verlag, Munich
Hofmann, Th. R. (1974), 'The nuclear model of clause structure; or,
    A study of the basic principles of grammar', mimeo
Huddleston, Rodney D. (1970), 'Some remarks on case grammar', *LIn* 1, 501-11
—— (1971), *The Sentence in Written English*, London & New York,
    Cambridge University Press
Hudson, R.A. (1970), 'On clauses containing conjoined and plural noun
    phrases in English', *Lingua* 24, 205-53
—— (1971), *English Complex Sentences*, Amsterdam, North-Holland
Ikegami, Yoshihiko (1970), *The Semiological Structure of the English
    Verbs of Motion: A Stratificational Approach*, Tokyo, Sanseido
—— (1973), 'A set of basic patterns for the semantic structure of the
    verb', *Linguistics* 117, 15-58
Inoue, Kazuko (1970), ' "Case" from a new point of view', in Jakobson
    & Kawamoto, 246-80
Ioup, Georgette (1975), 'Some universals for quantifier scope', in
    Kimball (1975), 37-58
Itkonen, Terho (1974-5), 'Ergatiivisuutta suomessa', *Virittäjä* (1974),
    379-98; (1975), 31-65
Jackendoff, Ray S. (1971), 'On some questionable arguments about
    quantifiers and negation', *Lg.* 47, 282-97
—— (1972), *Semantic Interpretation in Generative Grammar*,
    Cambridge, Mass, MIT Press
—— (1974), 'Introduction to the $\overline{\text{X}}$ convention', IULC
—— (1975) '*Tough* and the Trace Theory of movement rules', *LIn* 6, 437-47
—— & Peter Culicover (1971), 'A reconsideration of dative movements',
    FL 7, 397-412
Jacobs, Roderick A. & Peter S. Rosenbaum (1968), *English Transform-
    ational Grammar*, Waltham, Mass., Ginn
—— (eds.) (1970), *Readings in English Transformational Grammar*,
    Waltham, Mass., Ginn
Jacobson, Pauline & Paul Neubauer (1974), 'Extraposition rules and the
    cycle', *BS*³ 1
Jakobson, Roman (1936), 'Beitrag zur allgemeinen Kasuslehre:
    Gesamtbedeutungen der russischen Kasus', *TCLP* 6, 240-83
—— (ed.) (1961), *Structure of Language and its Mathematical Aspects*,

Providence, R.I., American Mathematical Society

—— & Shigeo Kawamoto (eds.) (1970), *Studies in General and Oriental Linguistics presented to Shiro Hattori,* Tokyo, TEC

Jespersen, Otto (1924), *The Philosophy of Grammar,* London, Allen & Unwin

Jessen, Marilyn E. (1973), 'Preliminaries to a theory of temporal journeys', *EWPL* 2, 109-26

—— (1974), *A Semantic Study of Spatial and Temporal Expressions in English,* Ph.D. thesis, University of Edinburgh

Johnson, David E. (1974), 'On the role of grammatical relations in linguistic theory', *CLS* 10, 269-83

Joseph, Brian D. (1975), 'Case marking and complementizers in Persian', *WPLU* 17, 141-4

Kastovsky, Dieter (1973), 'Causatives', *FL* 10, 255-315

Katz, Jerrold J. (1967), 'Recent issues in semantic theory', *FL* 3, 124-94

—— (1972), *Semantic Theory,* New York, Harper & Row

Kaufman, Terrence (1971), *Tzeltal Phonology and Morphology,* (= University of California Publications, Linguistics 61)

Keenan, Edward L. (1975), 'Some universals of passive in relational grammar', *CLS* 11, 340-52

——& Bernard Comrie (to appear), 'Noun phrase accessibility and universal grammar', *LIn*

Key, T.H. (1851), 'On the nature of the verb, particularly on the formation of the middle or passive voice', *PPhS* 5, 51-70

—— (1858), *A Latin Grammar,* London, Bell & Daldy

—— (1874), *Language: Its Origin and Development,* London, Bell

Kiefer, Ferenc (ed.) (1969), *Studies in Syntax and Semantics,* Dordrecht, Reidel

—— & Nicolas Ruwet (eds.) (1973), *Generative Grammar in Europe,* Dordrecht, Reidel

Kilby, David (1973*a*), *Deep and Superficial Cases in Russian,* Ph.D. thesis, University of Edinburgh

—— (1973*b*), 'Notational variance in Generative Semantics', *EWPL* 2, 66a-75

Kimball, John P. (ed.) (1972), *Syntax and Semantics,* vol.1, New York & London, Academic Press

—— (ed.) (1975), *Syntax and Semantics, 4,* New York, Academic Press

Kirkwood, Henry W. (1973), *Theme and rheme in English and German,* Ph.D. thesis, University of Edinburgh

Koutsoudas, Andreas (1971), 'Gapping, conjunction reduction, and coordinate deletion', *FL* 7, 337-86

—— (1972), 'The strict order fallacy', *Lg.* 48, 88-96
—— & Gerald Sanders (1974), 'On the universality of rules and rule-ordering constraints', IULC
Kretschmer, P. (1947), *Objektive Konjugation im Indogermanischen,* Vienna
Kullavanijaya, Pranee (1974), *Transitive verbs in Thai,* Ph.D. dissertation, University of Hawaii
Kuno, Susumu (ed.) (1968), *Mathematical Linguistics and Automatic Translation, Report NSF-20,* Cambridge, Mass., Computation Laboratory, Harvard University
—— (1972), 'Subject raising in Japanese', *Papers in Japanese Linguistics* 1
—— (1974), 'The position of relative clauses and conjunctions', *LIn* 5, 117-36
Kuryłowicz, Jerzy (1964), *The Inflexional Categories of Indo-European,* Heidelberg, Carl Winter
Lafon, René (1961), 'Sur les formes verbales basques qui contiennent un indice datif', *BSL* 56, 139-62
—— (1963), 'Notes explicatives à <Chanidze (1963)>', *BSL* 58, 27-40
—— (1971), 'Ergatif et passif en basque et géorgien', *BSL* 66, 327-43
Lakoff, George (1966), 'Stative adjectives and verbs in English', *Mathematical Linguistics and Automatic Language Translation, Report NSF-16,* Cambridge, Mass., Harvard University Computation Laboratory
—— (1968), 'Instrumental adverbs and the concept of deep structure', *FL,* 4-29
—— (1970a), *Irregularity in Syntax,* New York, Holt, Rinehart & Winston
—— (1970b), 'Global rules', *Lg.* 46, 627-39; reprinted in Seuren (1974c), 143-56
—— (1972a), 'Discussion of Grinder (1972), in Kimball (1972), 113-5
—— & Stanley S. Peters (1969), 'Phrasal conjunction and symmetric predicates', in Reibel & Schane, 113-42
—— & John R. Ross (1967), 'Is deep structure necessary? ', mimeo
Lakoff, Robin T. (1968), *Abstract Syntax and Latin Complementation,* New York, Holt, Rinehart & Winston
—— (1971), 'Passive resistance', *CLS* 7, 149-61
—— (1974), 'This and that', *CLS* 10, 345-56
Langacker, Ronald W. (1973), Review of Anderson (1971b), *JL* 9, 319-31
—— (1974), 'Movement rules in functional perspective', *Lg.* 50, 630-64

Langendoen, D. Terence (1969), *The Study of Syntax*, New York, Holt, Rinehart & Winston

—— (1970*a*), *Essentials of English Grammar*, New York, Holt, Rinehart & Winston

—— (1970*b*), 'On the accessibility of deep (semantic) structures', in Jacobs & Rosenbaum, 99-104

Lasnik, Howard & Robert Fiengo (1974), 'Complement object deletion', *LIn* 5, 535-71

Laurie, Simon S. (1859), *On the Fundamental Doctrine of Latin Syntax*, Edinburgh, Constable

Lee, David A. (1972), *Subjectivalization and Lexicalization in Case Grammar*, Ph.D. thesis, University of Kent

—— (1973), '*Stative* and case grammar', *FL* 10, 545-68

Lee, P. Gregory (1969), 'Subjects and agents', WPL 3, 36-113

—— (1971), 'Notes in defense of case grammar', *CLS* 7, 174-80

Leech, Geoffrey N. (1969), *Towards a Semantic Description of English*, London, Longman

Lees, Robert B. & Edward S. Klima (1963), 'Rules for English pronominalization', *Lg.* 39, 17-28

Lehmann, Twila (1972), 'Some arguments against ordered rules', *Lg.* 48, 541-50

Li, Charles N. (ed.) (1975), *Word Order and Word Order Change*, New York, Academic Press

Li, Paul Jen-kui (1973), *Rukai Structure*, Ph.D. dissertation, University of Hawaii

Lightfoot, David (1974), 'Indeterminacy in syntax', *CJL* 19, 150-66

—— (forthcoming), 'The theoretical importance of subject raising', Review of Postal (1974), *FL*

Ljung, Magnus (1970), *English Denominal Adjectives* , Lund, Studentlitteratur

Lyons, John (1966), 'Towards a "notional" theory of the "parts of speech" ', *JL* 2, 209-36

—— (1968), *Introduction to Theoretical Linguistics*, London & New York, Cambridge University Press

Maling, Joan W. (1972), 'On "Gapping and the order of constituents" ', *LIn*, 101-8

Manley, Timothy M. (1972), *Outline of Sre Structure* (= *Oceanic Linguistics* special publication 12), Honolulu, University Press of Hawaii

Marino, Matthew (1972), 'A strong deep case hypothesis', *PIL* 5, 568-603

Marr, N. & M. Brière (1931), *La langue géorgienne*, Paris, Firmin-Didot

Martinet, André (1962), *A Functional View of Language,* London,
    Oxford University Press
Matthews, G.H. (1965), *Hidatsa Syntax,* The Hague, Mouton
Matthews, Peter H. (1967), Review of Chomsky (1965), *JL* 3, 119-52
Matthews, Richard (1973), 'Active passivity', Ms.
Mattina, Anthony (1973), *Colville Grammatical Structure,* Ph.D.
    dissertation, University of Hawaii (*University of Hawaii Working
    Papers in Linguistics* 5, 4)
Meiklejohn, J.M.D. (1892), *A New Grammar of the English Tongue,*
    9th edn, London, Simpkin, Marshall, Hamilton, Kent & Co.
Mellema, Paul (1974), 'A brief against case grammar', *FL* 11, 39-76
Meščaninov, I.I. (1967), *Ergativnaja konstrukcija v jazykax raz ličnyx
    tipov,* Leningrad, Nauka
Miller, James E. (1973*a*), 'On the insertion of lexical items in a generative
    grammar', *EWPL* 3, 141-54 (revised version = Miller (1975))
—— (1973*b*), 'Deep structures without verbs', *EWPL* 2, 11-23
—— (1975), 'The parasitic growth of deep structures', *FL* 13, 361-89
Mittwoch, Anita (1971), 'Idioms and unspecified NP deletion', *LIn* 2,
    255-9
Moravcsik, Edith (1972), 'On case markers and complementizers',
    WPLU 8, 151-2
—— (1974), 'Object-verb agreement', *WPLU* 15, 25-140
Morgan, Jerry M. (1973), 'How can you be in two places at once when
    you're nowhere at all?', *CLS* 9, 410-19
Morin, Yves & Michael H. O'Malley (1969), 'Multi-rooted vines in
    semantic representation', *CLS* 5, 178-85
Macaulay, Ronald K.S. (1971), '*Aspect in English,* Ph.D. dissertation,
    UCLA
McCawley, James D. (1968), 'Lexical insertion in a transformational
    grammar without deep structure', *CLS* 4, 71-80; reprinted in
    McCawley (1973*b*)
—— (1970), 'English as a VSO language ', *Lg.* 46, 286-99; reprinted in
    McCawley (1973*b*), 211-28; also in Seuren (1974*c*), 75-95
—— (1971*a*) 'Prelexical syntax', *MSLL* 24, 19-33; reprinted in
    McCawley (1973*b*), 343-56; also in Seuren (1974*c*), 29-42
—— (1973*a*), Review of Chomsky (1972*b*), IULC
—— (1973*b*), *Grammar and Meaning: Papers on Semantic and
    Syntactic Topics,* Tokyo, Taishukan
—— (1973*c*), 'Syntactic and logical arguments for syntactic structures',
    in Fujimura, 259-376
McCoy, Ana M.B.C. (1969), *A Case Grammar Classification of Spanish*

Verbs, Ph.D. dissertation, University of Michigan

Newmeyer, Frederick J. (1971), 'The source of derived nominals in English', *Lg.* 47, 786-96

—— (1974), 'The precyclic nature of predicate raising', IULC

Nilsen, Don L.F. (1972), *Toward a Semantic Specification of Deep Case*, The Hague, Mouton

—— (1973), *The Instrumental Case in English*, The Hague, Mouton

Panevová, Jarmila (1974), 'On verbal frames in functional generative description, I', *PBML* 22, 3-40

Paris, Catherine (1969), 'Indices personnels et syntaxe de la phrase minimal dans les langues du caucase du nordouest', *BSL* 64, 104-83

Partee, Barbara Hall (1971), 'On the requirement that transformations preserve meaning', in Fillmore & Langendoen, 1-21

Pedersen, H. (1931), *Linguistic Science in the Nineteenth Century*, Cambridge, Mass.

Peranteau, P.M., J.N. Levi & G.C. Phares (eds.) (1972), *The Chicago Which Hunt*, Chicago, Ill., Chicago Linguistic Society

Perlmutter, David M. (1971), *Deep and Surface Structure Constraints in Syntax*, New York, Holt, Rinehart & Winston

Peters, Stanley (ed.) (1972), *Goals of Linguistic Theory*, New York, Holt, Rinehart & Winston

Pirejko, L.A. (1968) *Osnovnye voprosy ergativnosti na materiale indoiranskix jazykov*, Moscow, Nauka

Plank, Frans (1974), 'A belated case re cases versus coordination & identity deletion', *YPL* 4, 91-128

Platt, John T. (1971), *Grammatical Form and Grammatical Meaning*, Amsterdam, North-Holland

Porzig, W. (1934), 'Wesenhafte Bedeutungsbeziehungen', *BGDSL* 58, 70-97

Postal, Paul M. (1970), 'On coreferential complement subject deletion', *LIn* 1, 439-500

—— (1971), *Crossover Phenomena*, New York, Holt, Rinehart & Winston

—— (1972), 'On some rules that are not successive cyclic', *LIn* 3, 211-22

—— (1974), *On Raising: One Rule of English Grammar and its Theoretical Implications*, Cambridge, Mass., MIT Press

—— & John R. Ross (1971), 'iTough movement si, Tough deletion no!', *LIn*, 544-6

Pullum, Geoffrey K. (1975a), 'Contraction in English and the linear character of post-cyclic syntax' (Squibs on relational grammar, no.1)

—— (1975*b*), 'Ascension rules and essential variables' (Squibs on relational grammar, no.2)

—— (1975*c*), 'Reflexivization, linearization, and complex NP shift' (Squibs on relational grammar, no.3)

——(1975*d*), 'Is linearization cyclic, or is agreement postcyclic?' (Squibs on relational grammar, no.4)

—— (1975*e*), 'Word order universals and grammatical relations', mimeo

Quang Phuc Dong (1970), 'A note on conjoined noun phrases', *The Journal of Philosophical Linguistics* 2, 31-40; reprinted in Zwicky, Salus, Binnick & Vanek, 11-18

Radford, Andrew (1975), 'Pseudo-relatives and the unity of subject raising', *ArchL* 6, 32-64

Ramos, Teresita (1973), *The Case System of Tagalog Verbs*, Ph.D. dissertation, University of Hawaii

Reece, Laurie (1970), *Grammar of the Wailbiri Language of Central Australia*, University of Sydney, Australia

Reibel, David A. & Sanford A. Schane (eds.) (1969), *Modern Studies in English*, Englewood Cliffs, N.J., Prentice-Hall

Rigsby, Bruce (1975), 'Nass-Gitskan: An analytic ergative syntax', *IJAL* 41, 345-54

de Rijk, Rudolf P.G. (1972), 'Relative clauses in Basque – a guided tour', in Peranteau *et al.*, 115-35

—— (1974), 'A note on prelexical predicate raising', in Seuren (1974*c*), 43-74

Ringen, Catherine (1972), 'On arguments for rule ordering', *FL* 8, 266-73

Roberts, David (forthcoming), *A Study of 'Agency' in English and Other Languages*, Ph.D. thesis, University of Edinburgh

Robins, R.H. (1974), 'The case theory of Maximus Planudes', in *Proceedings of the XIth International Congress of Linguists*, Bologna, Mulino

Robinson, Jane J. (1970*a*), 'Case, category and configuration', *JL* 6, 57-80

—— (1970*b*), 'Dependency structures and transformational rules', *Lg.* 46, 259-85

Rogers, Andy (1974), 'A transderivational constraint on Richard? ', *CLS* 10, 551-68

Roldán, M. (1972), 'In defense of raising', *PIL* 5, 514-29

Rosenbaum, Peter S. (1967), *The Grammar of English Predicate Complement Constructions*, Cambridge, Mass., MIT Press

—— (1970), 'A principle governing deletion in English sentential complementation', in Jacobs & Rosenbaum, 20-9

Rosenberg Marc S. (1975), 'Generative vs. interpretive semantics',
   Review of Jackendoff (1972), *FL* 12, 561-82
Ross John R. (1967), *Constraints on Variables in Syntax*, Ph.D.
   dissertation, MIT (available from IULC)
—— (1970), 'On gapping and the order of constituents',
   in Bierwisch & Heidolph, 249-59
Ruhl, Charles (1972), ' "The grammar of hitting and breaking" revisited',
   Glossa 6, 147-54
Sanders, Gerald (1972), 'The simplex-feature hypothesis', IULC
Sandfeld, K. & H. Olsen (1936), *Syntaxe roumaine I: Emplois des mots
   à flexion*, Paris, Droz
Sandmann, Manfred (1954), *Subject and Predicate: A Contribution to
   the Theory of Syntax*, Edinburgh, Edinburgh University Press
Šaumjan, S.K. & P.A. Soboleva (1963), *Applikationaja poroždajuščaja
   model' i isčislenie transformacij v russkom jazyke*, Moscow, Izdatel'stvo
   Akademii Nauk SSSR
Schachter, Paul (1973), 'On syntactic categories: A critique of Lakoff's
   "Adjectives and Verbs", Ross's "Adjectives as Noun Phrases", and
   Bach's "Nouns and Noun Phrases" ', in Schachter & Bedell, 138-92
—— & George Bedell (1973), *Critiques of Syntactic Studies, II*
   (UCLA Papers in Syntax, no.4)
—— & Fé T. Otanes (1972), *Tagalog Reference Grammar*, Berkeley &
   London, University of California Press
Schank, Roger (1972), ' "Semantics" in conceptual analysis', *Lingua*
   30, 101-40
Seiler, Hansjakob (1973), 'The principle of concomitance: Instrumental,
   comitative, and collective', LAUT (published version: *FL* 12 (1974),
   215-47)
Seuren, Pieter A.M. (1969), *Operators and Nucleus: A Contribution to
   the Theory of Grammar*, London & New York, Cambridge University
   Press
—— (1973), 'Dative and predicate raising in French and sundry
   languages', LAUT
—— (1974a), Introduction to Seuren (1974c), 1-27
—— (1974b), 'Negative's travels', in Seuren (1973c), 183-208
—— (ed.) (1974c), *Semantic Syntax*, London, Oxford University
   Press
—— (1975) 'Referential constraints on lexical islands', LAUT
Sgall, Petr, Ladislav Nebeský, Alla Goralčíková & Eva Hajičová (1969),
   *A Functional Approach to Syntax in Generative Description of
   Language*, Amsterdam, Elsevier

Shaw, Patricia A. (1974), Review of Perlmutter (1971), *CJL* 19, 209-16

Shimizu, Midori (1975), 'Relational grammar and promotion rules in Japanese', *CLS* 11, 529-35

Skalička, V. (1962), 'Das Wesen der Morphologie und der Syntax', *Acta Universitatis Carolinae, Slavica Pragensia* 4, 123-7

Staal, J.F. (1967), *Word Order in Sanskrit and Universal Grammar*, Dordrecht, Reidel

Starosta, Stanley S. (1971*a*), Review of Lyons (1968), *Lg.* 47, 429-47

—— (1971*b*), 'Derivation and case in Sora verbs', *IL* 32, 194-206

—— (1971*c*), 'Lexical derivation in a case grammar', *University of Hawaii Working Papers in Linguistics* 3, 83-101

—— (1972), 'Case in the lexicon', Preprints for the XIth International Congress of Linguists, Bologna

—— (1973*a*), 'The faces of case', *Language Sciences* 25, 1-14

—— (1973*b*), 'Case forms and case relations in Sora', *University of Hawaii Working Papers in Linguistics* 5, 133-54

—— (1973*c*), 'Causative verbs in Formosan languages', Paper presented at the First International Conference on Austronesian Languages, Hawaii

—— (1974), 'A place for case', *Work in Progress* 7, 18-34 (Department of Linguistics, University of Edinburgh)

Steinberg, Danny D. & Leon A. Jacobovitz (eds.) (1971), *Semantics: An Interdisciplinary Reader,* London & New York, Cambridge University Press

Stewart, William (1975), 'The development of tense and aspect marking in English creoles', Paper presented at the annual meeting of the New York Academy of Sciences

Stockwell, Robert P., Paul Schachter & Barbara Hall Partee (1973), *The Major Syntactic Structures of English,* New York, Holt, Rinehart & Winston

Szamosi, M. (1973), 'On the unity of subject raising', *CLS* 9, 652-8

Talmy, Leonard (1973), *Semantic Structures in English and Atsugewi,* Ph.D. dissertation, University of California, Berkeley

Taylor, Harvey M. (1972), *Case in Japanese,* East Orange, NJ, Seton Hall University Press

Tchekhoff, Claude (1973), 'Parataxe et construction ergatif avec exemples en avar et tongien', *BSL* 68, 255-68

Teller, P. (1969), 'Some discussion and extension of Manfred Bierwisch's work on German adjectivals', *FL* 5, 185-217

Teng, Shou-hsin (1970), 'Comitative versus phrasal conjunction', *PIL* 2, 315-58

Tesnière, Lucien (1959), *Eléments de syntaxe structurale*, Paris, Klincksieck

Traugott, Elizabeth (1974), 'Explorations in linguistic elaboration: Language change, language acquisition, and the genesis of spatio-temporal terms', in J.M. Anderson & C. Jones (eds.) *Historical Linguistics*, vol.1, 263-304, Amsterdam, North-Holland

Trithart, Lee (1975), 'Relational grammar and Chicewa subjectivization rules', *CLS* 11, 615-24

Uhlenbeck, C.C. (1901), 'Agens und Patients im Kasussystem der indogermanischen Sprachen', *IF* 12, 170-1

Vater, Heinz (1973), Dänische Subjekt and Objektsätze: Ein Beitrag zur generativen Dependenzgrammatik, Tübingen, Niemeyer

Vendler, Zeno (1957), 'Verbs and times', *The Philosophical Review* 66, 143-60; reprinted in Vendler (1967), 97-121

—— (1967), *Linguistics in Philosophy*, Ithaca, NY, Cornell University Press

Vendryes, J. (1921), *Le langage*, Paris, La renaissance du livre

Vennemann, Theo (1974), 'Topics, subjects and word order: From SXV to SVX via TVX', in J.M. Anderson & C. Jones (eds.), *Historical Linguistics*, vol.1, 339-76, Amsterdam, North-Holland

Vestergaard, Torben (1973), 'A note on objective, instrumental and affected in English', *SL* 27, 85-9

—— (1974), 'Location, direction and aspect', Ms.

—— (1975), *Prepositional Phrases and Prepositional Verb: A Study in Grammatical Function*, Ms.

Visser, F.T. (1973), *An Historical Syntax of the English Language*, III, 2, Leiden, E.J. Brill

Walmsley, John B. (1971), 'The English comitative case and the concept of deep structure', *FL* 9, 493-507

Wang, Munç (1971), 'Copulative sentences in English: A Germanic language spoken in Northern Delaware', in Zwicky, Salus, Binnick & Vanek, 37-43

Washabaugh, William (1975), 'On the development of complementizers in creolization', *WPLU* 17, 109-40

Wexler, K. & P. Culicover (1974), 'Learning theoretic foundations of linguistic universals' (Social Sciences Working Paper 60), University of California, Irvine

Woodcock, E.C. (1959), *A New Latin Syntax*, London, Methuen

Wolff, Hans (1951), 'Comparative Siouan IV', *IJAL* 17, 197-204

Wurm, S.A. & D.C. Laycock (eds.) (1970), *Pacific Linguistics in Honour of Arthur Capell*, Canberra, Pacific Linguistics

302*Bibliography*

Zeyer, Louis (1974), 'Is English a VSO language? IULC

Žirkov, Lev Ivanovič (1948), *Tabasaransk jazyk,* Moscow & Leningrad

Zwicky, Arnold M. (1968), 'Naturalness arguments in syntax', *CLS* 4, 92-102

—— Peter H. Salus, Robert I. Binnick & Anthony L. Vanek (eds.) (1971), *Studies out in Left Field: Defamatory Essays presented to James D. McCawley on the occasion of his 33rd or 34th Birthday,* Edmonton & Champaign, Linguistic Research Inc.

AUTHOR INDEX

Abraham 281
Akmajian 283
Allen 250-1, 283
Anderson, J.M. 24, 30, 38, 41, 46,
 63, 64, 67-8, 69, 70, 78, 82, 84,
 85, 89, 91, 92, 95, 96, 98, 99,
 103, 107, 108, 110, 111, 115,
 119, 120, 126, 137, 160, 181,
 190, 205, 207, 219, 222, 256,
 266, 281, 282, 283
Anderson, J.M. & Jessen 96
Anderson, J.M. & Jones 137, 274,
 282
Anderson, S.R. 42, 48-57, 59, 81,
 152, 153
Andrews 281

Bach 72-3, 74-5, 77, 78, 79, 99
Baker 282
Baltin 77
Bang-Bang 127, 281
Bartsch & Vennemann 92, 95
Becker 26
Bedell 59
Bell 282
Bennett 101, 121, 282
Benveniste 207
Berman 79
Bernhardi 115
Bever 281
Binnick 166
Bogoras 122
Bowers 282
Brekle 281
Bresnan 105
Browne 135-6
Buckingham 281

Carden 283
Carnap 282
Catford 282
Chafe 281
Chanidze 263
Chomsky 12-19, 23, 42-5, 48, 49-50,
 51, 55, 57, 58, 59, 60, 70, 89, 97,
 99, 110, 169-70, 186, 207-9, 267,
 281, 282
Chvany 24, 128

Clark 117, 282
Comrie 256, 262-4, 267, 283
Contreras 281
Cook 281, 282
Cooper 282
Cruse 28, 281
Curry 71

Daneš 88
Darrigol 111
Dillon 89
Dirr 113
Dixon 253-6, 258-60
Dreike 282
Dumézil 251, 283

Emonds 31, 77, 79, 157, 176, 191
Evers 79-80

Fauconnier 248
Ferguson 282
Fillmore 13, 19-30, 37-55, 63, 64,
 65, 66, 67, 69, 81, 88, 96, 97-8,
 99, 110, 111, 113, 122, 125-7,
 129, 134, 142, 150, 281
Fischer & Marshall 28
Fletcher 46, 110
Fodor 23
Frajzyngier 101, 104
Fraser 49, 51, 53, 281
Freidin 13, 16, 19, 44, 65, 208,
 209-11, 281

Gaaf, van der 283
Gee 35-7, 195, 219
Gildersleeve & Lodge 10, 207
Givón 282
Gleitman 41, 169-70
Gonda 220
Gray 220
Green 13, 140, 143, 146-50, 157,
 195, 197-8, 281
Greenberg 78, 92, 95, 273
Grinder 77
Grosu 281
Gruber 26, 30, 31, 32, 34, 35, 103,
 111, 138, 227, 265, 281
Gundel 90-1, 187

Author Index

SUBJECT INDEX

(Common abbreviations for some of the items in the index are enclosed in square brackets; important page references are italicised.)